The Eucharist and Ecumenism

The theology of the eucharist has long been the subject of heated debate, particularly since the Reformation. George Hunsinger's book explores ways in which Christians might resolve their differences in this area. With the aim of fostering ecumenical convergence, he tackles three key issues dividing the churches about the eucharist: real presence, eucharistic sacrifice, and ordained ministry.

Hunsinger, a Protestant theologian in the Reformed tradition, brings Eastern Orthodox views more systematically into the discussion than has been common in the West. He also discusses the social significance of the eucharist. His detailed conclusion summarizes and clarifies the argument as a whole with an eye to explaining how the views proposed in the book could lead the churches, beginning with the Reformed church, closer to the day when obstacles to eucharistic sharing are overcome.

GEORGE HUNSINGER is Hazel Thompson McCord Professor of Systematic Theology at Princeton Theological Seminary. He is author of *Disruptive Grace: Studies in the Theology of Karl Barth* (2000) and *How to Read Karl Barth: The Shape of His Theology* (1991).

CURRENT ISSUES IN THEOLOGY

General Editor:

Iain Torrance
President and Professor of Patristics, Princeton Theological Seminary

Editorial Advisory Board:

David Ford   *University of Cambridge*
Bryan Spinks   *Yale University*
Kathryn Tanner   *University of Chicago*
John Webster   *University of Aberdeen*

There is a need among upper-undergraduate and graduate students of theology, as well as among Christian teachers and church professionals, for a series of short, focused studies of particular key topics in theology written by prominent theologians. *Current Issues in Theology* meets this need.

The books in the series are designed to provide a "state-of-the-art" statement on the topic in question, engaging with contemporary thinking as well as providing original insights. The aim is to publish books which stand between the static monograph genre and the more immediate statement of a journal article, by authors who are questioning existing paradigms or rethinking perspectives.

Other titles in the series:

Holy Scripture   John Webster
The Just War Revisited   Oliver O'Donovan
Bodies and Souls, or Spirited Bodies?   Nancey Murphy
Christ and Horrors   Marilyn McCord Adams
Divinity and Humanity   Oliver D. Crisp

GEORGE HUNSINGER

The Eucharist and Ecumenism

Let us Keep the Feast

CAMBRIDGE
UNIVERSITY PRESS

CAMBRIDGE UNIVERSITY PRESS
Cambridge, New York, Melbourne, Madrid, Cape Town, Singapore, São Paulo, Delhi

Cambridge University Press
The Edinburgh Building, Cambridge CB2 8RU, UK

Published in the United States of America by Cambridge University Press, New York

www.cambridge.org
Information on this title: www.cambridge.org/9780521719179

First published 2008

Printed in the United Kingdom at the University Press, Cambridge

A catalogue record for this publication is available from the British Library

Library of Congress Cataloguing in Publication data
Hunsinger, George.
 The Eucharist and ecumenism: let us keep the feast / George Hunsinger.
  p. cm.
 Includes bibliographical references and index.
 ISBN 978-0-521-89486-9 (hardback) – ISBN 978-0-521-71917-9 (pbk.)
 1. Lord's Supper and Christian union. I. Title.
 BX9.5.S2H86 2008
 234′.163–dc22   2008012864

ISBN 978-0-521-89486-9 hardback
ISBN 978-0-521-71917-9 paperback

Christ our Passover is sacrificed for us.
Therefore let us keep the feast.
The Book of Common Prayer
(1 Cor. 5:7–8)

In memoriam
Thomas F. Torrance
doctor ecclesiae
honoris causa ad gradum
with heartfelt thanks for his life and work

Contents

Acknowledgments

As an undergraduate I took a course on the Ecumenical Movement from Robert McAfee Brown, who had been an observer in Rome during Vatican II. It was Brown who first made me see that a divided church was intolerable, though I remained skeptical about solutions. When I went to seminary, the Jesuits saved my theological education. Frs. Gerald O'Collins and George W. MacCrae of the Weston School of Theology combined piety and learning in a way that often seemed lacking in the ethos across the commons at the divinity school where I was enrolled. For a young Presbyterian ministerial student, it was an exercise in practical ecumenism. Then during my doctoral studies, by the sheer force of his example and teaching, another former observer in Rome, George A. Lindbeck, made the ecumenical agenda seem inescapable, though for me it remained a matter of peripheral vision, as I was more preoccupied in those days with the sorrows and outrages of an unconscionable war.

The virtues of Mercersberg theology for the Reformed tradition, with its effort to retrieve a more catholic understanding of the eucharist through the work of John Nevin, were kept before my eyes by Howard G. Hageman, president of New Brunswick Theological Seminary, where I obtained my first academic post. Of course I had no idea at the time that these influences might be leading anywhere. Looking back, it seems that the turning point came in 1995 during a Lenten Bible study in my local congregation. Feeling that my New Testament Greek, never very good, was getting ever more rusty by the day, I took an interlinear volume with me to one of the sessions. To my surprise the word *koinonia* showed up in 1 Cor. 10:16. Could it be, I wondered, that the relationship between the bread and Christ's body might be one of mutual indwelling? Over time my hunch was reinforced by Luther, confirmed by Vermigli, and validated by Käsemann. I was headed down the trail that led to this book.

Through the kind invitation of Iain R. Torrance, later to become president at Princeton Theological Seminary, where I had joined the faculty, I was asked to lecture on the eucharist to the School of Divinity at the University of Aberdeen in 2003. Those lectures became the core of this volume. Great kindness was shown to my wife and me during our visit to the campus. I would especially like to thank John Webster, along with all the others, as well as Nicholas Thompson, whose guidance on the vexed matter of eucharistic sacrifice was most valuable. For assistance at various stages I would also like to thank my colleagues Sr. M. Paracleta Amrich, Brian Daley, Ralph Del Colle, Dawn De Vries, Theodor Dieter, George Parsenios, Michael Root, Bryan Spinks, Geoffrey Wainwright, Sarah Hinlicky Wilson, Randall Zachman, Philip Ziegler, and members of the Duodecim Theological Society. Kate Brett and Gillian Dadd, my savvy editors, oversaw the publication process with grace and seasoned judgment. Kathy Whalen aided greatly in the preparation of the diagrams. Finally, this work could never have been completed without the loving support and encouragement of my friend and colleague Deborah van Deusen Hunsinger, with whom I enjoy the added blessing of being married.

Three special influences stand out for me. Though I have remained only on the periphery of their work, the Center for Catholic and Evangelical Theology served to concentrate my mind. The interventions of Carl Braaten in particular helped me to see that Christian worship is essentially eucharistic worship or it is not Christian worship at all.

The Episcopal Church at Yale, through the innovative ministries of Richard Fabian and Donald Schell, enhanced my love for *The Book of Common Prayer* while also expanding my horizons about what a liturgy could be. The work they began in those days later morphed into San Francisco's St. Gregory of Nyssa Episcopal Church, where I was happy to rediscover them after a lapse of many years. Their insights, which have graced me with the richest eucharistic experiences of my life, are described in the conclusion.

Finally, towering in my mind above all others is Thomas F. Torrance. Without him I suspect that as a Reformed theologian, I might never have seen how to get from there to here regarding the eucharist, namely, from Karl Barth to something like the ecumenical center. Many of the leading themes in this book – *koinonia* relations, their formal structuring by the Chalcedonian pattern, transelementation, eucharistic sacrifice as the exclusive work of Christ, the dimension of depth, the imperative of women's ordination, the paschal mystery, the preeminence of Eastern Orthodoxy, and more – all have their roots in his work. The book is dedicated to his memory.

Introduction: Ecumenical theology

Ecumenical theology, as I understand it, differs from both enclave theology and academic theology. Although there are overlaps among these types, let me begin by differentiating them.

Three types of theology

By "enclave theology," I mean a theology based narrowly in a single tradition that seeks not to learn from other traditions and to enrich them, but instead to topple and defeat them, or at least to withstand them. Enclave theology is polemical theology even when it assumes an irenic façade. Its limited agenda makes it difficult for it to take other traditions seriously and deal with them with fairly. Whether openly or secretly, it is not really interested in dialogue but in rectitude and hegemony. It harbors the attitude that the ecumenical movement will succeed only as other traditions abandon their fundamental convictions, where they are incompatible with those of the enclave, in order to embrace the enclave's doctrinal purity. Because of its temptation to misrepresent or devalue traditions with which it disagrees, such theology is finally divisive and futile. With little chance of success beyond those already convinced, it mainly reinforces the ecumenical status quo. Enclave theology makes itself look good, at least in its own eyes, by making others look bad. It is in danger of what Paul rejected as "party spirit" or "works of the flesh," namely, enmity, strife, and factionalism (Gal. 5:20). In the ecumenical churches no tradition or communion is immune from this kind of dogmatism.

Ecumenical theology takes another approach. It presupposes that every tradition in the church has something valuable to contribute even if we cannot yet discern what it is. The ecumenical movement will succeed not when all other traditions capitulate to the one true church – whether centered in Geneva, Constantinople, Canterbury, Wittenberg or Rome – to say nothing of other symbolic locales like Lima, Cape Town, New Delhi, Canberra or Beijing. On the contrary, it will succeed only by a deeper conversion of all traditions to Christ. Ecumenical theology, though properly grounded in a single tradition, looks for what is best in traditions not its own. It seeks not to defeat them but to respect and learn from them. It earns the right to speak only by listening, and it listens much more than it speaks. When in the midst of intractable disagreements, it searches for unforeseen convergences. Its hope for ecumenical progress means that no tradition will get everything that it wants, each will get much that it wants, none will be required to capitulate to another, and none will be expected to make unacceptable compromises. Each will contribute to the richness of the whole, and all will be expected to stretch to accept some things that at first did not seem possible. Ecumenical theology, while unable to avoid speaking pointedly at times, seeks a charitable spirit which "bears all things, believes all things, hopes all things, endures all things" (1 Cor. 13:7).

Ecumenical theology must also differentiate itself from modern academic liberal theology. From an ecumenical point of view, perhaps the most striking aspect of this academic theology is its lack of allegiance to established confessional norms. Ecumenical councils like Nicaea and Chalcedon are written off as "definitive failures," full of contradictions and absurdities.[1] Holy Scripture is interpreted from every conceivable point of view – historicist,

---

[1] This is the view of Paul Tillich, for example, in *Systematic Theology*, vol. II (Chicago: University of Chicago Press, 1957), p. 142. See also pp. 91, 94, 143–45.

sociological, psychological, rationalist, metaphysical, etc. – except for the apostolic and the prophetic. Taking those latter viewpoints seriously would entail at least a *de iure* respect for their witness to something unanticipated, ineffable, and exclusively unique. It would mean respecting (if not necessarily embracing) the scandal of particularity – which, if true, would necessarily bring every modern secular method to its categorical limit. But that scandal – and with it the election of Israel and the bodily resurrection of Christ – is typically dismissed out of hand.

No real discussion is needed as long as modernist norms reign supreme. Unconditional allegiance to them is promulgated as ethical integrity. Theological discourse is said to be invalid if it does not conform to "common experience," or if it does not exemplify certain favored "metaphysical categories." Exclusive claims for the gospel are rejected as mythological, arbitrary and arrogant. Modern historical consciousness is said to require abandoning the claim to Christ's uniqueness. The biblical view of reality, like all human views, is seen as just one more culturally conditioned artifact, and religion becomes principally a matter of inwardness. Pluralism, relativism, and naturalism become the coin of the realm. When Christianity is reduced, through the looking glass of modern criticism, to being an ancient patriarchal religion of obscure Mediterranean provenance, it is little wonder that academic religionists should see themselves as "alienated theologians,"[2] and that historians should describe modern liberal theology as having increasingly lost touch with the churches.[3]

---

[2] See Van A. Harvey, "The Alienated Theologian," *McCormack Quarterly* 23 (May 1970), pp. 234–65. This conflicted figure is described as an academic professor of religion who is "concerned with the articulation of the faith of the Christian community but who is himself as much a doubter as a believer" (p. 235). Cited by Peter C. Hodgson in his "Editor's Introduction" to D. F. Strauss, *The Life of Jesus Critically Examined* (Philadelphia: Fortress Press, 1972), p. xv.

[3] "Liberal theologians, having been pushed to the left by liberationist and postmodern movements, found themselves speaking a language that had little currency in

Ecumenical theology, at its best, has never discarded the norms and critical methods of modern academic theology. It has indeed affirmed them, while rejecting only their purported supremacy. It has regarded them as a good servant but a bad master. It has welcomed the many valuable fruits of their application while subordinating them to the authority of the ecumenical councils (especially the first four). It is the councils, creeds, and confessions, not modernity, that provide a normative framework for the ecumenical understanding of Holy Scripture. The Nicene-Constantinopolitan Creed – commonly recited in eucharistic liturgies – is the most widely embraced standard in all of ecumenical Christianity.[4] Together with the Chalcedonian definition of Christ's person, it has protected the ecumenical churches, again and again, from the dangers of Arianism, Modalism, Nestorianism, and Docetism (to mention only the most important).[5] In modern liberal theology Arian and Nestorian tendencies are particularly evident, though not always unambiguously; yet they indicate a serious risk of propounding views of revelation and salvation, and therefore of

---

congregations." Gary J. Dorrien, "American Liberal Theology: Crisis, Irony, Decline, Renewal, Ambiguity," *Cross Currents* 55 (2005–6), p. 472. See now also Gary J. Dorrien, *The Making of American Liberal Theology: Crisis, Irony, and Postmodernity 1950–2005* (Louisville: Westminster/John Knox, 2006).

[4] As the only creed promulgated by any of the seven ecumenical councils, it is the only creed that is truly ecumenical and universal. In the Eastern Orthodox churches, it is simply the only creed, while in the Roman Catholic and other Western churches, it is often regarded, in effect, as the first among equals, alongside the Apostles' Creed. (The controversy over the *filioque* clause is discussed briefly in Part III on "Eucharist and ministry.") About half the world's Christian population is Roman Catholic while another quarter is Eastern Orthodox. See *Confessing the One Faith: An Ecumenical Explication of the Apostolic Faith as It Is Confessed in the Nicene-Constantinopolitan Creed (381)*, Faith and Order Paper 153 (Geneva: World Council of Churches, 1991).

[5] If, as is arguably the case, the historic "Nestorian" and "Monophysite" churches have also by and large conformed to the intentions of Nicaea and Chalcedon, as understood in the West, then their differences with the rest of ecumenical Christianity would at bottom be largely semantic rather than substantive.

worship – including eucharistic worship – that the ecumenical churches can ill afford to abide.[6]

Although modern academic theology, in its more polemical vein, has sometimes created the impression that no theologian could reject the supremacy of its preferred critical norms without lapsing into intellectual dishonesty, the list of modern theologians who have remained unpersuaded is long and distinguished. Any selection is bound to be arbitrary, but among the Roman Catholics one thinks, for example, of Hans Urs von Balthasar, Yves Congar and Monika Hellwig; among the Eastern Orthodox, of Georges Florovsky, John Meyendorff, and Nonna Verna Harrison; among the Anglicans of Benedicta Ward, Austin Farrer, and Rowan Williams; among the Lutherans, of Helmut Gollwitzer, Eberhard Jüngel, and Dorothea Wendebourg; among the Methodists, of E. Gordon Rupp, Georgia Harkness, and Geoffrey Wainwright; among the Baptists, of Nancey Murphy, Willie Jennings, and Timothy George; among the Reformed, of Heiko Oberman, J. Christine Janowski, and Karl Barth. The list, which is obviously selective, could be extended, but it should be enough to make the point. What these theologians – indeed this cloud of witnesses – have in common is a basic commitment to the historic standards of the ecumenical churches. While none of them disregarded modernity's critical norms, all of them, in one way or another, held Nicaea and Chalcedon to be superior. Over against the pressures of modernity, they refrained from absolutizing the relative and relativizing the absolute, as confessed by faith.

---

[6] Nicaea and Chalcedon are best understood, in Hans W. Frei's fine phrase, as "conceptual redescriptions of the narratives." They provide interpretive lenses through which the gospel narratives are to be read if their saving significance is to not to be missed. They offer second-order rules for reading, though they also make substantive claims. Most importantly, they are not replacements for the narratives, but attempts to make visible the deep structure within them, rendering explicit what is implicit. They bring out what is often depicted and assumed rather than stated in the New Testament witness to the uniqueness of Christ.

In practice the overlaps among enclave, academic, and ecumenical approaches to theology are of course untidy and complex. These distinctions are not meant as pigeonholes into which any one theologian's writings will neatly fit. They are rather categories of discernment by which trends and tendencies in any body of work can be picked out. There can obviously be enclave moments and modern-liberal-academic moments within an otherwise ecumenical theology as well as ecumenical moments within the other two types, and so forth.

Nor are these types necessarily exhaustive as though other schemes of classification were somehow superfluous. Enclave theology is perhaps best thought of as the shadow side of dogmatic or confessional theology, but confessional theology has an essential place in the churches that cannot be written off because of enclave abuses (which, if seen in the best light, are meant to uphold the integrity of the church). Dogmatic or confessional theology can advance the distinctive concerns of particular communions in ways that are often fruitful beyond them as well as for them.

Academic liberal theology, for its part, has done yeoman's service not only to save the ecumenical churches from fundamentalism and authoritarian ways of thinking, but also to advance the essential concerns of justice, freedom, and peace, and it has sometimes done so in circumstances where the rest of theology and church were asleep at the wheel.[7] It has also championed academic freedom in the study of theology, thus blocking the more stultifying effects of orthodoxy. It has evidenced a courageous openness to the new, even when not always doing justice to the old. In these and other respects its contribution has been essential.

---

[7] It will be a great day when liberation theologies are more fully developed within a Nicene and Chalcedonian framework. They will then have a better chance of breaking through the glass ceiling that tragically restricts their influence in the ecumenical churches. See my remarks in the "Introduction" to George Hunsinger, *Disruptive Grace* (Grand Rapids: Wm. B. Eerdmans, 2000), pp. 1–4. Also "Karl Barth and Liberation Theology," in *Disruptive Grace*, pp. 42–59.

In sum, the point of making these distinctions has not been to cover all the bases, but merely to highlight some of the distinctive aspects of ecumenical theology by using the other two types as a foil.

Promoting visible unity as a theological task

From the standpoint of ecumenical theology, with its goal of promoting visible unity as a theological task, at least three points emerge from this analysis.

First, insofar as academic theology fails to respect Nicaea and Chalcedon, it is in danger of mere sectarianism. Whatever inroads modern skepticism may have made into the mind of the church over the last 250 years, no communion has renounced, nor is any communion at all likely to renounce, the trinitarian faith of the ecumenical churches. Modernity has brought many blessings to the church, and promises to bring more still, but they have not always been unmixed.[8] Despite all ambiguities, complexities, and cross-currents, the prospect that ecumenical churches – by which I mean the Roman Catholic, Eastern Orthodox, Reformational, and anabaptist communions – will ever elevate "historical consciousness," relativism, pluralism, and naturalism (thus exaggerating the significance of inwardness[9]) into a position of overriding normative superiority remains what it has always been: near to zero. For academic theology, heterodox bishops, and friends of gnosticism to suppose otherwise would surely be illusory. Over the long haul, either there will be an increasing parting of the ways between modern liberal theology and the life of actual churches (to the detriment of each), or else a more robust integration of modernity's

---

[8] Perhaps I should mention that I regard "postmodernity," whatever if anything it may be, as a pendulum swing within modernity rather than a clean break from it; old wine in new bottles, so to speak.

[9] "Inwardness" is here used as shorthand for "profound religious experiences," etc., that supposedly remain untouched by modern critical inquiry.

contributions will take place within a normative theological framework viable for the church. (Some measure, though not an even measure, of both tendencies will probably be in evidence.) Ecumenical theology will continue to learn from academic theology, but whether the reverse is true remains to be seen.[10]

Second, ecumenical theology must cope not only with academic liberal theology to its left, but also with enclave theology to its right. Enclave theology confronts it with painful limits (as does academic theology when it adopts enclave-like behavior). Ecumenical theology can labor to turn contradictions into contrasts. It can search for possibilities where only impossibilities have prevailed. It can honor venerable convictions while striving toward a larger, more generous framework that might allow a new *modus vivendi* to emerge. It can untangle old misconceptions that have blocked the path to unity and challenge unnecessary exclusions. In can retrieve forgotten insights from the past to facilitate a more attractive future. It can dig for the truth embedded in error and for the error lurking in truth.

What it cannot do is uproot dogmatic attitudes that are deeply entrenched. It cannot, in and of itself, work as a solvent that loosens the deadlocked machinery of "theological correctness" (what the Germans call *Rechthaberei*).[11] If ecumenical theology has a role to play, it must work almost entirely at the level of ideas as opposed to attitudes. Among the barriers to eucharistic hospitality, for example,

---

[10] For an account of how world religions might be understood by ecumenical theology as here conceived, see my essay "Postliberal Theology," in *The Cambridge Companion to Postmodern Theology*, ed. Kevin J. Vanhoozer (Cambridge: Cambridge University Press, 2003), pp. 42–57; on pp. 53–57. See also my essay "Secular Parables of the Truth" in Hunsinger, *How to Read Karl Barth* (New York: Oxford University Press, 1991), pp. 234–80. For a sketch of Christianity in relation to Judaism, see my "Introduction" to *For the Sake of the World*, ed. George Hunsinger (Grand Rapids: Wm B. Eerdmans, 2004), pp. 3–7.

[11] The term *Rechthaberei* loosely translates as the state of thinking and behaving as if one were in the right and everyone else in the wrong. It carries connotations of sanctimony, self-congratulation, and humorlessness, combined with passive-aggressive traits.

perhaps none is more intractable than the question of what counts as validity in eucharistic ministry. (A modest attempt to address this question appears in Part III.) A great work of the Holy Spirit will surely be needed, beyond all human theologizing, and for which all must ceaselessly pray, if the churches seeking unity are ever to overcome the injuries of the past while being led to a deeper level of discernment. Distinguishing the wheat from the chaff – and therefore integrity from intransigence, generosity from gullibility, and faithfulness from foolishness – is finally a spiritual task. But it is an imperative that must be met – in integrity, generosity, and faithfulness – if the great high-priestly prayer of Jesus to his Father is at last to be fulfilled, "that they may be one, as we are one" (Jn. 17:22).

Finally, "ecumenical theology," as used here, has two senses, one broad, the other narrow. In the broad sense ecumenical theology is simply ecclesial theology, as beholden to norms grounded in Holy Scripture and clarified by conciliar and confessional traditions like Nicaea and Chalcedon. In the narrow sense, however, ecumenical theology involves a more specific set of goals and tasks. Since there is no such thing as a view from nowhere, ecumenical theology cannot be "ecumenical" in general, but will always be grounded in a particular tradition. It must think from a center in that tradition outward to an ecumenical circumference, and back again. On the divisive questions, it must weigh its own tradition in light of other traditions, and other traditions in light of its own. It must seek to preserve what is best and avoid what is worst while daring to be open to what is new. The most urgent and overriding goal, however, is not self-preservation but reunion.

Seven guidelines may be lifted up as informing ecumenical theology in its special vocation.

- Church-dividing views should be abandoned, especially in the form of false contrasts.
- No tradition, including one's own, should be asked to compromise on essentials.

- Where possible, misunderstandings from the past should be identified and eliminated.
- Real differences should not be glossed over by resorting to ambiguity; they will only come back to haunt theology and church.
- The range of acceptable diversity should be expanded as fully as possible within the bounds of fundamental unity.
- All steps toward visible unity should be taken which can be taken without theological compromise.
- No one church should be expected to capitulate to another or be swallowed up into it.

The possible tensions among these guidelines are obvious. What they might mean can only be determined by seeking to apply them on a case-by-case basis. In general, if a tradition holds a minority position or an unshared position over against the rest of ecumenical Christianity, a certain presumption will exist against it, though not necessarily an absolute presumption.[12] Perhaps it can be modified without essential compromise so as to become no longer church-dividing, and so to find a place within the scope of acceptable diversity, or even within a newly minted consensus. Candidates for this kind of ecumenical reconsideration might include the following (though drawing up such a list is risky): the primacy of the bishop of Rome, the *filioque* clause, the meaning of apostolic succession, the questions of married, female, and gay clergy, real presence in the eucharist, eucharistic sacrifice, the doctrine of justification by faith, believers' baptism, and Christian pacifism. This is not an exhaustive list, and it includes issues of different kinds. Some progress has been made on some of them over the course of the twentieth century, and more is still to be hoped for. But it is hard to see how future progress will be possible

---

[12] Of course it is not impossible that such a position may simply be correct and the rest of the churches flat-out wrong. It cannot be accepted, however, without the utmost scrutiny, and until every good-faith effort has been made to find a principled movement in the direction of ecumenical accommodation.

outside the scope of such guidelines. The point about taking all possible steps toward visible unity is a guiding principle of this essay as applied to the Reformed tradition.[13]

An ecumenical proposal on the eucharist

The essay at hand sets forth an ecumenical proposal on the eucharist. It is addressed to my own tradition, the Reformed tradition, and through it to the larger *oikumene*. It tries to show what respecting the suggested guidelines might mean if applied in a notoriously stubborn case. Regarding the eucharist I have tried to show how the Reformed tradition might be brought closer to Roman Catholic and Eastern Orthodox teachings without compromising Reformed essentials. If the argument is at all successful – though it makes no claims to be definitive and awaits the necessary corrections and contributions of others – I think it might also work for Lutherans, Anglicans, Methodists, and related communions. Of course, even that would be a lot to hope for, but what to do about those churches rooted in the anabaptist traditions, including charismatics and pentcostals, is beyond me. Any (hypothetical) success of my argument would be self-defeating if it led to insuperable barriers on that front. Nevertheless, I have had to make do with what little light I seemed to have.

In Part I, I offer a proposal about real presence. One way that ecumenical theology differs from dogmatic theology is by having to take authoritative church teachings into account, or at least by having to take them into account in another way. Whereas

---

[13] For a different though not incompatible perspective, see "What Is Ecumenical Theology?" in G. R. Evans, *Method in Ecumenical Theology* (Cambridge: Cambridge University Press, 1996), pp. 19–39. For a divergent perspective, see Michael Welker, *What Happens in Holy Communion?* (Grand Rapids: Wm. B. Eerdmans, 2000).

dogmatic theology might conclude that it is sufficient regarding the eucharist just to affirm "the real presence of Christ," ecumenical theology finds itself confronting a more demanding task. Because of authoritative teachings in the high sacramental communions, the question must be defined quite precisely. A position needs to be taken not merely on Christ's real presence, but on the real presence of his body and blood under the consecrated elements of bread and wine. Since few non-Catholics are ever likely to embrace transubstantiation, though for Roman Catholicism it is of course non-negotiable, the result would seem to be an ecumenical impasse.

However, it seems that Eastern Orthodoxy is not unacceptable to Roman Catholicism on this score, and that Orthodoxy allows but does not require the view of transubstantiation. Orthodoxy, which wishes to avoid being overly scholastic in its doctrinal formulations, permits a range of other possibilities, including the ancient patristic doctrine of "transelementation" (*metastoicheiosis*). The substance of this idea, as it turns out, can also be found in Luther as well as in the Reformed theologians Vermigli, Cranmer, and Bucer. Adopting it would perhaps not require a great adjustment in the views of Calvin. Here is a largely forgotten idea which, if officially embraced by the Protestant communions, could conceivably move them – at this momentous point – from a stance that was church-dividing to one within the bounds of acceptable diversity.

Eucharistic sacrifice is the theme of Part II. An examination of Aquinas and Trent shows them to be as explicit as could be desired in teaching that the eucharist was not a "repetition" of Christ's once-for-all sacrifice on the cross. Nevertheless, while Zwingli, Luther, and Calvin were not unaware that the idea of "repetition" was officially rejected by Catholicism, they doubted whether that was really the case, and they did so with almost shocking vehemence. Why such fierce doubts should have prevailed among them remains (as far as I can tell) unclear. Perhaps because of contrary currents in popular Catholicism, perhaps because of entanglements with the indulgence controversy, and perhaps because what official teaching rejected about repetition was clearer than what it affirmed, the Reformers would give no quarter.

Much of what Roman Catholicism included in its understanding of eucharistic sacrifice, however, can be found dispersed throughout the writings of Calvin, and was actually allowed, with qualifications, by Luther. Furthermore, the long-term effects in Protestantism of denouncing eucharistic sacrifice were not always cheering. A gradual erosion of comprehension set in regarding the ascended Christ's priestly intercession, and even worse, regarding the eucharist's paschal mystery. In more recent times Reformed theologians like B. B. Warfield, T. F. Torrance, and Max Thurian have grasped that the paschal aspect of the eucharist cannot be divorced from the idea of sacrifice. The way is therefore opened for revitalizing the Reformed tradition (and perhaps related traditions) on this point. At the same time, however, the high sacramental communions, while not wrong to posit a profound continuity between the cross and the eucharist, might learn something vital from the Reformation about their essential asymmetry and distinction as well.

The vexed question of validity in eucharistic ministry is tackled in Part III. Attention is given first to the official Roman Catholic judgment that the ministry of the Protestant churches is "defective." An attempt is made to take this charge seriously. At the same time doubts are raised about the self-exemption that Roman Catholicism so readily awards itself on this question. It is suggested that Protestant churches should set a good example by not rejecting the Catholic perception out of hand in the hopes that Catholicism might be spurred to a deeper level of self-examination. Five questions about ministry are then addressed in an effort to bring a measure of analytical clarity to the issues. A distinction is proposed between two types of theological imagination. Questions of admonition suggest that there is more than enough *defectus* to go around, not least in the refusal of the high sacramental churches to consider ordaining women.

Part IV includes two chapters on the eucharist and social responsibility. The first proposes to interpret the eucharist as Christ transforming culture. H. Richard Niebuhr's famous typology is defended against its recent critics, while his definitions of Christ, culture, and transformation are subjected to modification. The Messianic Banquet as a eucharistic feast defines not only the promised future, but also ethical responsibility here and now.

The next chapter discusses the relationship between the eucharist and peace. Recent criticisms of Nicene Christianity are addressed. Since the Nicene-Constantipolitan Creed has been so closely associated with the eucharist in the ecumenical churches, both historically and globally, it is a matter of concern when aspects of Nicene Christianity are accused by academic and liberationist critics of sponsoring violence, indifference, and abuse. The chapter argues that these accusations are overly broad.

The Conclusion summarizes the themes of this study while developing a few of them further. An authoritative ecumenical document, the *Catechism of the Catholic Church*, is examined for its teaching on the eucharist. The proposals advanced by this study are found to be in line with it, with the notable exceptions of transubstantiation and eucharistic ministry. The study has addressed the former by trying to expand the range of acceptable diversity, and the latter by calling for all parties (not just some) to work harder at eschewing church-dividing teachings. In a kind of coda the question of liturgy and architecture is then briefly discussed. The writings of Louis Bouyer and Pope Benedict XVI are examined in relation to San Francisco's Saint Gregory of Nyssa Episcopal Church. The innovative architecture at Saint Gregory's, which was designed to retrieve fourth-century liturgical practices, represents a creative attempt to embody some of the insights we find in Bouyer and the Pope. They suggest possibilities for renewal by which all churches could be enriched.

A word on Karl Barth

Finally, a word is in order about Karl Barth.[14] Readers familiar with my previous writings may wonder how anyone so steeped in Barth's theology could have arrived at the positions in this book. The most general answer is that I wish to align myself with the trajectory established by Thomas F. Torrance and Alasdair Heron, who have blazed a trail before me, moving not only with Barth and through Barth on the eucharist, but also beyond and against him. Also noteworthy in this regard is the work of Barth's student and close colleague, Helmut Gollwitzer, whose dissertation *Coena Domini* attempted, in important ways, to develop a high doctrine of the eucharist that would not be incompatible with Barth's theology. The more specific answer is twofold.

Barth arguably failed to exploit the full potential of his theology regarding the eucharist. One statement in particular helps to make this failing clear. In the midst of a fine comment on the Lord's Supper, Barth distances himself from the Roman Catholic mass. The eucharist is not to be seen, he says, as "a re-presentation and repetition" of Christ's sacrifice – "as in the Romanist doctrine of the mass" – but rather as "a simple and full enjoyment of its benefits," and in particular of "the eternal life won for us in him."[15]

From the standpoint of Barth's theology, this is an odd comment. It reflects standard Reformation polemic more than his own

---

[14] For some general assessments, see Michael Welker, "Karl Barth: From Fighter against the 'Roman Heresy' to Leading Thinker for the Ecumenical Movement," *Scottish Journal of Theology* 57 (2004): 434–50; Boniface A. Willems, "Karl Barth's Contribution to the Ecumenical Movement," in *Do We Know the Others?*, ed. Hans Küng (New York: Paulist Press, 1966), pp. 42–49.

[15] Karl Barth, *Church Dogmatics*, vol. III, part 2 (Edinburgh: T. & T. Clark, 1960), p. 502. Note that this remark was penned in 1948, well before the emergence of anything like Vatican II. Moreover, by "re-presentation" what Barth had in mind was probably something sacerdotal, not something effected by the living Christ himself.

best insights. It not only conflates re-presentation unnecessarily with repetition, but also divorces Christ from his benefits. These are two moves, however, that Barth has taught us to avoid.

First, Barth knew that Christ could not be enjoyed without his benefits, and that the reverse was also true, namely, that his benefits were unavailable without his person. Christ's benefits could be enjoyed only by way of *participatio Christi*. Moreover, Barth also knew that Christ's person was inseparable from his work, so that where Christ was present, his saving work was present as well. Humankind was not saved by the work of Christ *in abstracto*, Barth held, so much as by the person of Christ in his work. A separation of Christ's work of sacrifice on the cross from its benefits, as though the sacrifice were merely past while the benefits alone were present, fails to correspond with Barth's best insights. The very being of Christ was in his saving actions. Christ's sacrificial work on the cross belonged inseparably to his being as a person. His sacrificial work had no benefit that could be enjoyed apart from his person to which both the work and the benefit belonged.

Secondly, the idea that the being of Christ was in his work, and the work of Christ in his being, committed Barth to a doctrine of "re-presentation." Regardless of what one calls it (and it is not easy to find a satisfactory term), it is the actualistic idea that Christ's being in act involves a perfect work (*opere perfectus*) that is also a perpetual operation (*operatione perpetuum*).[16] The perpetual operation adds nothing new in content to the perfect work, which by definition needs no completion. Yet it belongs to the perfect work's perfection that it is not merely encapsulated in the past. On the contrary, it operates perpetually to make itself present for what

---

[16] Barth first used these terms, which he borrowed from Quenstedt, in his classroom lectures from 1924, which were posthumously published as Karl Barth, *Unterricht in der christlichen Religion* (Zurich: Theologischer Verlag Zürich, 1985), p. 148. See also Barth, *Church Dogmatics*, vol. i, part 1 (Edinburgh: T. & T. Clark, 1975), p. 427.

it is, again and again. Barth would sometimes articulate this idea in terms of Heb. 13:8: "Jesus Christ is the same yesterday and today and forever." The event of Jesus Christ, he would say, is not only "a past fact of history," but also "an event that is happening in the present here and now," as well as an event that "in its historical completeness" and "full contemporaneity" is also "truly future."[17]

The full contemporaneity of Christ's person in his work here and now, and of his work in his person, would have to take place, for Barth, primarily through Word and Sacrament. Yet it fell to T. F. Torrance, Barth's student, to make the connection that his mentor never quite managed to carry through: "The action of the Supper," wrote Torrance, "is not another action than that which Christ has already accomplished on our behalf, and which is proclaimed in the Gospel."[18] It is rather the very same action in a new and sacramental form. Ecumenical theology after Barth has every reason to exploit this insight.

It might be noted that the perpetual operation by which Christ makes himself present in and with his perfect work would seem to offer a solution to a eucharistic controversy that raged in Roman Catholic theology over the course of the twentieth century. Known as the question of the *Mysteriengegenwart der Heilstat Christi* – the mystery of the presence of Christ's saving work – it is associated with the name of Odo Casel. The Barthian view would side with Casel over against his critics, because of the way they tended to separate Christ's saving work and the event of the cross from the real presence of his person. Casel on the other hand affirmed (in at least some of his statements) the objective presence of Christ's saving work as belonging to his real presence in the liturgy. According to Jerome M. Hall, it is official Catholic teaching that Christ is present in the liturgy with his saving deeds, but that

---

[17] Barth, *Church Dogmatics*, vol. II, part 1 (Edinburgh: T. & T. Clark, 1975), p. 262.
[18] Thomas F. Torrance, *Conflict and Agreement in the Church*, vol. II (London: Lutterworth, 1960), p. 152.

nevertheless the controversy between Casel and his critics has never been adequately resolved. Neither side seemed to have a fully clear conception of the real presence of Christ's being in his act, and so of his act in his being.[19]

Finally, it may be noted that Barth's grasp of the ecumenical imperative left nothing to be desired.

> The plurality of churches ... should not be interpreted as something willed by God, as a normal unfolding of the wealth of grace given to [humankind] in Jesus Christ [nor as] a necessary trait of the visible, empirical Church, in contrast to the invisible, ideal, essential Church. Such a distinction is entirely foreign to the New Testament because, in this regard also, the Church of Jesus Christ is one. It is invisible in terms of the grace of the Word of God and of the Holy Spirit ... but visible in signs in the multitude of those who profess their adherence to her; she is visible as a community and in her community ministry, visible in her service of the word and sacrament ... It is impossible to escape from the visible Church to the invisible.
>
> If ecumenical endeavor is pursued along the lines of such a distinction, however fine the words may sound, it is philosophy of history and philosophy of society. It is not theology. People who do this are producing their own ideas in order to get rid of the question of the Church's unity, instead of facing the question posed by Christ ... If we listen to Christ, we do not exist above the differences that divide the Church: we exist in them ... In fact, we should not attempt to explain the plurality of churches at all. We should treat it as we treat our sins and those of others ... We should understand the plurality as a mark of our guilt.[20]

---

[19] See Jerome M. Hall, *We Have the Mind of Christ* (Collegeville: The Liturgical Press, 2001), pp. 1–37, esp. on p. 2.

[20] See Karl Barth, *Die Kirche und die Kirchen* (Munich: Chr. Kaiser, 1935), pp. 9–10. As quoted by Hans Urs von Balthasar, *Theo-Drama*, vol. III (San Francisco: Ignatius Press, 1992), pp. 443–44. Cf. Karl Barth, *The Church and the Churches*, (Grand Rapids: Wm. B. Eerdmans, 2005).

PART I

Real presence

1 | The bread that we break: controversies

No church should start down the road toward reunion, Hans Küng once remarked, without facing the imperative of conversion. He did not mean the conversion of one church to another, but a process that cut much deeper.

> The road to unity is not the return of one church to another, or the exodus of one church to join another, but a common crossroads, the conversion of all churches to Christ and thus to one another. Unity is not the subjection of one church to another, but the mutual regeneration and mutual acceptance of community through mutual giving and receiving.[1]

Greater mutuality among the churches through a deeper conversion to Christ, Küng believed, was the only way beyond the impasses of division. Ecclesial conversion would mean confronting significant challenges, sometimes painful, sometimes inspiring. Cherished traditions, venerable practices, hallowed institutions, and distinctive beliefs would need to be carefully scrutinized. No church should take the question of truth for granted. Here, again, Küng gave voice to the spirit of ecumenism. "All human truth," he stated, "stands in the shadow of error. All error contains at least a grain of truth. What a true statement says is true; what it fails to say may also be true. What a false statement says is false; what it means but does not say may be true."[2] Looking for the grain of

---

[1] Hans Küng, *The Church* (New York: Sheed & Ward, 1967), p. 293.
[2] Ibid., p. 343.

truth in every error, for the shadow of error in every truth, for the valid intention obscured in the false statement, and for the insight that has yet to be expressed – these are the practices necessary if the churches are to recover their visible unity in Christ.[3]

No point of division has been more disastrous than the disunity surrounding the eucharist, the very sacrament of unity itself. "The eucharist tastes bitter," declared George Lindbeck, "in a divided church."[4] If no question is more urgent, perhaps none is more intractable at the same time. The issues surrounding the eucharist not only are a morass in themselves, but also intersect with equally divisive questions about ministry, about the church, and even about the meaning of salvation. To submit that there is more actually existing unity regarding real presence than is commonly supposed (even in recent bilateral or multilateral dialogues), and that the potential for unity may be even greater still, is something that may at first seem far-fetched. Yet that is what Part I of this book would propose.

The proposal is at once descriptive and constructive. Representative figures from three ecumenical communions – the Roman Catholic, the Lutheran, and the Reformed – will first be examined. While the unity to be unearthed is far from perfect, the convergences, it will be argued, are far-reaching. Some of them will be

---

[3] The call to conversion has been echoed more recently by the Groupe des Dombes, *For the Conversion of the Churches* (Geneva: WCC Publications, 1993). "The Dombes theologians invite both Catholic and Protestant churches to the 'ecclesial conversion' they hold necessary for reconciliation ... Doctrinal change must be rooted in a conversion of attitude on each side and concretized ... in the prayer, preaching, and catechesis of each tradition." See Catherine E. Clifford, *The Groupe des Dombes: A Dialogue of Conversion* (New York: Peter Lang, 2005), pp. 146, 233. Vatican II's "Decree on Ecumenism" (*Unitatis Redintegratio*) means much the same thing when it speaks of the need for purification and renewal. See *The Documents of Vatican II*, ed. Walter M. Abbott (New York: Guild Press, America Press, Association Press, 1966), pp. 341–66.

[4] George Lindbeck, "The Eucharist Tastes Bitter in a Divided Church," *Spectrum* 19/1 (Spring 1999), pp. 1, 4–5.

actual, others merely potential. The more they are potential, the more the weight will have to fall on the constructive side of the argument.

At the center of the proposal is an analogy between the Incarnation and the eucharist. This analogy is nothing new, and is in fact a standard item in the ancient, authoritative sources of the undivided church. Moreover, it extends well into Eastern Orthodoxy today. Nevertheless, in ecumenical dialogues it has not been exploited as fully as might be wished. Like the Chalcedonian Definition, which did not stabilize the church's understanding of the Incarnation without also generating lasting dissent, the incarnational analogy will undoubtedly leave dissent in its train. But it may also lay the groundwork for a significant measure of convergence – one that may help the churches move beyond the current impasse that still dogs the question of real presence.

Real presence according to Aquinas

As a point of entry into the Roman Catholic tradition, let us begin with Thomas Aquinas. Aquinas was able to accomplish something that neither Luther nor Calvin ever quite managed. He was able to hold together, convincingly, a robust definition of "real presence" with an equally robust definition of "local presence." He was able, that is, to satisfy two conditions that are indispensable for any proposal that would hope to resolve eucharistic conflicts.

When it came to technical precision, Aquinas' affirmation of Christ's real human body in heaven – of its "local presence" – left nothing to be desired. Yet this affirmation served merely as background for the point that really mattered to him – the eucharistic presence of Christ in the reality of his body and blood. Real presence was the sacramental means by which the risen Lord drew near. "He joins us to himself in this sacrament," wrote Aquinas, "in the reality of his body and blood ... Hence this sacrament, because it joins

Christ so closely to us, is the sign of his supreme love and lifts our hope on high."[5]

Real presence, Aquinas continued, had to be kept distinct from local presence. "The body of Christ is not in this sacrament in the way a body is located in a place. The dimensions of a body in a place correspond with the dimensions of the place that contains it. Christ's body is here in a special way that is proper to this sacrament" (*ST* 3.75.1) Or again, Christ's body was in the sacrament "[not] as if it were present in the way that is natural for a body to be present, that is, visibly in its normal appearance ... [but] a spiritual, non-visible presence, in the way of a spirit and by the power of the Spirit" (*ST* 3.75.1).

Christ's bodily presence, Aquinas continued, was spiritual, and it came about only by the power of the Holy Spirit. Nevertheless, although lacking in spatial dimensions, it was also substantial. "The substance of Christ's body or of his blood is in the sacrament as a result of the sacramental sign; not so the dimensions of his body or of his blood ... The whole substance of the body and the blood of Christ is contained in this sacrament" (*ST* 3.76.1). Real presence, reiterated Aquinas, meant nothing less than substantial presence – the actual presence of Christ's body, though in a spiritual mode without dimensions. "The body of Christ is here as if it were just substance, that is, in the way that substance is under its dimensions, and not in any dimensive way ... The manner of presence is controlled by considerations of what it means to be there just as substance" (*ST* 3.76.3). Aquinas' point was that substantial presence did not require local presence, but occurred precisely without it. "The body of Christ is not under the dimensions of the bread locally ... Hence, Christ's body in this

---

[5] Thomas Aquinas, *Summa Theologiae* 3.75.1 All quotations throughout the present volume are from the Blackfriars edition (New York: McGraw-Hill Book Co., 1964–). (Hereafter cited in the text according to convention by part, question, and section.)

sacrament is in no way localized" (*ST* 3.76.5). Christ's body was, as it were, in but not of the sacrament; that is, properly speaking, it was in heaven yet also sacramentally present at the same time.

> Christ's body is not in this sacrament in the sense of being restricted to it. If that were so, it could only be on that altar where the sacrament is actually being consecrated. But it is always in heaven in its proper appearance, and it is on many other altars under its sacramental appearance ... So it does not follow that the body of Christ is in this sacrament as localized.
>
> (*ST* 3.76.6)

In his *Summa Theologiae*, Aquinas did not reach for an incarnational analogy to explain how the substance of Christ's body was related to the sacramentally consecrated bread, or his blood to the consecrated wine. When he did think about the Incarnation in relation to the eucharist, it was to establish his doctrine of concomitance. According to that teaching, "wherever the body of Christ may be, you must have the godhead with it" (*ST* 3.76.1). Concomitance thus establishes the presence of the whole Christ in the eucharist, his deity in and with his humanity. But the possibility of an analogy between two different relationships – between Christ's deity and humanity, on the one hand, and between eucharistic sign and reality, on the other – was not considered.

Instead, the analogy Aquinas drew was, rather strikingly, to the doctrine of creation. The famous doctrine of transubstantiation was conceived, it is important to see, as a miraculous change comparable only to the divine work of *creatio ex nihilo*. In fact, Aquinas noted, the extraordinary change, or *conversio*, that occurred in transubstantiation, involved "far more difficulties than does creation" (*ST* 3.75.8). For whereas creation involved "just the one difficulty that something comes from nothing"(*ST* 3.75.8), transubstantiation involved at least two difficulties. First, the substance of one entity, the consecrated element, was totally transformed into that of something else, namely, the body or the blood of Christ. The second difficulty was that nonetheless the "accidents" or appearances of the consecrated element remain even after "their substance has disappeared" (*ST* 3.75.8).[6]

For our purposes, two points are worthy of note. First, the analogy to creation could not be drawn more explicitly. "This change," Aquinas explained, "does not occur because of passive ability in the creature to be this or that, but solely through the active power of the Creator" (*ST* 3.75.8). Second, Aquinas believed that transubstantiation was the only possible way that real or substantial presence could occur in the eucharist without local presence. "There is no other way," he wrote, "in which the body of Christ can begin to be in this sacrament except through the substance of the bread being changed into it" (*ST* 3.75.3).[7] Because of this change, the body of Christ was substantially contained under the accidents of the consecrated bread.

The idea that the substance of the consecrated element did not remain, but was changed into Christ's body, became, of course, the official teaching of the Council of Trent.[8] It thus remains normative, in some strong sense, for the Roman Catholic church right down to the present day.[9] What that normative sense might be

---

[6] Several other difficulties exist as well, all thoroughly discussed by Aquinas, that need not detain us here.

[7] More recently this view has been echoed by Karl Rahner, "The Presence of Christ in the Sacrament of the Lord's Supper," in *Theological Investigations*, vol. IV (London: Darton, Longman & Todd, 1966), pp. 287–311; on p. 300.

[8] Trent, in turn, was only reaffirming the official teaching of the Roman Catholic Church, as promulgated by the Fourth Lateran Council in 1215. However, it is important to note that not until Trent was transubstantiation officially defined as involving the conversion of one "substance" into that of another – a definition taken almost word for word from Aquinas. By contrast, the Fourth Lateran Council had not mentioned "substance" but wrote only of "the bread being changed (*transubstantiatio*) by divine power into the body, and the wine into the blood." Conversion is one thing, replacement quite another. See H. J. Schroeder, *Disciplinary Decrees of the General Councils: Text, Translation and Commentary* (St. Louis: B. Herder, 1937), p. 236.

[9] "Since the dogma of transubstantiation," writes Rahner, "even in its explicit formulation, has stood for centuries in the faith of the Church, the Church would

today will be taken up later, along with the question of whether it might also be open to augmentation. In official Roman Catholic teaching, however, the idea of real or substantial presence is always inseparable from two ideas: that of sacramental conversion and that of sacramental containment.

Before moving on, a glance needs to be taken at the effect of the sacrament as Aquinas understood it. The eucharist, he noted, looked to the past, the present, and the future. Looking back to the past, it commemorated Christ's passion, and so was called a sacrifice. Looking forward to the future, it prefigured "that enjoyment of God which will be ours in heaven" (*ST* 3.73.4). And looking to the present, the eucharist established what it signified, and signified what it established, namely, the unity of the church (*ST* 3.73.4).

In particular, the sacrament led those who received it toward "spiritual perfection" by bringing them into union with Christ and so with one another (*ST* 3.73.3). In other words, for those not in a state of mortal sin, it brought an increase of grace[10] – the grace which forgave venial sins, formed habits of virtue, and led to acts of charity (*ST* 3.79.5). Grace was conferred and received according to the measure of faith and devotion in the recipient (*ST* 3.80.2). Through regular participation in the sacrament, the communicant was drawn gradually into an ever-greater conformity with Christ.

Finally, the question of efficacy can be illuminated by considering the case of reception by an unbeliever. Here Aquinas made a suitably complex judgment. Although sinners received Christ's body sacramentally, he explained, they did not receive it spiritually. Sacramental reception seems to have been objective, while spiritual reception, in turn, was subjective. Christ's body was indeed given and eaten objectively, under the species of the consecrated bread,

---

have had to deny its own being, as it understood itself to be, if it gave up this doctrine." Rahner, "The Presence of Christ," p. 297 (*supra* n. 7).

[10] "In this sacrament, however, grace is increased and the life of the spirit perfected and made whole by union with God." Aquinas, *ST* 3.79.1.

but it brought no spiritual benefit, and indeed, tended only to destruction. In the absence of faith the body of Christ could be received and eaten only improperly, and in a sense was not eaten at all (*ST* 3.80.3). But with faith (understood as assent to the articles of belief), and especially with devotion, Christ himself was received and his health-giving virtue was conferred, both sacramentally and spiritually, under the species of the bread and the wine (*ST* 3.80.5).

Real presence according to Luther

In contrast to Aquinas and Calvin, it was Luther who set forth the incarnational analogy. In doing so he retrieved a long-standing patristic tradition that had gradually fallen into eclipse. For Luther the analogy functioned as an alternative to the doctrine of transubstantiation. In *The Babylonian Captivity of the Church*, he wrote:

> Thus, what is true in regard to Christ is also true in regard to the sacrament. In order for the divine nature to dwell in him bodily [Col. 2:9], it is not necessary for the human nature to be transubstantiated and the divine nature contained under the accidents of the human nature. Both natures are simply there in their entirety, and it is truly said: "This man is God; this God is man." Even though philosophy cannot grasp this, faith grasps it nonetheless. And the authority of God's Word is greater than the capacity of our intellect to grasp it. In like manner, it is not necessary in the sacrament that the bread and wine be transubstantiated and that Christ be contained under their accidents in order that the real body and real blood may be present. But both remain there at the same time, and it is truly said, "This bread is my body; this wine is my blood," and vice versa.[11]

[11] Martin Luther, *The Babylonian Captivity of the Church*, in *Luther's Works*, American Edition, vol. 36 (Philadelphia: Fortress Press, 1959), p. 35. (Works from this series hereafter cited in the text as *LW*.)

Luther based the analogy, in part, on an interpretation of 1 Cor. 10:16: "The bread that we break, is it not a [participation]" – the Greek word is *koinonia* – "in the body of Christ?"[12] According to this verse, as Luther read it, the relationship of the body of Christ to the eucharistic bread was one of participation or *koinonia*.

The formal pattern in the analogy thus consisted of two terms and a relationship. As in the Incarnation, so also in the eucharist, the relationship was one of participation or *koinonia* – a relationship that hinged on the mystery of mutual indwelling. Just as the divine nature dwelt in Christ bodily, so also did his life-giving flesh come to dwell, so to speak, in the consecrated bread, and vice versa. Regardless of whether reason could understand it, both entities in the relation were simply there in their entirety. Consequently, just as one could point to the human Jesus and say without equivocation, "This man is the Lord," so also could one take the consecrated bread and say without equivocation, "This is the body of Christ." The predications were true by participation, and for Luther the idea of participation invalidated the idea that one substance was transformed into another. Real presence meant that Christ's life-giving flesh was substantially present in, with, and under the bread, whose substance remained that of bread.

Unfortunately, Luther did not exploit the incarnational analogy he had revived. Instead, he relied more heavily on two other arguments. The one we might call the argument from literalism, the other the argument from ubiquity. Let us take up the ubiquity argument first.

Although Luther never denied the idea of local presence, as it had been so carefully defined, for example, by Aquinas, his argument from ubiquity understandably undermined the confidence of his opponents in the Reformed theological camp. However, the Reformed never appreciated that Luther attributed no more to ubiquity than secondary importance. For him it

---

[12] Ibid., p. 34.

was no more than a kind of background belief designed to show that real presence was not, as some had supposed, impossible. Luther's ubiquity argument was that if Christ is seated at God's right hand, and if God's right hand is a metaphor for God's power, and if God's power is ubiquitous, then Christ's body is also ubiquitous. Real presence, therefore, was not impossible.

To the Reformed, however, it looked as though the Lutheran position boiled down to the alarming error that Christ's body was locally present in the eucharist, yet no more than substantially present in heaven. "Tell me," Zwingli asked at the Marburg Colloquy, "is the body of Christ in a place?" To which the Lutheran Brenz retorted: "It is without place."[13] Luther, to my knowledge, never made such an unqualified statement. When Zwingli insisted, "Christ is finite as we are finite," Luther replied, "I admit that."[14] It seems fair to say that in the highly charged atmosphere of those years, the Lutherans were so concerned to assert real presence in the eucharist that the idea of local presence in heaven, so important to the Reformed, suffered by comparison. The Lutherans had a robust doctrine of real presence but, in contrast to someone like Aquinas, not an equally robust doctrine of local presence.

And yet the account cannot rest there. In a little-known proposal drafted hurriedly by Luther just before the Marburg Colloquy dissolved, the makings of an adequate solution were set forth. The sentence, "This is my body," Luther proposed, meant that Christ's body was present in the eucharist truly but not locally. "Truly" meant "substantively and essentially," he explained, while "not locally" meant "not according to ordinary qualities" and "not quantitatively." The Reformed were asked to affirm real presence

---

[13] Quoted in Hermann Sasse, *This Is My Body* (Philadelphia: Fortress Press, 1959), pp. 261–62.

[14] Ibid., p. 256.

on these terms, while the Lutherans would reject local presence with respect to the eucharist.[15]

Luther's last-minute proposal rose nearly to the level of Aquinas. While it lacked the latter's careful analytical precision, and made no mention of local presence in heaven, it nonetheless brought a degree of clarity to the Marburg Colloquy that had not been previously attained. Unfortunately, the proposal was rejected by the Reformed and immediately discarded, apparently even by a figure like Bucer, who had himself been present at Marburg, and who persisted long afterwards in striving for reconciliation, as if Luther's proposal had never been made or its wording was unknown.

In the "Wittenberg Concord" of 1536,[16] however, Bucer went on to adopt the important term "sacramental union" from Luther.[17] Three items were rejected: an essential change in the elements, local presence in the eucharist, and permanent union apart from use. It was affirmed that "through sacramental union the bread is the body of Christ," and that "the unworthy also eat." The Lutherans did not insist on a statement that Christ's flesh was

---

[15] Ibid., pp. 266–67.

[16] Though sometimes attributed to Bucer, the document was actually drafted by Melanchthon in collaboration with Bucer. It was mainly Bucer who managed to gain its acceptance by Wittenberg and Southern Germany. See Randall Zachman, *John Calvin as Teacher, Pastor, and Theologian* (Grand Rapids: Baker Academic, 2006), pp. 25, 31–33; Ernst Bizer, *Studien zur Geschichte des Abendmahlsstreits im 16. Jahrhundert* (Darmstadt: Wissenschaftliche Buchgesellschaft, 1962).

[17] Luther had introduced the term in his 1528 "Confession Concerning Christ's Supper": "Why then should we not much more say in the Supper, 'This is my body,' even though bread and body are two distinct substances, and the word 'this' indicates the bread? Here, too, out of two kinds of objects a union has taken place, which I shall call a 'sacramental union,' because Christ's body and the bread are given to us as a sacrament. This is not a natural or personal union, as is the case with God and Christ. It is also perhaps a different union from that which the dove has with the Holy Spirit, and the flame with the angel, but it is also assuredly a sacramental union" (*LW* 37, pp. 299–300).

eaten even by open unbelievers, and the Reformed forewent an avowal that the sacrament was essentially a memorial.[18]

The Wittenberg Concord, whose continuing ecumenical significance should not be underestimated, was signed by Luther, Melanchthon, Musculus, and Bucer, while also being accepted later by Calvin. Agreement had thus been reached among the key cities of Wittenberg, Augsburg, Strasbourg, and Geneva. For a full evangelical consensus, it remained only to bring Zurich into the fold. After Bucer and Capito were unsuccessful, it fell to Calvin to gain acceptance for something like the Wittenberg Concord among the Swiss. His efforts came to naught when the "Zurich Consensus" (1549), which he hammered out with Bullinger, met with fierce rejection by some Lutherans and, perhaps most bitterly, silence from Melanchthon.[19]

What Luther wanted more than anything else was to take seriously Christ's statement, "This is my body." Although it is often said that Luther interpreted this statement "literally," it would be better to say that he interpreted it "realistically." For he explicitly described the statement as a synecdoche.[20] While Luther wanted to rely on the words of Christ and nothing else, he knew that Christ's flesh was not literally present in the eucharist, as he

---

[18] The most important part of the Wittenberg Concord is included in the "Solid Declaration" of the Lutheran "Formula of Concord," thus giving it a kind of Lutheran confessional status. See *The Book of Concord*, ed. Theodore G. Tappert (Philadelphia: Fortress Press, 1959), pp. 571–72. For background, see Zachman, *John Calvin*, pp. 25, 32–36 (*supra* n. 16); Hastings Eells, *Martin Bucer* (New Haven: Yale University Press, 1931), pp. 191–204; Martin Greschat, *Martin Bucer* (Louisville: Westminster/John Knox Press, 2004), pp. 132–42. For a detailed account of its history and reception, see Bizer, *Studien* (*supra* n. 16); Walther Köhler, *Zwingli und Luther*, vol. II (Gütersloh: C. Bertelsmann Verlag, 1953), pp. 432–525.

[19] See Zachman, *John Calvin*, pp. 26, 49–51. On the "Zurich Consensus," see Paul Rorem, *Calvin and Bullinger on the Lord's Supper* (Bramcote: Grove Books Ltd, 1989).

[20] The term "synecdoche," as used by Luther, was later adopted in the "Apology of the Formula of Concord" (1583). This acceptance had been anticipated in the "Formula of Concord" (1577). See *The Book of Concord*, p. 576 n. 1 (*supra* n. 18).

once colorfully put it, like pork on a plate. According to Luther, synecdoche was a figure of speech such that when two realities were present so that the one was contained in the other, either could be used to refer to the other. The statement, "This is my body," was a synecdoche, because the word "bread" was used to refer to the body, yet the bread that did the containing was not identical with the body it contained, and vice versa. Together they formed a unity-in-distinction, with the emphasis falling on their unity.[21]

The efficacy of the eucharist, according to Luther, was no different from that of the Word, because the content imparted by both was identical. For Luther the eucharist was a particular form of God's Word, not something independent of or alongside it. "The same thing is present in the sermon," he stated, "as in the sacrament" (*LW* 36, p. 348). "The sacraments ... contain nothing but God's words, promises and signs" (*LW* 42, p. 109). As a visible form of the Word, the eucharist testified concretely that Christ came also for the communicant in particular (*pro me*). It gave "a sure sign" that "Christ's death overcame my death in his death, that his obedience blotted out my sin in his suffering, that his love destroyed my hell in his forsakenness" (*LW* 42, p. 109).

What finally made the substance of the Word and the eucharist identical, according to Luther, was that each imparted "the entire Christ."[22] Christ himself was mediated no less through the Word than through the sacrament. The Word of God, explained Luther, always "brings with it everything of which it speaks, namely, Christ with his flesh and blood and everything that he has and is" (*LW* 36, p. 278). Christ "has put himself into the Word," he continued, "and through the Word he puts himself into the bread [and wine] also" (*LW* 36, p. 343). Christ's real presence in the eucharist was thus a special form of his presence in the Word. Just as Christ was

---

[21] Ibid., pp. 163, 254.
[22] Luther, "The Large Catechism," in *The Book of Concord*, p. 442.

imparted through the Word, so was he also imparted, though in a different form, "corporeally in the bread and wine" (LW 36, p. 343).

Since Christ had only one body, Luther reasoned, it was the body that was born of the Virgin Mary and that had suffered on the cross that was made present in the eucharist. Luther followed the medieval tradition, as seen, for example, in Aquinas, to this extent: while rejecting the idea of conversion as transubstantiation, he retained the idea of containment. In the eucharist the body of Christ appeared in the form of bread. It could not be eaten spiritually without also being eaten physically at the same time. Yet even this physical eating was somehow distinctively spiritual, since the substance of Christ's flesh could not be "cut into pieces, divided, chewed, digested, consumed and destroyed" (LW 37, p. 130). While all who participated, whether believers or impious, received Christ's flesh in the form of bread, faith (understood as *fiducia* more than *assensus*) was always necessary if Christ was to be eaten and received spiritually (LW 37, p. 132). "As we eat him," wrote Luther, "he abides in us and we in him. For he is not digested or transformed but ceaselessly he transforms us, our soul into righteousness, our body into eternal life" (LW 37, p. 132). Through their eucharistic union with Christ, believers were transformed as whole persons, body and soul, that they might dwell with him and he with them to all eternity.

Real presence according to Calvin and Vermigli

Whereas Aquinas had upheld a robust distinction between real and local presence, and Luther had retrieved the incarnational analogy, Calvin made a contribution at a different point. First, he assigned to the Holy Spirit a more prominent role in the eucharist than had usually been common (in the West); and second, he introduced into the discussion what might be called the upward vector. That is, whereas theologians like Aquinas and Luther, and the traditions they represented, had thought primarily of a movement from heaven to earth, Calvin introduced the complementary idea of a movement from earth to heaven. For Calvin, the Holy Spirit served as the mediator of communion between heaven and earth. By the Spirit's ineffable operation, not only was Christ made really present to believers in the eucharist, but at the same time they were made really present to him in heaven.

The mediation of the Spirit was, in effect, Calvin's alternative to Luther's idiosyncratic doctrine of ubiquity. Like Aquinas, and like the entire Reformed theological camp, Calvin was profoundly concerned not to undermine the idea of the risen Christ's possessing a real, and therefore finite, human body. Also like Aquinas, Calvin sought a way to affirm the real presence of Christ in the eucharist without jeopardizing Christ's local presence in heaven. Unlike both Aquinas and Luther, however, Calvin distanced himself from the notion of containment. He agreed that real presence meant substantial presence, but disagreed that substantial presence meant containment; in other words, that Christ's body was contained in the bread. Whether Calvin rejected this idea categorically, however, or only under a certain aspect, is not easy to decide.

For Calvin, as for almost all the Reformed, the idea of containment veered too close to the idea of local eucharistic presence. In effect Calvin argued not so much that Christ's body was in the bread as that the bread was the instrument by which the Spirit presented and imparted the life-giving flesh of Christ to faith. Calvin's resort to the upward vector was closely related to his fear that containment meant local presence.

> But greatly mistaken [he wrote] are those who conceive no presence of flesh in the Supper unless it lies in the bread. For thus they leave nothing to the secret working of the Spirit, which unites Christ himself to us. To them Christ does not seem to be present unless he comes down to us. As though, if he should lift us to

himself, we should not just as much enjoy his presence! The question is therefore only of the manner, for they place Christ in the bread, while we do not think it lawful to drag him down from heaven ... Since this mystery is heavenly, there is no need to draw Christ to earth that he may be joined to us. (*Inst.* IV.17.31)[23]

At the moment of distribution, according to Calvin, the body of Christ was exhibited and offered to the recipient "with" the bread, although sometimes he could also say "in" and "through" it as well. The bread was therefore not an empty sign. In the act of reception, however, the bread alone was in the mouth, while the life-giving flesh of Christ, and so Christ in person himself, entered into the believer's heart by faith. The believer carried away from the eucharist no more than he or she collected with the vessel of faith (*Inst.* IV.17.33). Those without faith were like an empty bottle that cannot be filled with liquid as long as it is corked and sealed.[24] In other words, while the impious may receive the bread, they receive nothing of Christ's life-giving flesh.[25]

Like Luther, Calvin believed that the content of the gospel and that of the eucharist were the same – the living Christ himself – differing only in their forms of presentation and reception, and therefore, to some extent, in their function. Roughly speaking, while the gospel's function was to awaken faith and instruct it, the eucharist was designed to nourish faith and renew it. The eucharist had to be seen, Calvin believed, within the larger context of the gospel. That meant within the context of our union with Christ, or *participatio Christi*, as established by the Holy Spirit through faith.

---

[23] John Calvin, *Institutes of the Christian Religion*, ed. John T. McNeill, tr. Ford Lewis Battles (Philadelphia: Westminster, 1960). (Hereafter cited from this edition in the text.)

[24] Calvin, "Confession of Faith in the Name of the Reformed Churches of France," in *Tracts and Treatises*, vol. II, ed. Henry Beveridge (Grand Rapids: Baker Book House, 1983), p. 158.

[25] I owe the previous two citations to Brian Gerrish, *Grace and Gratitude* (Minneapolis: Fortress Press, 1993), p. 161 n. 10.

As in Aquinas and Luther, the main point of the eucharist for Calvin was union and communion with Christ:

> The Lord bestows this benefit upon us through his Spirit, so that we may be made one in body, spirit, and soul with him. The bond of this connection is therefore the Spirit of Christ, with whom we are joined in unity, and is like a channel through which all that Christ himself is and has is conveyed to us. For if we see that the sun, shedding its beams upon the earth, casts its substance in some measure upon it in order to beget, nourish, and give warmth to its offspring – why should the radiance of Christ's Spirit be less in order to impart to us the communion of his flesh and blood? On this account, Scripture, in speaking of our participation with Christ, relates its whole power to the Spirit. But one passage will suffice for many. For Paul, in the eighth chapter of Romans, states that Christ dwells in us only through his Spirit [Rom. 8:9]. Yet he does not take away that communion of his flesh and blood which we are now discussing [Rom. 8:9], but teaches that the Spirit alone causes us to possess Christ completely and have him dwelling in us.
>
> (*Inst.* IV.17.12)

Although Calvin has been criticized for identifying the "substance" of Christ's flesh with its life-giving virtue or power, no great difference would seem evident in this respect between Calvin and Aquinas, both of whom could use the terms "substance" and "virtue" interchangeably. Regardless of whether they had exactly the same definitions for these terms, the similarities seem more important than any differences. Calvin did not use the term "substance" in the technical sense of a substratum that could be detached from its accidents, or to indicate corporeal reality in the merely physical sense. For him "substance" meant something like an entity's fundamental reality or power.[26] Calvin clearly intended

---

[26] See Helmut Gollwitzer, *Coena Domini* (Munich: Chr. Kaiser Verlag, 1937), pp. 120–25; Max Thurian, *The Eucharistic Memorial*, vol. II (London: Lutterworth, 1961), p. 111.

to affirm not only the real presence but also real reception of Christ's life-giving flesh in the eucharist.

> The same body which Christ has offered as a sacrifice is extended in the Supper.
>
> (*Inst.* IV.17.34)

> In short, he feeds his people with his own body, the communion of which he bestows upon them by the power of his Spirit.
>
> (*Inst.* IV.17.18)

> I freely accept whatever can be made to express the true and substantial partaking of the body and blood of the Lord, which is shown to believers under the sacred symbols of the Supper.
>
> (*Inst.* IV.17.19)

It seems fair to say that Calvin agreed in principle with Aquinas and Luther on the fact of real and objective presence, but disagreed with them about the modes of presence and reception. For Calvin, unlike Aquinas and Luther, reception took place, as has been noted, by faith alone, not also orally by the mouth. Reminiscent of Luther, however, Calvin at least hinted at the possibility of an incarnational analogy. Yet where Luther's christological sensibilities were Alexandrian, Calvin's were more Antiochian. In describing how he thought Christ's body was related to the eucharistic bread, Calvin was fond of using the formula "distinction without separation" – a clear allusion to Chalcedon.[27] As in christology, so also with the

---

[27] As pointed out by Gerrish, p. 137 n. 41. Although Calvin was aware of the term "sacramental union," he did not use it apart from polemical contexts. See, for example, John Calvin, *A Harmony of the Gospels*, vol. III (*Comm. on* Matt. 26:26 and par.) (Grand Rapids: Wm. B. Eerdmans, 1972), p. 135; and Calvin, "The True Partaking of the Flesh and Blood of Christ in the Holy Supper," in *Tracts and Treatises*, vol. II, p. 559. Like most of the Swiss, he was so skittish about local presence in the eucharist that he would not "place Christ in the bread" (*Inst.* IV.17.31). But he meant this stricture against a crude local enclosing or a carnal infusing, which none but perhaps extreme Lutherans like Westphal had ever

incarnational analogy, Calvin seemed to differ from Luther in emphasis, but not in principle. Where Luther stressed the inseparable unity, Calvin affirmed the abiding distinction. Yet with respect to affirming the Incarnation, both theologians arguably fell, despite their differing emphases, within the bounds of Chalcedonian orthodoxy. If we were to subject the incarnational analogy to a Chalcedonian interpretation, might not the same be said of their views of the eucharist as well?

Within the Reformed tradition the incarnational analogy found perhaps its strongest representative not in Calvin, but in his friend and correspondent Peter Martyr Vermigli. An unjustly neglected figure, Vermigli emerges as a weighty thinker whose ideas today seem full of ecumenical promise. Calvin went so far as to state of him that "the whole [doctrine of the eucharist] was crowned by Peter Martyr, who left nothing more to be done."[28]

Vermigli developed the incarnational analogy in an extremely suggestive way.[29] In particular, without losing the distinctive Reformed concern about local presence, he suggested how the idea of *conversio,* so important to Aquinas, and the idea of participation, so important to Luther, might be combined. Since the history of the eucharistic controversies is arguably a history of false alternatives, the potential advance here was considerable.

suggested. Significantly, the term was eventually adopted by the Westminster Confession of Faith in 1646: "There is, in every sacrament, a spiritual relation, or sacramental union, between the sign and the thing signified: whence it comes to pass, that the names and effects of the one are attributed to the other" (ch. 27, "Of the Sacraments").

[28] Calvin, "True Partaking of the Flesh and Blood of Christ in the Holy Supper," in *Selected Works of John Calvin: Tracts and Letters*, vol. II (Grand Rapids: Baker Book House, 1983), p. 535. Quoted by Frank A. James, "*Nunc Peregrinus Oberrat*: Peter Martyr in Context," in *Peter Martyr Vermigli and the European Reformations: Semper Reformanda*, ed. Frank A. James (Leiden: Brill, 2004), p. xxiii.

[29] See Nick Needham, "Peter Martyr and the Eucharistic Controversy," *Scottish Bulletin of Evangelical Theology* 17 (1999), pp. 5–25.

Vermigli, it might be said, retained Calvin's focus on the eucharistic role of the Holy Spirit, while upgrading his view of the incarnational analogy. The sacrament was not so much a "means of grace," he taught, as an "instrument of the Spirit."[30] By means of the consecrated elements, the Spirit united the communicants to Christ and Christ to them. The primary union and communion in the eucharist were always between Christ and the communicants, not between Christ and the elements. As instruments by which that communion was actualized, however, the elements were by no means empty signs.

Like Luther, Vermigli posited an incarnational analogy between "the bread that we break" and Christ's life-giving flesh. A careful thinker, he realized that this analogy could be no more than an analogy. The sacramental union, as he called it, between the eucharistic bread and Christ's flesh was not, and could not possibly be, a hypostatic union. For one thing, the eucharistic union was between two realities that were creatures (bread and flesh), not, as in the Incarnation, between a divine reality and a human. For another thing, the union, once formed, was of limited duration, not perpetual. With such qualifications as these in mind, however, the Chalcedonian pattern might be applied. The eucharistic bread and the life-giving flesh were brought together by the Spirit to form a unity-in-distinction. They were related without separation or division and without confusion or change. That was their formal relation.

Materially, on the other hand, the word that Vermigli used for this relation was the carefully chosen but rather inelegant term "transelementation."[31] Transelementation meant that the bread

---

[30] Peter Martyr Vermigli, *The Oxford Treatise and Disputation, On the Eucharist, 1549*, ed. Joseph C. McLelland (Kirksville: Truman State University Press, 2000), p. 93. (Hereafter cited in the text.) Calvin could also speak of the sacraments as "instruments of the Spirit." For examples, see Ronald S. Wallace, *Calvin's Doctrine of Word and Sacrament* (Edinburgh: Oliver & Boyd Ltd, 1953), p. 170.

[31] Ibid., pp. 90–91, 218. For a discussion of transelementation in Vermigli, see Joseph C. McLelland, *The Visible Words of God* (Edinburgh: Oliver & Boyd, 1957), pp. 132, 164–68, 193–96.

itself was transformed by virtue of its sacramental union with, and participation in, Christ's flesh. Vermigli retrieved this term for the eucharist, drawing upon an ancient image that went back to Gregory of Nazianzus and Cyril of Alexandria, who had themselves applied it to both the eucharist and the Incarnation. Vermigli, however, did not seem to be aware of these early precedents. He referred instead to a relatively obscure figure named Theophylact, Archbishop of Bulgaria (eleventh century), from whom he apparently learned of the term.[32]

The image which illustrated transelementation was that of an iron rod thrust into the fire.[33] Just as the iron was transformed by its participation in the fire, so was the consecrated element transformed by its sacramental union with Christ's flesh. In and with this transforming union, the distinction between the two was maintained. Just as the iron did not cease to be iron, or the fire fire, so did the bread not cease to be bread, or Christ's flesh his flesh. In the mystery of their sacramental union they formed a unique distinction-in-unity and unity-in-distinction.[34]

---

[32] Steven Runciman describes Theophylact as being, like Anselm, "one of the most distinguished scholars of his time ... Unfortunately for him, his friend the Patriarch Nicholas III, who had a high regard for his abilities, appointed him to take over the administration of the Bulgarian Church. It was an important post, but it obliged him to move to a little town in the depths of Macedonia; and there he remained for the rest of his life, wistfully regretting the libraries and the lecture-rooms of the capital and writing innumerable letters to his many friends." See Runciman, *The Eastern Schism* (Oxford: Clarendon Press, 1953, 1997), p. 72.

[33] Interestingly, Vermigli associated this image not with Theophylact but with Lutheran teaching; see Vermigli, *Oxford Treatise*, p. 107 (*supra* n. 30).

[34] According to Hermann Sasse, "Gregory of Nazianzus was the first to use the simile of iron and fire to illustrate the relationship of the two natures [of Christ] (which later was used to explain the relationship between the bread and the body in the sacrament)" (*This Is My Body*, p. 150 n. 34 [*supra* n. 13]). For Cyril of Alexandria, see Steven A. McKinnon, *Words, Imagery, and the Mystery of Christ* (Leiden: Brill, 2000), pp. 207–12.

On these grounds Vermigli was prepared to admit real sacramental conversion and the objective presence of Christ's life-giving flesh:[35]

> We admit Theophlyact's terms changing, transforming, and transelementing, because of the sacramental change. Where he affirms that the bread sanctified upon the altar is the body of Christ, we allow it. For it is proved by Augustine to Boniface that the sacrament of the body of Christ in a way both is and is called the body of Christ ... it is transformed by an ineffable operation ... Doubtless it is the kind of inexpressible work that the Holy Spirit performs.[36]

> I don't deny that the body of Christ is given in some way: what is given is both; namely, bread and Christ's body.[37]

Vermigli was not the only Reformed theologian to cast a favorable eye toward Theophylact and transelementation. Similar judgments are on record from Martin Bucer and Thomas Cranmer. It is not unlikely that their statements reflect Vermigli's influence.

Bucer could endorse eucharistic conversion with reference to the idea of transelementation.

> Certainly the Holy Fathers understood ... no other change in the elements than one by which the bread and wine ... in the permanence ... of their natural characteristics, were changed from their usual and ordinary use and were, as we might say, "transelemented" so that they became symbols of the body and blood and thus of the whole Christ.[38]

---

[35] For the complexities in how Vermigli regarded Christ's bodily presence in the elements, see John Patrick Donnelly, "Christological Currents in Vermigli's Thought," in *Vermigli and the European Reformations*, pp. 177–96; on 178–79.

[36] Vermigli, *Oxford Treatise*, p. 218 (*supra* n. 30).   [37] Ibid., p. 215.

[38] Martin Bucer, *Censura*, in *Martin Bucer and the Book of Common Prayer*, ed. E. C. Whitiker (Great Wakering: Mayhew-McCrimmon, 1974), p. 56.

Bucer elsewhere stated that the elements of bread and wine were converted "into the substance of [Christ's] body and blood by his word," without losing their natural properties, through a kind of "transelementation."[39] What troubled Bucer was not that the bread and wine should be converted into the substance of Christ's body and blood, but that they should lose their natural properties in the process. Once the latter point was clarified for him, he could endorse the idea that the elements were substantially converted into the reality they signified.

The image that conveyed the idea of transelementation was known and approved by Cranmer:

> As hot and burning iron is iron still, and yet hath the force of fire; and as the flesh of Christ, still remaining flesh, giveth life, as the flesh of him that is God; so the sacramental bread and wine remain still in their proper kinds; and yet to them that worthily eat and drink them, they be turned not into the corporeal presence, but into the virtue of Christ's flesh and blood.[40]

Noting that he learned this imagery from Theophylact, Cranmer continued:

> And although Theophylactus spake of the eating of the very blood of Christ, and the drinking of his very blood ... calling the bread not only a figure, but also the body of Christ, giving us by those words to understand, that in the sacrament we do not only eat corporally the bread, which is a sacrament and figure of Christ's body; but spiritually we eat also his body, and drink his very blood. And this doctrine of Theophylactus is both true, godly and comfortable.[41]

---

[39] See Nicholas Thompson, *Eucharistic Sacrifice and Patristic Tradition in the Theology of Martin Bucer, 1534–1546* (Leiden: Brill, 2005), pp. 240–41.

[40] Thomas Cranmer, "A Defence of the True and Catholic Doctrine of the Sacrament of the Body and Blood of Our Saviour Christ," in *The Work of Thomas Cranmer*, ed. G. E. Duffield (Philadelphia: Fortress Press, 1965), p. 187.

[41] Ibid.

In another passage, this time with reference to Cyprian, Cranmer again seems to affirm, though not without ambiguities, both the incarnational analogy and eucharistic conversion:

> Which words of Cyprian do manifestly show ... that sacramentally the divinity is poured into the bread and wine, the same bread and wine still remaining: like as the same divinity by unity of person was in the humanity of Christ, the same humanity still remaining with the divinity [the incarnational analogy].
>
> And yet the bread is changed, not in shape, nor substance, but in nature, as Cyprian truly saith, not meaning that the natural substance of the bread is clean gone, but that by God's word there is added thereto another higher property, nature, and condition, far passing the nature and condition of common bread ... so that now the said mystical bread is both a corporal food for the body, and a spiritual food for the soul [eucharistic conversion along the lines of transelementation].[42]

What makes the passage ambiguous are the words omitted by the second ellipsis: "that is to say, that the bread doth show unto us, as the same Cyprian saith, that we be partakers of the Spirit of God, and most purely joined unto Christ, and spiritually fed with his flesh and blood."[43] Elsewhere he could describe eucharistic conversion as no more than a change in use.[44] At points like these, it seems better to chart the tensions in Cranmer's theology than merely to resolve them one way or another, as is often done by modern interpreters. What he meant by "spiritual" in eucharistic contexts is not a simple matter. Wanting to exclude "transubstantiation" while still allowing for "true" or "real" presence, he seems to have lacked the technical apparatus he needed to state his mind without ambiguity.

Like Bucer, Cranmer could sometimes endorse a strong view of eucharistic conversion as long as it did not entail the idea that the

---

[42] Ibid., p. 108.   [43] Ibid.   [44] Ibid., p. 181.

sacramental bread and wine lost their "proper kind" in the process. The bread and wine, though not crudely corporeal, were turned into the "virtue" of Christ's flesh and blood.

The ancient image could also be used by Luther.

> And why could not Christ include his body in the substance of the bread just as well as in the accidents? In red-hot iron, for instance, the two substances, fire and iron, are so mingled that every part is both iron and fire. Why is it not even more possible that the body of Christ be contained in every part of the substance of the bread? (*LW* 36, p. 29).[45]

Zwingli rebuffed Luther for taking this image from the Incarnation and applying it to the eucharist. Referring to patristic theologians who had used it as an analogy for the two natures of Christ, Zwingli attacked: "This metaphor you took from them if you confess it. If you deny it, you pilfered it and twisted it to support the notion of the flesh in the bread, Luther."[46] Zwingli was evidently unaware that the image had been used by patristic writers for the eucharist as well.

The Reformed interest in Theophylact and transelementation should not be pressed too far. The point is not that Vermigli, Bucer, and Cranmer integrated this understanding of sacramental conversion systematically into their doctrines of the eucharist. They did not. The point is that they clearly found nothing objectionable in it. They did not see it as contradicting their fundamental theological convictions. From time to time they discussed it openly and favorably. Vermigli in particular embraced it in a way that converged strongly with the historic views of

---

[45] Theophylact's view of the eucharist does not seem to have been known by Luther. It is mentioned favorably, though only in passing, in "The Apology of the Augsburg Confession," Article X. See *The Book of Concord*, p. 179.

[46] See Zwingli, "Friendly Exegesis," in *Writings of Huldrich Zwingli*, vol. II, ed. H. Wayne Pipkin (Allison Park: Pickwick Publications, 1984), p. 321.

Eastern Orthodoxy. The suggestion being made here is that this ancient view of eucharistic conversion and real presence, if embraced by Protestant churches today, would be fraught with ecumenical significance.[47]

---

[47] The patristic idea of transelementation is noted favorably by T. F. Torrance in *Theology in Reconciliation* (Grand Rapids: Wm. B. Eerdmans, 1975), p. 162. See also Iain R. Torrance, *Christology After Chalcedon* (Norwich: Canterbury Press, 1988), p. 77.

2 | The iron in the fire: a proposal

A proposal for resolving ecumenical controversies about sacramental conversion and real presence can now be developed under six captions: mode of bodily presence, mode of rhetoric, mode of reception, mode of conversion, mode of duration, and mode of consecration. The first three involve suggestions primarily for non-Catholics, with special attention to the Reformed tradition. The second three address the possibility that the views of Catholics and non-Catholics could be diverse without being church-dividing.

Mode of bodily presence

Following Aquinas and others, any viable ecumenical resolution would need to affirm that no real presence of Christ's body occurs in the eucharist at the expense of its local presence in heaven. Conversely, no local presence of his body in heaven could be admitted that would prohibit its real presence in the eucharist. For a position to be ecumenically viable, both modes of bodily presence – real in the eucharist and local in heaven – would need to be upheld at the same time. None of the four major traditions examined – Roman Catholic, Lutheran, Reformed, and Eastern Orthodox – would deny what this assertion intends, though the Reformed, especially the more Zwinglian, might have the most problems with parts of it.[1]

[1] The local presence of Christ's body in heaven was affirmed in the East as well as in the West. See Jaroslav Pelikan, *The Spirit of Eastern Christendom* (600–1700)

The idea of "local presence in heaven" is ecumenically mandatory. Whatever it might mean, the integrity of Christ's humanity, and therefore of his human body, cannot be defined out of existence in its final, glorified state. Moreover, whatever "real, substantial presence" might mean, it cannot be conceived in such a way that Christ's "local presence in heaven" would be undermined.

In principle the idea of "local presence in heaven" was generally understood as involving some form of analogical discourse. What was crucial was that in his ascended and glorified state, Christ not be thought to lose the defining properties of his human nature. The position sometimes taken on "ubiquity" – that Christ's body in heaven is ubiquitous, because heaven is as ubiquitous as God himself – does nothing to address this concern. The Lutheran idea that Christ's human body is "ubiquitous" and the Zwinglian idea of Christ's "disembodied" spiritual presence, though extreme polar opposites, are in some ways reverse mirror images of one another.

As Reformed theologians, Calvin, Vermigli, Bucer, and Cranmer all stood with the broad ecumenical consensus that "real, substantial presence" is, in some sense, inalienable from the mystery of the eucharist.

Although historic Reformed confessions naturally reflect the polemics and limitations of their times, openings in the direction of real substantial presence are evident in the following excerpts:

> The French Confession of 1559:
> Although he is in heaven until he comes to judge the world, we believe that he gives us life and nourishes us with the substance of his body and blood. This takes place in the unfathomable and incomprehensible power of his Spirit.[2]

(Chicago: University of Chicago Press, 1974), p. 47. Examples are given by Darwell Stone, *A History of the Doctrine of the Holy Eucharist*, vol. I (New York: Longmans, Green, & Co., 1909), pp. 138, 177, 179.

[2] *The French Confession of 1559*, ed. Joseph D. Small (Louisville: The Presbyterian Church USA, 1998), p. 16.

The Scots Confession of 1560:
Notwithstanding the distance between his glorified body in heaven and mortal [humanity] on earth, yet we must assuredly believe that the bread that we break is the communion of Christ's body and the cup which we bless the communion of his blood. Thus we confess and believe without doubt that the faithful ... eat the body and drink the blood of the Lord Jesus.[3]

The Heidelberg Catechism of 1563:
His crucified body and blood are the true food and drink of our souls for eternal life ... We come to share in his body and blood through the working of the Holy Spirit.[4]

The Second Helvetic Confession of 1566:
... the flesh and blood of Christ are the food and drink of the faithful, and are received by the faithful unto eternal life.[5]

The Belgic Confession of 1618:
Truly we receive into our souls, for our spiritual life, the true body and true blood of Christ, our only Savior.[6]

The Westminster Larger Catechism of 1648:
They that worthily communicate feed upon his body and blood, to their spiritual nourishment and growth in grace.[7]

These excerpts are not meant to represent the documents in their full tenor and content. A moment's notice will show that much countervailing material has been left out. Only the French Confession, under the strong influence of Calvin, goes so far as to

[3] *The Scots Confession of 1560*, ed. G. D. Henderson (Edinburgh: Saint Andrew Press, 1960), p. 75.
[4] The Heidelberg Catechism in Philip Schaff, *The Creeds of Christendom*, vol. III (New York: Harper & Row, 1931), pp. 334–35.
[5] The Second Helvetic Confession in ibid., p. 892.
[6] The Belgic Confession in ibid., p. 429.
[7] The Westminster Larger Catechism, in *The Book of Confessions* (Louisville: The Presbyterian Church USA, 1999), pp. 223–24.

include the disputed term "substance." Yet even in a tradition not noted for its openness to affirming real presence, a consistent recognition is evident that, in some sense, Christ's body and blood are made available and received in the sacrament.[8] The Reformed did not wish to deny real presence absolutely. But they could affirm it only insofar as it seemed compatible with Christ's integral human body in its heavenly state.

In more recent times the larger Reformed and Lutheran churches in the USA have adopted "A Formula of Agreement" (1997),[9] allowing them to overcome historic divisions and engage in eucharistic sharing with one another across denominational lines. An earlier document, arising from an international process of dialogue, the Leuenberg Agreement of 1973, formed the basis on which this eucharistic sharing eventually became official.[10]

The Leuenberg Agreement (III.1.18):

In the Lord's Supper the risen Jesus Christ imparts himself in his body and blood, given for all, through his word of promise with

[8] See also the 1549 *Book of Common Prayer*: "Grant us therefore, gracious Lord, so to eat the flesh of thy dear Son Jesus Christ, and to drink his blood in these holy mysteries, that we may continually dwell in him and he in us." *The First English Prayer Book* (Harrisburg: Morehouse Publishing, 1999), p. 32. In the revision of 1559 these words were preserved with no significant change. At the distribution, the words of the priest in the first prayer book were: "The body of our Lord Jesus Christ which was given for thee, preserve thy body and soul unto everlasting life." The 1559 revision retained these sentences while adding: "Take and eat this in remembrance that Christ died for thee, [and] feed on him in thine heart by faith, with thanksgiving." The addition brought a "Reformed" note to the more "Catholic" original wording without deleting it. See *The Book of Common Prayer, 1559: The Elizabethan Book of Prayer*, ed. John Booty (Charlottesville: University of Virginia Press, 1975).

[9] *A Formula of Agreement between the Evangelical Lutheran Church in America, the Presbyterian Church (USA), the Reformed Church in America, and the United Church of Christ*, (Louisville: The Presbyterian Church USA, 1998).

[10] The Leuenberg Agreement in *The Leuenberg Agreement and Lutheran–Reformed Relationships*, ed. William G. Rusch and Daniel F. Martensen (Minneapolis: Augsburg, 1989).

bread and wine. He thus gives himself unreservedly to all who receive the bread and wine; faith receives the Lord's Supper for salvation, unfaith for judgment.

The Leuenberg Agreement (III.1.19):
We cannot separate communion with Jesus Christ in his body and blood from the act of eating and drinking. To be concerned about the manner of Christ's presence in the Lord's Supper in abstraction from this act is to run the risk of obscuring the meaning of the Lord's Supper.[11]

As important as these points of agreement are, they leave open questions vital to other ecumenical dialogue partners, including more conservative Lutheran and Reformed churches, on the one hand, and high sacramental churches on the other (Roman Catholic, Eastern Orthodox, and so on). Each of these groupings would be concerned, though in different ways, about how the two modes of bodily presence are more precisely ordered and defined.

A third dialogue, whose results were made public in 1984, urged moving toward a deeper appreciation of the sacramental mystery based on the consensus already achieved:

Appreciating what we Reformed and Lutheran Christians already hold in common concerning the Lord's Supper, we nevertheless affirm that both of our communions need to keep on growing into an ever-deeper realization of the fullness and richness of the eucharistic mystery.[12]

The idea of transelementation, as represented by Vermigli, Bucer, and Cranmer (and based on patristic sources), would today allow the Reformed churches to maintain their historic concern for

---

[11] The idea of real presence as inseparable from sacramental action raises questions that are discussed below under "Mode of conversion."

[12] *An Invitation to Action*, ed. James E. Andrews and Joseph A. Burgess (Philadelphia: Fortress Press, 1984), p. 14.

Christ's bodily integrity while moving closer to the high sacramental traditions on real presence. It would mean a further step toward healing intolerable ecumenical divisions. Nothing essential would be lost for the Reformed, while something valuable would be gained. Nothing would be compromised, but something unexpected would be embraced. Finding a principled way to accept views which it had been previously thought necessary to reject is the soul of the ecumenical project.

Mode of rhetoric

When Christ's two modes of bodily presence are taken into account – "local" in heaven, "substantial" in the eucharist – it becomes evident that what it would mean for a "literal" statement to be made about his "real presence" in the eucharist is far from clear-cut. The problem is compounded by whether the bread and wine must be thought to lose their "substance" for Christ's body and blood to be present in them. In any case, it is obvious that Christ's body and blood cannot be in the eucharist in exactly the same manner as in heaven. Though present in "substance," their "dimensionality" in the eucharist would be, as Aquinas argued, somehow inseparable from that of the elements. All traditions would agree that a gross, carnal or "Capernaitic" presence in the eucharist is out of the question.

Nevertheless, it was "corporeal" presence in the crude sense that the Protestants ascribed to the Catholics, and that the Reformed suspected of the Lutherans.

Cranmer is instructive on this matter. He noted that Theophylact, whose views he affirmed, spoke – in a potentially problematic way – not only about the eucharistic elements being converted into Christ's body and blood, but also about them as being eaten and drunk. Cranmer continued: "Yet he meaneth not of a gross, carnal, corporeal, and sensible conversion of the bread and wine, nor of a like eating and drinking of his flesh and blood."[13]

What he meant, Cranmer continued, was rather a sacramental conversion, and a sacramental eating and drinking – where the word "sacramental" stood in apposition to "true" rather than crudely "corporeal." "And this doctrine of Theophylactus," concluded Cranmer with approval, "is both true, godly, and comfortable."[14] Here at least Cranmer approved of a view which affirmed a true and substantial presence of Christ's body and blood as present in and through the consecrated elements.

It is well known that Cranmer saw the statement "This is my body" as being "figurative," but not that he was essentially making a rhetorical judgment. As the following analysis shows, however, figurative judgments need not rule out – but are indeed compatible with – factual judgments that Christ's body is substantially present in the eucharist and imparted by it. Regardless of whether that presence is called "real" or "true," rhetorical judgments need to be kept distinct from "factual" judgments. Confusing the rhetorical and the factual levels has historically been a bane of the discussion.[15]

An initial conclusion follows from these observations. Since Catholicism did not teach a "gross, carnal, corporeal, and sensible" (i.e. Capernaitic) conversion and eating in the sacrament, and since for the Catholics the "substantial" element was also somehow "spiritual" or "mystical," the differences, on this point, between a Reformer like Cranmer and a Catholic like Aquinas were by no means so great as it seemed to many in the sixteenth century, with

[13] Thomas Cranmer, "A Defence of the True and Catholic Doctrine of the Sacrament of the Body and Blood of Our Saviour Christ," in *The Work of Thomas Cranmer*, ed. G. E. Duffield (Philadelphia: Fortress Press, 1965), p. 187.

[14] Ibid.

[15] For Cranmer, see Peter Brooks, *Thomas Cranmer's Doctrine of the Eucharist* (New York: Seabury Press, 1965). On his figurative rhetorical judgment, see p. 89 n. 1; on his factual judgment of "true" presence, see pp. 72–111. On "true" presence as "substantial" presence, see p. 116.

lasting influence. This would not be the first time in the history of Christian theology where the controversies were vexed by semantic problems about finding the right terminology and making it understood.

From a semiotic point of view, statements about "real presence" are difficult to classify, even when meant "literally." It is almost impossible for the mode of rhetoric not to remain "figurative" in some sense as long as the difference is taken seriously between the heavenly and eucharistic modes of Christ's presence.

The rhetorical problem has often focused on the liturgical use of Jesus' statement at the Last Supper, "This is my body." Luther, who believed the statement was literal, nonetheless classified it as a synecdoche, while Calvin allowed for it to be either a synecdoche or a metonymy (though he preferred the latter). Roman Catholics, if rarely commenting directly on the rhetoric, apparently took it as being "literal." For their part, the Eastern Orthodox, who exemplified a variety of viewpoints, could sometimes regard it from the standpoint of "realistic symbolism" or "symbolic realism." Upon reflection, it is the latter assessment that would seem most suitable to the complexities.[16]

If the statement were a synecdoche, as Luther held, then the word "this" would apparently be related to "my body" as a container is related to what it contains, on the supposition that a synecdoche is a figure of speech by which a part can be put for the whole in which it is included. The relationship of signifier to signified would then be one of combination and integration. "Bread" and "body" would be two ways of looking at one integral reality. The bread would be evident to the senses, with the body

---

[16] For the rhetorical distinctions that follow, see Hayden White, *Metahistory* (Baltimore: Johns Hopkins University Press, 1973), pp. 31–37; Richard A. Lanham, *A Handlist of Rhetorical Terms* (Berkeley: University of California Press, 1969); Gerhart B. Ladner, "Medieval and Modern Understanding of Symbolism: A Comparison," *Speculum* 54 (1979), pp. 223–56.

being hidden in or under it, so that the body would be "contained" by the bread, while neither would lose its defining properties.[17]

In fact, however, for Luther, their oneness was actually that of identity and difference, or of dialectical identity, not strictly of container and contained; and so the term "synecdoche" did not quite fit the case. A synecdoche can put the part for the whole, the whole for the part, the species for the genus, the genus for the species, or the materials used for the thing made. In each case one term is more inclusive than the other. For Luther the bread is the "includer" and the body is the "included," yet the bread is not a "part" belonging to the body as the relevant "whole." The dialectical identity of the bread and the body would actually be a relation between two wholes, not between a part and a whole, or between one part and another. In the nature of the case, the container/contained analogy (which at best relates a part to a whole) breaks down.

If the statement were a metonymy, as suggested by Calvin, then the word *this* would be related to the word "body" by a process of association.[18] A metonymy uses the name of one thing for something else with which it is associated. "Bread" and "body" would in some sense be external to one another – Calvin did not want to see the body as "localized" or "contained" by the bread – and yet in medieval usage "metonymy" could imply not only contact or contiguity, but also participation.[19]

The idea of "containment" was ambiguous. On the one hand, it could mean that Christ's body was contained in the eucharist at the expense of its presence in heaven. (That is part of what Calvin feared

---

[17] For passages where Luther reverts to the term "synecdoche," see "Confession Concerning Christ's Supper," *Luther's Works*, vol. 37 (Philadelphia: Fortress Press, 1961), pp. 301–2; and Hermann Sasse, *This Is My Body* (Philadelphia: Fortress Press, 1959), pp. 163, 254–55.

[18] For passages where Calvin uses "metonymy," see *Inst.* IV.17.21, pp. 1385–86; *Comm.* on 1 Cor. 11:24, in *The First Epistle of Paul to the Corinthians* (Grand Rapids: Wm B. Eerdmans, 1960), p. 205.

[19] Ladner, "Medieval and Modern," pp. 250–51 (*supra* n. 16).

about the Catholic and Lutheran teachings.) Or it could mean, on the other hand, that only the "substance" of Christ's body was "localized" in the bread and made available with it. Calvin's close association of the substance of Christ's body with the bread was not always far from the latter idea. What Calvin wanted was a close association of body and bread, and perhaps even a participation of the former in the latter, but not a real identification between them.

Insofar as Calvin thought of the body as being given "with" the bread, a "parallelism" was implied between two external though contiguous and separable realities given in the eucharist at the same time, the bread to the mouth, the body to faith. However, as implied by his occasional statements that the body was given "in" the bread, Calvin sometimes veered toward an "instrumentalism" where the body was given by means of the bread.[20] "Christ distinctly offers his body in the bread," Calvin could write, "and his blood in the wine."[21] "The body of Christ is given in the bread, and through the bread, and is received with the bread," he could state, and yet the bread was not converted into the body "in an absolutely literal sense" so as to remove all distinction between them.[22] "In Calvin's view," writes Gerrish, "it [was] the nature of the sacraments to cause and communicate (*apporter et communiquer*) what they signify."[23] In the end Calvin assumed a sacramental

---

[20] Gerrish distinguishes among symbolic memorialism (Zwingli), symbolic parallelism (Calvin), and symbolic instrumentalism (Luther), regarding how the sign is related to the reality. Yet as Gerrish points out, Calvin's view of the relationship between sign and reality was more fluid, ambiguous and reticent than a strict application of these categories would suggest, so that he could also approximate Luther's instrumentalism. See Gerrish, "The Lord's Supper in the Reformed Confessions," *Theology Today* 23 (1966), pp. 224–43.

[21] Calvin, "The True Partaking of the Flesh and Blood of Christ in the Holy Supper," in *Tracts and Letters*, vol. II, ed. Henry Beveridge (Grand Rapids: Baker Book House, 1983), p. 516.

[22] Calvin, "Second Defence in Answer to the Calumnies of Joachim Westphal," in ibid., p. 272.

[23] Gerrish, "Lord's Supper," p. 230; cf. p. 234 (*supra* n. 20).

union between the sign and the thing signified, without wishing to specify the nature of the union too precisely.[24] With the sign was joined a true possession of the reality.

The term "metonymy" – whose semantic range included the ideas of both contact and participation – was therefore satisfactory only as it preserved the ambiguous overlap between "parallelism" and "instrumentalism," while to some degree concealing it. Nevertheless, for Calvin, bread and body were in some sense related by a sacramental union. They formed a differentiated unity of contiguous or perhaps parallel particulars as opposed to a dialectical identity.[25] The "signified" (the substance of Christ's life-giving flesh) was present in and with the "signifier" (the consecrated bread), though not inseparably fused with it.[26]

If the liturgical use of "This is my body" were taken "literally," as Roman Catholicism seemed to require, then the word "this" would stand in a *syntactical* relation of identity with the word "body." Yet *semantically* this identity-relation was subject to complex metaphysical qualifications. Not only was the bread not identical with the body in its ascended, heavenly form, but the eucharistic relation itself was closer to being one of container and contained than of strict identity. In the eucharist the bread kept its local dimensionality while losing its substance, whereas the body kept its substance while losing its local dimensionality.

---

[24] Of Calvin on the eucharist, Gerrish writes: "His language is complex; it could lead in more than one direction, and it is not easy to harmonize all his different assertions." See Gerrish, *The Old Protestantism and the New* (Chicago: University of Chicago Press, 1982), p. 106.

[25] For a passage where Calvin seems to reject the idea of "contiguity," see *Inst.* IV.17.19. What he is mainly rejecting, however, is local presence.

[26] It would be false to say, as one sometimes reads in conservative Lutheran polemics, that for Calvin the Lord's Supper merely strengthens faith but does not offer Christ and his blessings to believing reception. These polemics seem to have as hard a time dealing fairly with Calvin as conservative Reformed polemics sometimes have in dealing fairly with Luther and the Lutheran confessions. To have difficulty in making fair and discriminating judgments is the hallmark of enclave theology.

The substance of the body was contained within the dimensions of the bread by which it was imparted. Whether in heaven or in the eucharist, the indivisible substance of Christ's life-giving flesh was one and the same. But in the eucharist it assumed the form of bread.

After the consecration, while the whole body (and, concomitantly, the whole Christ) was eucharistically present under a particular aspect (dimensionless substance), the bread was present only in a form that was metaphysically odd, since only its "accidents" (or "species") were retained. The substance of Christ's body was by no means "identical" with the accidents or species of the bread.[27] The signified was present in the signifier, and inseparable from it, but they did not stand in a relation of equivalence.

In these terms, the statement "This is my body" was true in a "real," though (and this is the point) not strictly a "literal," sense. The two terms being related were neither two "parts" nor two "wholes," but rather one "whole" ("body") in a particular aspect ("substance") and an outward "form" ("accidents" or "species") subsisting without its ordinary substance ("bread"). This was not a relation of dialectical identity between two wholes, nor was it a union of two distinct wholes in temporal contiguity. It was a metaphysically peculiar union, so to speak, of contentless form with formless content.

If the rhetorical terms "synecdoche," "metonymy," and "literalism" all turn out to be less than fully perspicuous, that should not be allowed to obscure a more basic point. In each case – whether through the ideas of dialectical identity, contiguous union, or containment – a semantic and conceptual attempt is being made to affirm the mysterious reality of Christ's life-giving flesh as present with the bread in the eucharist. The mystery of this presence seems

[27] To avoid tying the church too closely to a particular metaphysics, the Council of Trent chose the non-technical term "species" as opposed to "accidents" as used by Aquinas.

to elude statements that can be described in ordinary terms. The proposed modes of real relation are not easily squared with standard modes of rhetorical classification. This is a point worth making for the sake of ecumenical discussion. Because the term "literal" is essentially a rhetorical category entangled in a very problematic semantics, it would probably be better to leave it to one side. Matters that are already very difficult are only hopelessly obscured if one discussion partner claims to have a "literal" view of "real presence" which is supposedly superior for that reason to the views of others.

The final proposal to be considered, though it could not be adopted in its fullness by official Catholicism, could be accepted by many non-Catholics, and in fact has been accepted by many of them. If it were more widely articulated in official church teachings and liturgies, it would be an advance toward ecumenical convergence. Because it is essentially a view found within Eastern Orthodoxy, and because Eastern Orthodox views are not intolerable to Roman Catholicism, it promises not to be church-dividing. It seems to be well within the orbit of Lutheranism, Anglicanism, and Methodism, and it has distinguished Reformed adherents (at least in some of their statements). It could be embraced by the Reformed churches without any fundamental compromise, though it would require a serious effort at rethinking old polemics and opening up new horizons. It is the view – affirmed by Vermigli, Bucer, and Cranmer – known in Eastern Orthodoxy as "transelementation." How this view might comport with transubstantiation is discussed later under "Mode of conversion." What needs to be set forth now is one of the major premises of this study.

There is arguably an irreducible minimum that must be met with respect to the question of "real presence." Meeting this minimum would not be enough for new eucharistic sharing to begin, but no such sharing will be possible without it. It represents a necessary condition, though not a sufficient one, for removing the unacceptable divisions that persist in the churches around the eucharist. Putting aside for the moment all questions of theoretical elaboration – like "transubstantiation" or "transelementation" – a specific assertion is ecumenically necessary for all churches to make about the consecrated elements of bread and wine. It pertains to the liturgical use of the statement "This is my body." Ecumenically, it is not enough to interpret it either as "This signifies my body" or as "This contains my body," even if, at some level, the ideas of signification and containment need not be entirely ruled out. It must be possible for all traditions to assert – without equivocation – at the level of first-order discourse as found in the liturgy, that the relation of "This bread" to "my body" is actually one of real predication.

The Wittenberg Concord of 1536, as affirmed by Luther, Melanchthon, Bucer, and Calvin, contained the words: "Through sacramental union the bread is the body of Christ." In principle therefore no obstacle should stand in the way of accepting this ecumenical minimum by the Reformed. Even the Zwinglians among them could accept it if they would agree to the proposal made below about "symbolic realism." They would not renounce what they affirm (the symbolic aspect) but would enrich their position by accepting what they thought they had to reject (the realist aspect).[28]

A real predication of syntactical equivalence must be possible regardless of how it is explained. Even if the predication were also symbolic as well as real, as would be the case in what is being proposed, a merely symbolic predication would not be enough. For the Reformed churches and others to suppose the contrary would amount to a counsel of despair. It would mean, in effect, that for them the divisions are for ever beyond healing. If there is in fact a way for real predication to be affirmed without compromise by churches that have historically resisted it, then every reason exists for them to take a reconciling step forward here.

[28] See above, nn. 26 and 27.

At least three tendencies can be discerned in Eastern Orthodoxy with respect to the rhetorical question. (Because the question is not usually addressed by them directly, these tendencies have to be inferred.) The first is to rest content simply with first-order predication; the second is to insist that the predication is real though not symbolic; and the third is to allow that the predication, while real, is nonetheless symbolic as well. While any of these views might be ecumenically viable in the sense of not being church-dividing (except perhaps for the second), it is the third view that holds the most promise. For not only would it seem to comport better with the actual complexities, but it would also create a space in which other traditions, like the Reformed, might be able to make an important advance.

Resting content with first-order predication undoubtedly has its appeal. Given the holy mystery at stake, it would be unnatural not to feel that there is something repellent about the kind of conceptual analysis attempted in this essay. The wager being made is that it must nevertheless be attempted for the sake of overcoming the divisions of the past. Not everyone, however, will need an exercise of this sort or benefit from it.

Insisting that the predication is real though not symbolic was a tendency that became prominent in the East at around the time of the iconoclastic controversy in the eighth century. It was then argued that before the consecration the elements were an image, but that afterwards they ceased being an image and became the actual body.[29] John of Damascus[30] and the Seventh Ecumenical

---

[29] Stone, *History of the Doctrine of the Holy Eucharist*, vol. 1, p. 192 (*supra* n. 1).

[30] "This denial [by John of Damascus] that the consecrated elements are figures was probably due partly to an instinctive dislike of language which might be interpreted so as to be inconsistent with the doctrine that the consecrated elements are the body and blood of Christ, and partly to the stress of the iconoclastic controversy and the fear that if the consecrated elements were described as figures this might lead to a view that they were no more the body and blood of Christ than the image of a saint is a saint." Stone, ibid., pp. 147–48.

Council[31] reflected this view. The ideas of the "figurative" and the "real" were felt to be mutually exclusive.[32]

It was not always so. From the second through at least the fourth and fifth centuries, the ideas of the real and the symbolic were not seen as contradicting each other. Adolph von Harnack writes:

> What we now-a-days understand by "symbol" is a thing which is not that which it represents; at that time "symbol" denoted a thing which in some kind of way, really is what it signifies; but, on the other hand, according to the ideas of that period, the really heavenly element lay either in or behind the visible form without being identical with it.[33]

> What we now call a "symbol" is something wholly different from what was so-called by the ancient church.[34]

Authorities associated with this general tendency – where symbol and reality were at once identical and yet also different – would include Theodoret of Cyprus, the Cappadocians, and Cyril of Alexandria.[35]

When the liturgical use of the statement "This is my body" is understood rhetorically as a form of "symbolic realism," then the word *this* is related to the word *body* by a pattern of identity and difference. (Luther would have been right about the pattern but

---

[31] "The [Seventh Council's] statement about the eucharist, which ... does not possess the authority of the formal decree, is apparently historically in error in saying that the fathers had used the word antitype only of the unconsecrated elements." Stone, ibid., p. 150.

[32] According to John Meyendorff, using the terms "symbol," "figure," and "image" for the consecrated elements largely disappears from Byzantine Christianity. Meyendorff, *Byzantine Christianity* (New York: Fordham University Press, 1974), p. 204.

[33] Adolph von Harnack, *History of Dogma*, vol. II (New York: Dover Publications, 1961), pp. 144–45.

[34] Ibid., vol. IV, p. 289 n. 2.

[35] See Stone, *History of the Doctrine of the Holy Eucharist*, vol. I, pp. 64, 67, 71–73, 103–6 (*supra* n. 1).

wrong about the rhetorical category.) "Bread" and "body" would be two wholes in dialectical relation. The bread would be identical with the body in one way while remaining different from it in another. The relation between them would be one of mutual indwelling. While the bread would contain the body, the body would also, more importantly, contain the bread, and the relation would not be symmetrical.

The body, not the bread, would emerge more clearly as the primary reality. The bread would be assimilated into Christ's real, transcendent body more than the other way round.[36] It would be eucharistically converted by its consecration yet without losing its "substance" or ordinary phenomenological characteristics. The bread would at once symbolize and yet also be the mystery that it imparts. "The symbol *is* the mystery," wrote Harnack of the ancient view, "and the mystery was not conceivable without the symbol."[37] The inherent density of the mystery would be reflected in a complex rhetorical classification. It is this very complexity that the idea of "transelementation" intends and permits.

In recent theology Alexander Schmemann has revived the ancient pattern. About how the symbol is related to the mysterious presence of Christ's flesh, he wrote: "The symbol does not so much 'resemble' the reality that it symbolizes as it participates in it and therefore it is capable of communicating it in reality."[38] For Schmemann, the symbol (*signum*) participates in the mysterious reality (*res*) that it communicates. The bread is the instrument by which Christ bestows himself. Through his having joined it to his life-giving flesh, the two are one. On the basis of "transelementation," the historic conflict between "symbolic" and "realistic" readings of "This is my body"

---

[36] Salvador Dali's famous painting *The Sacrament of the Last Supper* might be taken as an attempt to depict this point.

[37] Harnack, *History of Dogma*, vol. II, p. 144 (italics added) (*supra* n. 33).

[38] Alexander Schmemann, *The Eucharist* (Crestwood: St. Vladimir's Seminary Press, 1988), p. 38.

can be transcended and overcome. As John Zizioulas writes: "The symbol is a form of paradox: it at once is not and is the reality."[39]

Mode of reception

Even if the Reformed churches could accept the idea of transelementation, they would still have difficulty in embracing the position that Christ's flesh is received orally, even by unbelievers. The conversion of the bread into Christ's life-giving flesh would be affirmed, and the controlling pattern of the sacramental union would be one of identity and difference (not just contiguous or parallelistic union). Nevertheless, more than one possible mode of reception would still be conceivable. On the basis of symbolic realism, it could still be supposed that Christ's flesh is received only as Christ himself is received – not orally, but spiritually as an indivisible whole, by faith alone.

All four traditions (Catholic, Orthodox, Lutheran, and Reformed) would agree that whatever is visible of the bread is physically consumed, but that the substance of Christ's life-giving flesh is not so consumed. It is often stated in the tradition that it is our bodies and souls which are transformed by the substance of Christ's flesh, not the other way round. As Gregory of Nyssa once explained, just as food is assimilated to our bodies and not our bodies to the food, so our bodies are "assimilated" to Christ's living-giving flesh, not the other way round, so as to become immortal, for that is how Christ's own earthly flesh had been "transmade" or "transelemented" into incorruption (and so "deified") through its union with the eternal Word.[40] The view of John of Damascus is broadly representative:

---

[39] John Zizioulas, "Symbolism and Realism in Orthodox Worship," *Sourozh* 79 (2000), pp. 3–17; on p. 3.

[40] Gregory of Nyssa, "The Great Catechism," ch. 37 in *The Nicene and Post-Nicene Fathers*, vol. 5, ed. Philip Schaff and Henry Wace (Grand Rapids: Wm. B. Eerdmans, 1954), pp. 504–6. Vermigli, following Theophylact, adopts the

It is Christ's body and blood entering into the composition of our soul and body without being consumed, without being corrupted, without passing into the privy – God forbid! – but into our substance for our sustenance, a bulwark against every sort of harm and a purifier from all uncleanliness.[41]

The familiar sixteenth-century accusation against the Lutherans, that they made Christ's flesh pass through the privy, etc., was not a highpoint in Reformed polemics. On the other hand, what John of Damascus writes suggests that the worry about a "Nestorian" tendency among the Reformed in their view of the sacrament can be overdrawn. Since all who follow John of Damascus believe that the substance of Christ's flesh is not digested with the bread, the difference between them and the Calvinist Reformed would appear to be merely relative. It would come down to whether Christ's flesh separates from the bread immediately before or immediately after the oral reception.

If the only possible vehicle of reception were faith – as insisted by Calvin, Vermigli, and virtually all the Reformed – then, according to transelementation, Christ's flesh would be received by faith as the bread is received; but without faith neither Christ himself nor his life-giving flesh would be obtained. Belief would receive Christ in his flesh along with the bread; unbelief would receive only the bread. The real presence of Christ's flesh in and with the bread would be objectively offered to all, but unbelief would lack the capacity to receive it, and this incapacity would manifest the divine judgment.

Affirming the real presence of Christ's body not only with, but in the bread would seem vastly more important than affirming its

same line of thought: "We are transelemented into Christ." See Peter Martyr Vermigli, *The Oxford Treatise and Disputation on the Eucharist, 1549* (Kirksville: Truman State University Press, 2000), pp. 215–19; on p. 216.

[41] John of Damascus, *The Orthodox Faith* in *Saint John of Damascus: Writings* (Washington, DC: Catholic University of America Press, 1958), p. 360.

oral reception. Logically, as will be explained, the former need not depend on the latter. Therefore, the question arises as to whether a traditional Reformed position on "oral reception" might not fall within the bounds of acceptable diversity.

The reverse question also arises. Is there a version of oral reception that might be embraced without compromise by the Reformed? A brief overview of the historic Lutheran/Reformed controversy will help to answer this question. The Lutherans affirmed that Christ's body was received orally, even by unbelievers; the Reformed denied both unbelieving and oral reception.

Luther in 1528:

Thus also it is correct so say, "He who takes hold of this bread, takes hold of Christ's body; and he who eats this bread, eats Christ's body; he who crushes this bread with teeth or tongue, crushes with teeth or tongue the body of Christ." And yet it remains absolutely true that no one sees or grasps or eats or chews Christ's body in the way he visibly sees and chews any other flesh. What one does to the bread is rightly and properly attributed to the body of Christ by virtue of the sacramental union.[42]

Calvin in 1559:

And this is the wholeness of the sacrament, which the whole world cannot violate: that the flesh and blood of Christ are no less truly given to the unworthy than to God's elect believers. At the same time, it is true, however, that just as rain falling upon hard rock flows off because no entrance opens into the stone, the wicked by their hardness so repel God's grace that it does not reach them. Besides, to say that Christ may be received without faith is as inappropriate as to say that a seed may germinate in fire.[43]

[42] Luther, "Confession Concerning Christ's Supper," in *Luther's Works*, vol. 37 (Philadelphia: Fortress Press, 1961), p. 300.
[43] Calvin, *Inst.* IV.17.33; p. 1407.

The "Formula of Concord" condemned the following errors in 1577:

That in the holy sacrament the body of Christ is not received orally with the bread, but that with the mouth we receive only bread and wine and that we receive the body of Christ only spiritually by faith . . . That in the Holy Supper unbelieving and impenitent Christians do not receive the body and blood of Christ, but only bread and wine.[44]

The "Westminster Confession of Faith" in 1646:

Although ignorant and wicked men receive the outward elements in this sacrament, yet they receive not the thing signified thereby; but by their unworthy coming thereunto are guilty of the body and blood of the Lord, to their own damnation. Wherefore all ignorant and ungodly persons, as they are unfit to enjoy communion with him, so are they unworthy of the Lord's table, and can not, without great sin against Christ, while they remain such, partake of these holy mysteries, or be admitted thereunto.[45]

Calvin stood opposed to both Zwingli and Luther. Against Zwingli he denied that Christ's flesh and blood were present only to faith, affirming instead that in the sacrament they were objectively present to unbelievers and believers alike. Against Luther, on the other hand, he denied that Christ's flesh and blood were received orally by anyone, affirming that they could only be received spiritually by faith.

The doctrine of transelementation would modify Calvin's position by moving it away from contiguous union or symbolic parallelism toward mutual coinherence and dialectical identity. The sacramental union would shift from the notion that Christ's body was somehow divisible from the bread at the moment of reception. Contrary to Lutheran polemics, Calvin did not maintain

---

[44] The Formula of Concord (Epitome, Article VII, nos. 5 and 16) in *The Book of Concord*, ed. Theodore G. Tappert (Philadelphia: Fortress Press, 1959), pp. 485–86.

[45] Schaff, *Creeds of Christendom*, vol. III, pp. 666–67 (*supra* n. 4).

the "subjective" (Zwinglian) view that Christ was present in the sacrament only to faith. But in line with general Reformed sensibilities, he did tend toward a "Nestorian" understanding of the sacramental union. In effect, he presumed that though Christ's body was joined with the bread, the two were separable at the moment of reception.[46]

At least one passage exists where Calvin seems to approach the idea of transelementaton:

> Because [the Greek Fathers][47] say that in consecration a secret conversion [arcanam conversionem] takes place, so that there is now something other than bread and wine ... they do not mean by this that the elements have been annihilated, but rather that they now have to be considered of a different class from common foods intended solely to feed the stomach, since in them is set forth the spiritual food and drink of the soul.
>
> (Inst. IV.17.14)

Calvin finds nothing objectionable here: "This we do not deny."[48]

"Transelementation" would rectify any existing Nestorian imbalance. By conceiving of the sacramental union in terms of the incarnational analogy, it would uphold the historic Reformed concern that no "confusion or mix" be allowed between the substances of Christ's body and the bread (as if in sacramental Monophysitism). Moreover, by allotting sole efficacy to Christ as the acting subject (thus denying a synergistic relation between

---

[46] For a rather pronounced Reformed expression of this "Nestorian" tendency in another context, see The Heidelberg Catechism, Questions 47 and 48, in Schaff, Creeds of Christendom, pp. 322–23. See also Barth's strictures against these particular questions in Church Dogmatics, vol. II, part 1 (Edinburgh: T. & T. Clark, 1957), p. 489.

[47] Although Calvin refers only vaguely to the "ancients," the position he describes fits more readily with the Greek than the Latin Fathers.

[48] Does this passage, which did not appear until the 1543 edition of the Institutes, perhaps show the influence of Vermigli?

Christ and the minister presiding at the eucharist), it would support the Reformed concern to block any form of sacramental "Pelagianism." Nevertheless, it would also guard the sacramental union against "separation and division." Christ's body would not be separated or divided from the bread at the moment of reception. Christ would be received by faith in the form of bread.

As Eastern Orthodoxy shows, this understanding of sacramental union need not become a warrant for "adoration of the host" outside the scope of the liturgy.[49] But it would concede merit to the traditional Lutheran teaching of a twofold eating.[50] The spiritual eating of faith would not exclude an oral reception of Christ's body with the bread.[51] For the body would be connected with the bread by a pattern of unity-in-distinction. The unity would be inseparable even as the abiding distinction remained. Unbelief would not prevent an oral reception of Christ's body with the bread any more than it would prevent an aural reception of the gospel when within earshot of preaching. The manner of the sacramental union would be what it has always been: incomprehensible. Nestorian and Monophysite distortions would both be ruled out.

A careful distinction was made by Aquinas between spiritual and non-spiritual ways of receiving Christ's body in the eucharist.

---

[49] Both Timothy Ware and Alexander Schmemann make this clear. "The eucharist is essentially a meal," writes Ware, "and so the significance of the consecrated elements becomes distorted if they are used outside the context of eating and drinking." Ware, *The Orthodox Church*, 2nd edn. (Harmondsworth: Penguin Books, 1993), p. 285. See also Schmemann, *Eucharist*, p. 226. I am assuming that in any reunion of the churches with eucharistic sharing, adoration of the host, as a Roman Catholic practice, would need to fall within the scope of what is not church-dividing and in need of further discussion. For a thoughtful (though to me unconvincing) defense of the practice, see E. L. Mascall, *Corpus Christi* (London: Longmans, Green, & Co., 1953), pp. 168–77.

[50] See Heinrich Schmid, *Doctrinal Theology of the Evangelical Lutheran Church* (Minneapolis: Augsburg Publishing House, 1899; repr. 1961), pp. 568–71.

[51] Luther's extravagant language at this point may be regarded with restraint.

Spiritual receiving did not pertain to unbelievers. To that extent Aquinas upheld what would later be Calvin's concern. At the same time, he allowed that unbelievers would nevertheless receive Christ's body orally with the bread in a non-spiritual way. To that extent, he upheld Luther's position. Like Luther, he refused to disconnect Christ's body from the bread in either type of reception. He asked whether the unbeliever received Christ's body "sacramentally." If the term "sacramentally" qualified the verb as to what was eaten, the answer was yes; but if it qualified it as to the eater, the answer was no. Christ's body was received orally with the bread by the unbeliever in a sacramental but unspiritual way. The doctrine of transelementation would allow the Reformed to accept these distinctions in line with Catholic, Orthodox, Lutheran, and other traditions.[52] The Reformed would shift from a "Nestorian" to a more "Chalcedonian" view of the sacramental union at the moment of reception.

Ecumenical theology seeks to reconcile divided traditions. It seeks to show that divisions can sometimes be overcome by turning incompatibilities into compatibilities. Moreover, it seeks to show that this kind of reorientation can occur without any participant having to relinquish fundamental convictions. What was positively affirmed is still affirmed. But what was once ruled out as incompatible is re-envisioned. The incompatible becomes compatible without compromise when needless exclusions are overcome.

For example, in the eucharist, the altar is also a table, and the table also an altar, so that the ideas of "table" and "altar" are not mutually exclusive. "Altar" is a priestly image while "table" is a royal image. There is no need to choose between them, because they supplement and complement each other. Eastern Orthodoxy points the way when it adopts the term "altar table." In this chapter it has been shown that traditional eucharistic exclusions of

---

[52] Aquinas, *Summa Theologiae* 3.80.3.

the "symbolic" from the "real," and of the "real" from the "symbolic," can also be overcome. Again, Eastern Orthodoxy points the way when it draws upon the ancient patristic conception of "symbolic realism." Finally, it has been shown, especially by the careful distinctions of Aquinas, that "substantial presence" in the eucharist need not exclude "local presence" in heaven, nor need "non-reception" exclude "oral reception" in the case of unbelievers.

The ideas of an "altar table," of "symbolic realism," of "substantial" eucharistic presence as not undermining "local" presence in heaven, and of "non-reception" as not excluding "oral reception" all pose special challenges for the Reformed tradition. They would require accepting ideas it was thought necessary fervently to reject. The doctrine of transelementation, as rediscovered by certain sixteenth-century Reformed theologians, is the pivot on which these moves would turn. Accepting them would be a great step toward ecumenical healing. Yet where full agreement cannot be achieved, convergence might sometimes be possible. Can "transelementation" be thought to coexist peaceably with "transubstantiation"?

Mode of conversion

Because of its allegiance to the Fourth Lateran Council and the Council of Trent, the Roman Catholic Church is committed to transubstantiation. It is a dogma that can be interpreted but not revoked. Few non-Catholics, however – including, it would seem, most of the Eastern Orthodox – are ever likely to affirm transubstantiation in any strong way. What seems to be needed at this point, ecumenically, is a range of viewpoints that would not be church-dividing. As it turns out, Eastern Orthodoxy is not unacceptable to Roman Catholicism on the eucharist. On the contrary, despite an official invitation extended by the Second

Vatican Council, it is the Orthodox who refuse to accept eucharistic sharing with the Catholics.[53] The Orthodox refusal, however, evidently rests on matters other than transubstantiation.[54]

The suggestion being made here is that if non-Catholics can move closer to the Eastern Orthodox on real presence, and if on this point the Orthodox are not unacceptable to the Catholics, then a non-Catholic convergence around the Orthodox promises to resolve this particular aspect of the eucharistic controversies. Again it needs to be stressed that this outcome would depend on at least three corollaries. First, while this move would be necessary, it would not be sufficient for eucharistic sharing to begin across the historic divisions. Second, at the level of first-order discourse, the liturgical use of "This is my body" would need to be affirmed by all without equivocation. The third is that in order for this affirmation to be possible, transelementation (or something like it), as a view within Orthodoxy, would need to be accepted by traditions like the Reformed.

The term "transelementation" was not uncommon among the Greek patristic theologians. Gregory of Nyssa could write of Christ, for example: "He gives these gifts by virtue of the benediction through which He transelements [*metastoicheioen*] the natural quality of these visible things to that immortal thing."[55] Darwell Stone, who relies on Nyssa as a benchmark, notes that he also used the term "transmade" (*metapoiesis*) in a parallel sense.[56] Theodoret, Chrysostom, Cyril of Alexandria, John of Damascus, and others are then mentioned as anticipating or corresponding to Nyssa.[57]

---

[53] See *The Documents of Vatican II*, ed. Walter M. Abbott (New York: Guild Press, America Press, Association Press, 1996), pp. 357–61.

[54] This refusal is discussed in Chapter 6.

[55] Nyssa, "Great Catechism" xxxvii, in *Nicene and Post-Nicene Fathers*, vol. 5, series 2, ed. Philip Schaff (Grand Rapids: Wm. B. Eerdmans, 1954), p. 506.

[56] Stone, *History of the Doctrine of the Holy Eucharist*, vol. 1, pp. 72–73, 103–4.

[57] Ibid., pp. 99–100, 104–6, 147–48.

John Meyendorff sums up the spirit of this trajectory:

> The Eucharist is Christ's transfigured, life-giving, but still human, body, en-hypostasized in the Logos and penetrated with divine "energies." Characteristically, one never finds the category of "essence" (*ousia*) used by Byzantine theologians in a Eucharistic context. They would consider a term like "transubstantiation" (*metousiosis*) improper to designate the Eucharistic mystery, and generally use the concept of *metabole*, found in the canon of John Chrysostom, or such dynamic terms as "trans-elementation" (*metastoicheiosis*) or "re-ordination" (*metarrhythmisis*).[58]

Although after the thirteenth century the term "transubstantiation" is scattered through Eastern Orthodoxy, it was rarely used speculatively, but only to affirm Christ's glorified humanity as present in the eucharist.[59]

Bishop Kallistos (Timothy) Ware concurs: "While Orthodoxy has always insisted on the reality of the change, it has never attempted to explain the manner of the change: the Eucharistic Prayer in the Liturgy simply uses the neutral term *metaballo*, to 'turn about,' to 'change,' to 'alter.'"[60] A commitment to scholastic distinctions has been resisted. Ware concludes:

> Today a few Orthodox writers still use the word transubstantiation, but they insist on two points: first, there are many other words which can with equal legitimacy be used to describe the consecration, and, among them all, the term transubstantiation enjoys no unique or decisive authority; secondly, its use does not commit theologians to the acceptance of Aristotelian philosophical concepts.[61]

---

[58] John Meyendorff, *Byzantine Theology* (New York: Fordham University Press, 1979), p. 203.

[59] Ibid., p. 204.

[60] Timothy Ware, *The Orthodox Church*, 2nd edn. (Harmondsworth: Penguin Books, 1997), p. 283.

[61] Ibid., p. 284.

The Greek Orthodox Archbishop of Aksum, Methodios Fouyas, writes:

> The Orthodox Church uses the word "transubstantiation" not to define the manner ... but only to insist on the fact that the bread truly ... becomes the ... body of the Lord ... The difference between Orthodox and Romans is this: the latter used this word to mean the special theory according to which the change is made, but the Orthodox used it to mean the fact of the change, according to the patristic conception.[62]

Orthodox conceptions stay closer to first-order than second-order discourse.

Nevertheless, transubstantiation differs from transelementation in several respects.

- Transubstantiation focuses mainly on the idea of descent; transelementation, on that of elevation.
- Transubstantiation asserts that one substance is transmuted into another; transelementation, that one object is suffused with another's reality and power.
- Transubstantiation concentrates mainly on the agency of the priest as exercised through the words of institution; transelementation, on the agency of the Holy Spirit as invoked by the prayer of *epiclesis*.
- Transubstantiation envisions a more fixed relation, transelementation a more dynamic relation, between the living Christ and the conse crated element.
- For transubstantiation the relation is that of one-sided containment; for transelementation, of mutual indwelling.
- Transubstantiation asserts that the body of Christ is enclosed in the consecrated bread; transelementation, that Christ by his

---

[62] Mathodios Fouyas, *Orthodoxy, Roman Catholicism and Anglicanism* (New York: Oxford University Press, 1972), p. 189.

Spirit assimilates the consecrated bread to his life-giving flesh so that it becomes one with the bread by which it is imparted.

- For transubstantiaiton the process of how the elements are converted is conceived along causal lines (with Aristotelian metaphysics in the background); for transelementation, along more purely mystical lines (with no particular metaphysical commitments).

- For transubstantiation the relation between Christ's flesh and the consecrated elements is one of substance and accidents (or species); for transelementation, of two unabridged objects.

- For transubstantiation the whole (the substance of Christ's flesh) is contained by the part (the accidents of the bread), or is contained at least under a particular aspect or species. For transelementation, the lesser object (the consecrated element) is contained by the greater object (Christ's flesh), which at the same time allows itself to be contained by the lesser object as well.

- For transubstantiation the sacramental union occurs between a whole and a part (or between a whole and an aspect), by an indirect analogy with *creatio ex nihilo*; for transelementation, between two interpenetrating wholes, according to the incarnational analogy, with its aspects of unity, distinction, and above all asymmetry (with precedence belonging at every point to the living Christ in the power of the Spirit).

- In short, transubstantiation is a theory of descent and replacement; transelementation, a theory of ascent and enhancement.

Are these contrasts mainly a matter of emphasis or are they more fundamental? To some extent they would seem to be a matter of emphasis. There is no reason why transubstantiation could not incorporate the idea of elevation as a supplement to the idea of descent. This move might have the desirable effect of de-centering the agency of the priest while making clearer that the central acting subject is always the living Christ in the power of the Spirit. Some recent Roman Catholic theology seems to move in this direction.

Other matters are less certain. Could transubstantiation really allow for the idea of mutual indwelling or asymmetrical mutual containment? Could it allow for Christ and his flesh as the superior factor by which the consecrated element is itself contained, along with the traditional dogma that Christ's flesh is contained by the element? That would seem to entail shifting to a more dynamic relation in which Christ was – and more clearly remained – the sovereign acting subject in the sacrament.

The sticking point would apparently be the Aristotelian (or quasi-Aristotelian) metaphysics hovering in the background of "transubstantiation." If it is accepted that no metaphysical object can have more than one substance at the same time, then transubstantiation would be an ingenious way of making the essential point.[63] It would be a way of stating unequivocally that "This bread is the body of Christ." While non-Catholics might wonder why the church should be expected to take on such metaphysical commitments, they could at least take the view that what is intended is sacramentally sound.

Roman Catholics, in turn, would also need to take a charitable view. They would need to acknowledge that the idea of "transelementation," as here described, is not church-dividing. They would need to recognize that it differs markedly from other views with which it might be confused (and has been confused in the past). They would need to accept the following clarifications about transelementation:

- that it is not a matter of "transfinalization," because more is at stake when the elements are consecrated than simply a change in purpose;
- that it is not a matter of "transignification," because consecrating the elements does more than simply change their meaning;

---

[63] For a defense of this principle, see Karl Rahner, "The Presence of Christ in the Sacrament of the Lord's Supper," in *Theological Investigations*, vol. IV (London: Darton, Longman & Todd, 1966), pp. 299–300.

- that it is not a matter of "consubstantiation," because it does not see a "local" (three-dimensionally circumscribed, present with weight or mass) presence of Christ's flesh in the consecrated elements, or two substances merely coexisting with one another;
- that it is not a matter of "impanation," because it does not hold that the substance of the bread is hypostatically united to Christ, or that Christ's body has "become bread" (for the reverse is true), or (as was sometimes said) that "God has become bread";
- that it is not a matter of "companation," because it does not see one substance being formed out of two mixed substances (a "monophysite" tendency), or the substance of the bread as connected in some external way to the body of Christ (a "Nestorian" tendency).

Transelementation does not require the idea of "substance" at all. (It is perhaps no longer entirely clear just what this metaphysical term might mean – a point about which at least some contemporary Catholic authorities would agree.)

Transelementation simply holds:

- that the consecrated bread becomes the body of Christ, by virtue of the *epiclesis* and the words of consecration, in the mode of a sacramental union;
- that this sacramental union involves a *koinonia* relation of inseparable unity, abiding distinction, and fundamental asymmetry (cf. 1 Cor. 10:16);
- that it is a matter of mutual indwelling between sign and reality, but with the living Christ himself as the active and preeminent factor in the Spirit;
- that the elements are objectively elevated, empowered, and transfigured by the Holy Spirit into a wholly new form beyond themselves without relinquishing their ordinary characteristics;
- that those characteristics are not destroyed but mystically reconfigured and contained by the new higher reality that supersedes them;

- that the conversion of the elements is fundamental while yet also being mystical and ineffable;
- that the consecrated elements are "effective signs," which really convey what they signify.

It would seem that "transubstantiation" and "transelementation" could at least live together in a kind of peaceful coexistence, if not more. A unity of believers and communions could be achieved within the margins of this diversity. Attention may be drawn to a few hopeful signs.

First, in the papal encyclical *Mysterium Fidei*, promulgated in 1965 by Pope Paul VI, at least two points germane to our discussion were made.[64] Not only was it acknowledged that "greater clarity of expression" with regard to real presence is "always possible" as long as the essential meaning is retained (no. 25), but a gesture toward some version of "transelementation" was also explicitly in evidence. The Fathers knew, said the Pope, that in the sacrament we should not attend to the senses, which perceive only the properties of the bread and the wine, but to the words of Christ, which have the power "to change, transform, 'transelementize' the bread and the wine into his body and blood" (no. 47). This statement, made merely in passing, would hardly commit the encyclical to the full definition offered here, but it would indeed seem to bring it within hailing distance.

Second, another hopeful sign appeared in the official Vatican response of 1987 to the World Council of Churches milestone document, *Baptism, Eucharist and Ministry* (1982).[65] While insisting that a real conversion of the elements must be upheld, so that

---

[64] Pope Paul VI, encyclical *Mysterium Fidei* (September 3, 1965), in International Committee on English in the Liturgy, *Documents on the Liturgy, 1963–1979: Concilliar, Papal, and Curial Texts* (Collegeville: Liturgical Press, 1983), Document 176, pp. 378–92.

[65] *Baptism, Eucharist and Ministry*, Faith and Order Paper No. 111 (Geneva: World Council of Churches, 1982).

an intrinsic change is affirmed, the Vatican also stated that it was open to "possible new theological explanations as to the 'how' of the intrinsic change."[66] Edward Kilmartin interpreted the Vatican outlook in the official response as pointing toward something like what this essay has called "transelementation." He wrote:

> This outlook . . . is not unlike the patristic view that the sanctifying action of the Holy Spirit elevates the bread and wine to their ultimate relational possibility: Through this action the bread and wine are so related to the risen Lord, that they become his body and blood, while remaining elements of this earth.[67]

The aspects of elevation, intrinsic change, and yet preservation would all be compatible with what has been set forth here as transelementation.

Finally, Pope Benedict XVI has also written of eucharistic conversion in terms of elevation (over and above one substance replacing another), while also capturing the important sacramental aspects of dynamism, ineffability, and christological sovereignty.

> It cannot be the case that the Body of Christ comes to add itself to the bread as if bread and Body were two similar things that could exist as two "substances," in the same way, side by side. Whenever the Body of Christ, that is, the risen and bodily Christ comes, he is greater than the bread, other, not of the same order. The transformation happens, which affects the gifts we bring by taking them up into a higher order and changes them, even if we cannot measure what happens . . . The Lord takes possession of the bread and wine; he lifts them up, as it were, out of the setting of their normal existence into a new order, they have become profoundly

---

[66] Cited by Edward J. Kilmartin, SJ, "The Official Vatican Response to BEM: Eucharist," in *Ecumenical Trends* 17 (1988), pp. 37–40; on p. 39.

[67] Ibid., p. 40. Kilmartin pursues these ideas in his book *The Eucharist in the West* (Collegeville: Liturgical Press, 1998). See especially pp. 51–58, 180–83, 145–53.

different even if, from a purely physical point of view, they remain the same.[68]

The body of the living Lord is here said to be greater than the bread. He transforms the earthly elements by elevating them to a new and higher order. The transformation they undergo is ineffable, while at the physical level they remain earthly and the same. It would seem that the idea of intrinsic change is emerging in some authoritative Roman Catholic statements as more important than the medieval ideas of substantial replacement and containment. While these latter points are not denied, they no longer seem to be as predominant as they once were. It is not the bread and wine that take possession of Christ, but he who takes possession of them. In all their earthliness they have become the higher reality that they signify, the life-giving flesh of Christ.[69]

Not only would it seem that transelementation is not church-dividing from a Roman Catholic standpoint, but the possibility seems to exist that some aspects of it are already being incorporated into official Catholic teaching. In any case the promise of transelementation is that it could be accepted today by ecumenically minded Reformational churches without theological compromise, as the sixteenth-century precedents in Luther, Calvin, Vermigli, Bucer, and Cranmer show, while also meeting the remaining concerns of contemporary Roman Catholicism. It seems to be sufficient "to remove," as the Vatican requires, "all ambiguity regarding the mode of the real presence which is due to a substantial change in the elements."[70]

---

[68] Joseph Cardinal Ratzinger [Pope Benedict XVI], *God Is Near Us: The Eucharist, The Heart of Life* (San Francisco: Ignatius Press, 2003), p. 86.

[69] The question of transubstantiation is revisited in the Conclusion of this book.

[70] "The Official Roman Catholic Response to the Final Report of ARCIC I (1991)," in *Anglicans and Roman Catholics: The Search for Unity*, ed. Christopher Hill and E. J. Yarnold (London: SPCK/CTS, 1994), pp. 156–66; on pp. 162–63.

The Catholic Church holds that Christ in the Eucharist makes himself present sacramentally and substantially when under the species of bread and wine these earthly realities are changed into the reality of his Body and Blood, Soul and Body.[71]

According to transelementation the substantial change occurs more nearly by enhancement than by replacement, but the gifts are seen as taken up into a higher order where they are intrinsically and objectively changed into the reality of Christ's body and blood. If, as affirmed by Vatican II, the Roman Catholic church is indeed open to various theological formulations beyond those that are traditional, then a resolution of the historic divisions about real presence would not seem entirely out of reach.[72]

Mode of duration

Still another issue needs to be examined. Although mentioned in passing in the section on reception, it must now be taken up more directly. It pertains to an unresolved question in the ecumenical dialogues – surprisingly, one that threatens to unravel the existing areas of consensus. It is the question of whether the sacramental union persists beyond the celebration of the sacrament itself.

Consider how this question was addressed by *Baptism, Eucharist and Ministry* (*BEM*), which after twenty-five years is still the chief document of multilateral convergence:

> It is in virtue of the living Word of Christ and by the power of the Holy Spirit that the bread and wine become sacramental signs of Christ's body and blood. They remain so for the purposes of communion.[73]

---

[71] Ibid., p. 163.
[72] For tensions in what the Vatican has said it requires, see Francis Sullivan, "The Vatican Response to ARCIC I (1992)," in ibid., pp. 298–308.
[73] *Baptism, Eucharist and Ministry*, "Eucharist," para. 15.

From the standpoint of "transelementation," this statement could be made stronger and perhaps more precise. It could be said that in the Word and by the Spirit, the bread and wine "become Christ's body and blood in the form of sacramental signs." It could be said that according to transelementation, the sign becomes the reality without ceasing to be a sign, even as the reality becomes a sign without ceasing to be the reality. In short, the bread and wine become Christ's body and blood in sacramental form.

Whether this sort of reformulation might help to remove some existing objections is not clear.

One objection comes from the high sacramental communions. In 1984 an "Agreed Statement" on *BEM* was issued by the Eastern Orthodox/Roman Catholic Consultation in the United States. It finds much to applaud in *BEM* while also holding many points in abeyance. On the matter of duration, a question is posed.

> We note that *Baptism, Eucharist and Ministry* mentions the practice of reservation of the eucharist without presenting an adequate theological rationale for it. For the Roman Catholic and Orthodox churches, it is our faith that the bread and wine become and remain the body and blood of Christ that allows us to reserve the sacrament. We would therefore welcome further elaboration on this point.

The official Roman Catholic response was even more pointed:

> We have to ask what it means for the understanding of real presence and the reality of the transformation, when someone denies the persistence of the real presence after the celebration.[74]

---

[74] The Secretariat for the Promotion of Christian Unity, with the Congregation for the Faith, *Response to "Baptism, Eucharist and Ministry"* (1987), III.B.2. Quoted in Robert W. Jenson, *Unbaptized God* (Minneapolis: Fortress, 1992), p. 28. Jenson's book offers a rare summary of where agreement and dissent can be found as a result of the many and various official ecumenical dialogues.

A divergent, typically Protestant line of objection was registered by the Presbyterian Church of Wales:

"Consecration" signifies the setting apart of the elements for the purpose of communication, with the result that the method of disposal is an irrelevance.[75]

The Protestant objection would seem to be twofold. On the one hand, consecration takes place for a particular purpose. Let us call it eucharistic communion with Christ in his self-offering to the Father for the sake of the world – a communion that extends, confirms and deepens the grace of forgiveness and new life. On the other hand, the sacramental union of sign and reality is not only real but also living and active. If it persisted beyond the eucharistic celebration, it would seem as though the door were opened first, to some purpose other than communion (e.g., adoration of the host),[76] and second, to some sort of static, thing-like presence of Christ in the elements.

Robert Jenson comments:

Disagreements about what the elements are after the celebration does in fact turn out to unravel consensus about what they are during it ... Disensus on the persistence of Christ's presence as the elements casts doubt on consensus that in the [sacrament] the elements truly become the body and blood of Christ.[77]

---

[75] Quoted by Jenson, *Unbaptized God*, p. 29 n. 15.

[76] The Vatican response to ARCIC I seemed to make adoration the touchstone for whether consensus obtained on the question of reservation. Since adoration is a matter that separates Roman Catholicism from Eastern Orthodoxy as well as from Protestantism, it is not clear why it should impede unity, as long as the Roman view were not ruled out as intolerable. This is a point that requires further discussion. See "Official Roman Catholic Response," in Hill and Yarnold, *Anglicans and Roman Catholics*, p. 163.

[77] Jenson, *Unbaptized God*, pp. 29–30 (*supra* n. 74).

From the standpoint of "transelementation" several observations are in order.

- First, using the consecrated elements for any purpose other than communion is disapproved of not only by Protestants, but also by the Eastern Orthodox. In the Orthodox churches eucharistic adoration is unknown outside the liturgy itself. It would seem that the Orthodox position is not regarded as church-dividing by Roman Catholicism.
- Second, in Orthodox churches the sacrament is reserved only for purposes of future communion, usually for the sick.[78] This kind of reservation is not unknown in some Protestant churches at the present time, though without an adequate theological basis. Restricting the use of the reserved sacrament to communion would go a long way toward addressing Protestant concerns.
- Third, theoretically it would not be incoherent to accept transelementaiton and yet a merely eucharistic duration for the union. Affirming transelementation – and therefore the real and objective conversion of the elements for purposes of communion – would seem to address at least some of the concerns expressed by the sacramental churches.
- Lastly, transelementation would allow the very idea of "eucharistic duration" to extend beyond the celebration of the sacrament. In the Word and by the Spirit, the sacramental union once accomplished would persist, because Christ by his Spirit would have joined himself to the elements for eucharistic purposes of communion. In the reserved sacrament the union would not be static but would continue to be living and operative albeit in a quiescent state. It would be "at rest," so to speak. It would persist without becoming crudely lifeless or "thing-like." It would represent Christ's enduring commitment to attest and impart himself by means of the consecrated elements.

---

[78] Not all Orthodox churches observe this practice.

In short, the promise of transelementation might be, if not to resolve the remaining differences, at least to lessen them to the point where they would not be church-dividing. No doubt would need be cast on the central point: the Holy Spirit's conversion of the elements into Christ's body and blood for the purposes of communion. The eucharistic conversion would be objective and real, regardless of whether the union persisted, under the Lordship of Christ, beyond the celebration.

When the issue is posed in this way, it might be possible for many Protestants to see wisdom in the Eastern Orthodox position. Why should eucharistic conversion and duration be merely temporary? Why should they not be seen as permanently elevating the earthly gifts into what J. M. R. Tillard, the Roman Catholic ecumenist, has called "a sacramental world" with its own inner laws?[79]

What that "world" might entail was once suggested by E. B. Pusey, the nineteenth-century patristics scholar and dignitary of the Oxford movement:[80]

> The Fathers ... assert ... that what is consecrated and what we receive, are the Body and Blood of Christ ... not in any physical or carnal way, but spiritually, sacramentally, Divinely, mystically, ineffably, through the operation of the Word of Christ, and of God the Holy Ghost.
>
> ... Several of the Fathers use such words as transmute, trans-make, transform, trans-element, reorder, of the working of the [eucharistic] consecration ...

---

[79] Quoted by Jenson, *Unbaptized God*, p. 30 n. 17.

[80] Pusey compiled a very extensive catalogue, apparently the most extensive ever published, of patristic quotations documenting the Eastern view of transelementation and related concepts. See E. B. Pusey, *The Doctrine of the Real Presence as Contained in the Fathers* (Oxford: John Henry Parker, 1855). This 722-page volume was published in support of the already very substantially documented sermon cited in the next footnote.

All these words are also, by the very same Fathers, used of spiritual changes, which do not involve change of substance ...

In the same context, in which a Father speaks of the sacramental change, he says, using the same word, "The Body [of Christ] by the indwelling of God the Word, was transmade, *metepoiethe*, into the Divine dignity."

More largely, the Fathers speak of the change and "transmaking of the human nature into the Divine;" they say that "the Lord's Body was trans-elemented into incorruption;" "the Flesh of our Lord becometh Christ and Lord;" the Flesh of the Manhood was transmade into the Divine Nature;" "what was visible became Christ and Lord." More frequently yet do they use the words of a change which is wholly spiritual, the change of regeneration. "Our nature is by Baptism," they say, "transformed from corruptible to incorruptible;" "spiritually trans-elemented from a foul to a better state;" "trans-elemented to the ancient image through the Spirit;" "trans-elemented to that which was above nature" ...

They use the illustration, "iron (red hot) becometh fire." They say, "we are changed into the substance of angels;" "the body passeth into the nature of the soul;" "nature is changed into a heavenly substance;" "saints are changed into angels;" "Christians are wholly trans-elemented into Christ. Who hath power to impart life."[81]

These observations may cast light on the question of duration. If the Incarnation were taken as the reference point, it would seem that the sacramental union would persist. This is the view of the high sacramental churches. On the other hand, if the image of iron in the fire were the controlling idea, the sacramental union, though real and objective, might endure only for as long as the eucharistic

---

[81] E. B. Pusey, *The Presence of Christ in the Holy Eucharist: A Sermon Preached Before the University, in the Cathedral Church of Christ, in Oxford, on the Second Day after Epiphany, 1853* (Oxford: James Parker & Co., 1871; Whitefish: Kessinger Publishing, LLC, 2004), pp. 46, 43–45.

celebration, as though the iron were then removed from the fire. This might be the view of some Protestant churches.

Certainly it would be a very important ecumenical gesture for those not reserving the sacrament to ensure that it was humanly consumed with reverence. But if, as transelementation would suggest, the consecrated gifts are elevated by the Holy Spirit into the sacramental realm of holiness, immortality, and incorruption, that is, into the realm of Christ's heavenly presence, then it would not be implausible to hold, with the sacramental churches, that the union once instituted would not disappear. The sacrament would be reserved for the sick and otherwise consumed with reverence.

Why should the consecrated gifts not persist in representing the risen Christ's ongoing, irreversible and continually renewed commitment to join his people to himself in his once-for-all atoning sacrifice and eternal intercession? Why should the gifts once elevated not permanently retain the higher predication they have gained in the Spirit for purposes of communion with Christ? In short, why should the sacramental union once instituted not continue – not only *in usu*, but also *extra usum*, though still *pro usum*?

Mode of consecration

The *epiclesis* is an ancient prayer of invocation, rooted in Eastern liturgies, which calls upon the Holy Spirit in the eucharist. From a theological point of view, three disputed questions exist about the use of this prayer: the objects of consecration, the moment of consecration, and the agency of consecration. (Liturgically, a dispute also exists about where the prayer should be placed in the liturgy.)

The first question, arising from within traditional Protestantism, is whether the Spirit's blessing should be invoked upon the gifts of bread and wine or rather only upon those persons gathered to receive them. The other two questions point to tensions between Eastern Orthodoxy and Roman Catholicism. Certain papal statements made recently by John Paul II, though they cannot be discussed here, raise concerns about whether traditional Catholic/Orthodox differences about the *epiclesis* have been resolved as fully as was widely supposed. *Epiclesis* as a key to the consecration of the gifts, it may be noted, makes the divine operation of the Holy Spirit central in a way that relativizes what can be contributed by the priest.[82]

The focus here is, again, on whether "transelementation" can shed light on this matter.

Any Protestant restriction of the *epiclesis*, or something like it, to the blessing of persons alone has precedents in the early Reformation. Cranmer, for example, at first included the following prayer in the 1549 Communion Service:

> Hear us, O merciful Father, we beseech thee, and with thy Holy Spirit and Word, vouchsafe to bless and sanctify these thy gifts and creatures of bread and wine, that they may be unto us the body and blood of thy most dearly beloved Son Jesus Christ.[83]

What happened next is described by Bryan D. Spinks: "Although its intended Reformed theology could be expressed and expounded by someone of the caliber of Peter Martyr, [the Roman Catholic] Bishop Gardiner drew attention to the fact that the doctrine of transubstantiation could also be expressed in

---

[82] See Patrick Regan, "Quenching the Spirit: The Epiclesis in Recent Roman Documents," *Worship* 79 (2005), pp. 386–404. For a more general survey, see Robert F. Taft, "Ecumenical Scholarship and the Catholic–Orthodox Epiclesis Dispute," *Ostkirchlichen Studien* 45 (1996), pp. 201–26.

[83] Quoted in Bryan D. Spinks, " 'And with thy Holy Spirite and Worde': Further Thoughts on the Source of Cranmer's Petition for Sanctification in the 1549 Communion Service," in *Cranmer: A Living Influence for 500 Years*, ed. Margot Johnson (Durham: Turnstone Ventures, 1990), pp. 94–102; on p. 94. I have modernized the spelling in the prayer.

similar phraseology. Thus reference to sanctification by Word and Spirit did not survive the 1552 revision."[84] Such scruples persist in contemporary Protestantism. While many Protestant churches affirmed the prominent role for the Holy Spirit included in the eucharistic proposal of *BEM*, not all could accept an invocation of the Spirit upon the gifts. "Some of them," Geoffrey Wainwright has noted, "remain hesitant about the *epiklesis* in a technical liturgiological sense (particularly as an invocation of the Holy Spirit upon the elements)."[85]

An acceptance of transelementation would of course go hand in hand with an acceptance of the *epiclesis* of the Spirit's blessing upon the gifts. Vermigli took it for granted that the Spirit's primary role in the eucharist was to transform believers by bringing them into communion with Christ. Yet he also accepted a role for the Spirit in the transformation of the gifts themselves. It belongs to the Holy Spirit, he argued, to change the symbols of bread and wine into "the state and condition of sacraments."[86] "Indeed," states Joseph McLelland, "he posits a definite sacramental mutation [i.e., transelementation] in the elements deriving from and analogous to the mutation in the communicants themselves."[87]

That the gifts themselves might be blessed along with the people is now the regular subject of eucharistic prayer across a wide range of churches and traditions.

Liturgy of St. Chrysostom:
For the precious gifts here offered, let us pray to the Lord ... make us fit to offer You spiritual gifts and sacrifices for our sins ... Make us worthy to find grace in your eyes.

---

[84] Ibid., p. 100. A version of the original prayer was eventually restored and remains in use to the present day.

[85] Geoffrey Wainwright, "Word and Sacrament in the Churches' Responses to the Lima Text," *One in Christ* 24 (1988), pp. 304–27; on p. 312.

[86] Vermigli, *Oxford Treatise*, p. 85 (*supra* n. 40).

[87] Joseph C. McLelland, *The Visible Words of God* (Edinburgh: Oliver & Boyd, 1957), pp. 32–33.

Liturgy of St. Basil:
Bless this offering and . . . accept it on your altar in heaven. In your goodness and love for mankind, remember both those who offer it and those for whom it is offered.

The Lima Liturgy (1982):
May the outpouring of this Spirit of Fire
transfigure this thanksgiving meal
that this bread and wine may become for us
the body and blood of Christ.

Novus Ordo Missae (Paul VI, 1975):
In memory of his death and resurrection, we offer you, Father, this life-giving bread, this saving cup. We thank you for counting us worthy to stand in your presence and serve you. May all of us who share in the body and blood of Christ be brought together in the unity by the Holy Spirit.

The Book of Common Prayer
Sanctify [these gifts] by your Holy Spirit . . . Sanctify us also . . .

The Great Thanksgiving C, PCUSA:
Pour out your Holy Spirit upon us and upon these your gifts of bread and wine. Make them to be for us the body and blood of Christ.

Although these prayers differ in language, content, and emphasis, they all have one thing in common. They all pray for a divine blessing upon both the eucharistic gifts and those gathered to receive them. The Liturgy of St. Basil in particular is notable for the way it sees the liturgy on earth as sharing in the great liturgy of heaven. The prayers of the Protestant churches tend generally to emphasize sanctification, communion with Christ, and being equipped for service.

Admittedly, the prayer cited from the Presbyterian Church (USA), though certainly promising, is still not typical of its eucharistic prayers. Nevertheless, from an ecumenical perspective, it points in the right direction. Such prayers might help to lead the Reformed churches toward an acceptance of transelementation, which in turn would surely lead to the use of more such prayers. A beginning is at least in evidence: *lex orandi, lex credendi.*[88]

Conclusion

To conclude: this book tries to achieve two goals. It tries to develop a position on the eucharist (1) that would not be church-dividing and (2) that could be adopted by the Reformed tradition without theological compromise. It would seem that the doctrine of transelementation meets these conditions.

(1) The doctrine seems not to be church-dividing. Along with other terms of similar meaning, "transelementation" has a secure place within the first five centuries of the undivided church, at the least. It continues to represent the main position of Eastern Orthodoxy today, which the Roman Catholic Church does not consider to be divisive.[89] Since few non-Catholics are likely to embrace the doctrine of transubstantiation, an alternative that is not unacceptable to Roman Catholicism is greatly to be desired. It would seem that transelementation could be embraced by a wide variety of non-Catholics.

(2) It also seems that the doctrine could be adopted by the Reformed tradition. It was actually approved in the sixteenth century, in one way or another, by Vermigli, Bucer, and Cranmer. It would perhaps not take a great adjustment in Calvin's doctrine to bring it into alignment. Whereas Calvin seemed to posit a relationship of contiguous conjunction or symbolic parallelism between sign and reality, he nonetheless allowed for a "secret conversion" whereby the gifts were taken up and changed into a higher order of reality.

---

[88] For a discussion of this formula as revived by Geoffrey Wainwright, see James F. Kay, "The *Lex Orandi* in Recent Protestant Theology," in *Ecumenical Theology in Worship, Doctrine, and Life,* ed. David S. Cunningham *et al.* (New York: Oxford University Press, 1999), pp. 11–23.

[89] For how traditional Roman Catholic theology evaluated "transelementation" and related terms, see Pusey, *Doctrine of Real Presence,* pp. 161–72.

Vermigli and the others were open, more explicitly, to a relationship of eucharistic elevation, conversion, and mutual indwelling, along the lines of the iron in the fire. Once the idea of the corporeal is clarified so as to exclude local presence in the sacrament (which no one ever wanted anyway), the substantial presence of Christ's life-giving flesh in, with, and as the consecrated elements should not be out of reach for ecumenically minded Calvinists.

In line with the Fathers of the fourth and fifth centuries, and Eastern Orthodoxy today, the Reformed would retain their traditional view that the eucharistic sign is indeed a sign, but would stretch to adopt the position that the sign, without ceasing to be a sign, also becomes primarily – in the Word and by the Spirit – the reality that is signified. (The name of Zwingli, which so far has been conspicuously absent from this discussion, will be introduced in the next chapter on eucharistic sacrifice, where his concerns can be more readily addressed.)

"Once the question of the elements has been raised," observes Geoffrey Wainwright, "it will not go away."[90] He therefore issues a pertinent challenge:

> It would be important that the Orthodox Churches explain to others what they mean by the transformation of the elements (*metabole*); that the Roman Catholic Church explore with others how what is "most aptly called transubstantiation" (Council of Trent) may otherwise be expressed; that those Protestants who deny any "essential change" in the elements state what they are thereby affirming. Here the dialogue remains open after the Lima text.[91]

The proposal made here is one that has taken up Wainwright's challenge at precisely these points in order that the dialogue may possibly go forward.

---

[90] Wainwright, "The Eucharist in the Churches' Responses to the Lima Text," *One in Christ* 25 (1989), pp. 53–74, on p. 65.
[91] Ibid., pp. 65–66.

PART II

Eucharistic sacrifice

3 | The sacrifice we offer: controversies

A sacrifice of thanks and praise: the Reformers on eucharistic sacrifice

Nothing was denounced more vehemently by the Reformation than the Roman Catholic view of the mass as a "propitiatory sacrifice." To the Reformers almost everything wrong with Catholicism seemed to coalesce at this point. The Catholic mass combined several distinct abuses. They were mercenary, because masses for the dead were shamelessly bought and sold. They were ecclesiological, because the priesthood had usurped an illicit role at the expense of Christ's people. Above all, they were soteriological, because the Roman church had arrogated powers to itself that did not belong to it, but only to Christ. Zwingli, Luther, and Calvin were relentless, in the grand sixteenth-century style, in exposing these interlocking evils.

The focus of attention here will be the soteriological question, and again the approach will be ecumenical. While full agreement may not be possible, a greater measure of common ground exists among the divided churches than might first meet the eye. Today's heirs of the Reformation arguably have much to learn from sacramental traditions like Catholicism about eucharistic sacrifice. A fresh consideration could enrich their understanding of the Lord's Supper. At the same time, many historic Reformation concerns no longer seem incompatible with contemporary Catholic teaching, especially as expressed in official church documents. An attempt will be made to lay some groundwork for decreasing, if not eliminating, the distance separating the churches. A case will be made that the Reformed tradition in particular could move toward a new understanding of the eucharist by reflecting on the meaning of Passover.

The discussion will proceed in three parts. In the first, the Reformation critique will be examined. In the second, this critique will be juxtaposed with the positions taken by Thomas Aquinas and the Council of Trent. Questions will be raised, directly and indirectly, about the extent to which the Reformation understood Catholicism correctly. A glance at recent Catholic theology will show reasons for ecumenical hope. A constructive proposal will be developed in the next chapter.

The Reformation critique: Zwingli

If Huldrych Zwingli was sure of anything, it was that the cross of Christ had been a real sacrifice, but that the Lord's Supper most assuredly was not. "If Christ is a unique high priest," argued Zwingli, "who sacrifices nothing but himself, it is impossible for him to be frequently offered up for us ... He cannot be sacrificed more than once."[1] Christ's high-priestly sacrifice was unrepeatable, because it was in fact "a perfect sacrifice" (DRF p. 92). It was perfect for at least two reasons: first, because of the one who had offered it; and second, because of what it had accomplished.

The one who had offered it was Christ himself and Christ alone. "And as Christ suffered and died only once," Zwingli wrote, "he has also been offered up only once. For no one can make the offering but Christ alone who offers himself" (DRF p. 97). "Who has ever offered up Christ?" the Reformer asked. "When Christ was offered up on the cross and died, no one offered him up but he

---

[1] Huldrych Zwingli, *The Defense of the Reformed Faith* (Allison Park: Pickwick Publications, 1984), p. 92. (Hereafter cited in the text as *DRF.*)

himself" (*DRF* p. 97). "No person could have been found to do this except Christ."[2] No one else could have done it, because he alone was God incarnate. "Christ is our salvation by virtue of that part of his nature by which he came down from heaven, not of that by which he was born of an immaculate virgin, though he had to suffer and die by this part; but unless he who died had also been God he could not have been salvation for the whole world."[3] In short, the perfection of this unique sacrifice was grounded in the divine-human person who had offered it (*DRF* p. 98).

At the same time, the sacrifice was also perfect because of its effect. As "a surety, price and payment for our sin," Zwingli wrote, Christ's high-priestly death on the cross was "sufficient and inexhaustible for all eternity" (*DRF* p. 95). Christ's saving work was finished at the cross. "There our salvation and his testament were fully perfected" (*DRF* p. 96). "By this one death he purified and paid for the sins of the whole world for eternity" (SCI p. 71). The efficacy of this sacrifice involved no imperfection. "Christ, who is true God and human," Zwingli urged, "is so high and valuable that his death offered only once is rich and precious enough to pay for all the world's sin for eternity; for he is eternal God. Therefore, his suffering is also unceasingly fruitful for eternity" (SCI p. 72). This unique sacrifice, once offered, was final and all-sufficient, being universal in its scope and valid to all eternity.

Zwingli found it to be intolerable that the Roman mass should attempt to repeat the unrepeatable. Christ himself had destroyed all sin when he had offered himself once for all. If his sacrifice were to be repeated, that could only mean it was not perfect, and that its efficacy was not eternal. "If, now," Zwingli objected, "the priesthood claims that they sacrifice for sin, then that must mean that

---

[2] Huldrych Zwingli, "Short Christian Instruction," in *In Search of True Religion: Reformation, Pastoral and Eucharistic Writings* (Allison Park: Pickwick Publications, 1984), p. 71. (Hereafter cited in the text as SCI.)

[3] Zwingli, *On True and False Religion* (Durham, NC: Labyrinth Press, 1981), pp. 205–6. (Hereafter cited in the text as TFR.)

Christ did not complete salvation perfectly with his suffering – or that it is no longer powerful" (SCI p. 72). To those who insisted that Christ must be offered on the altar each day, because we sin each day, Zwingli retorted: "But that is a belittling and degrading of the offering" (DRF p. 94). For Christ was such a perfect sacrifice that he – offered but once – sufficed for all eternity, even as he perfected all those who believed in him (DRF p. 94). "If Christ has to be offered up daily, it must be because his being offered once on the cross is not sufficient for all time" (TFR p. 325).

To think that the mass could somehow expiate sin was absurd. "We all wanted to attain salvation by masses," noted Zwingli, "when yet the Lord's Supper, even if celebrated according to Christ's institution of it, would not expiate sin; for that belongs to Christ alone" (TFR p. 238). Any attempt to repeat Christ's unrepeatable sacrifice was therefore blasphemous. "For if we believe that he, once sacrificed, has redeemed and paid for all eternity for us ... then it must be blasphemy to undertake it again, just as if it had not been previously accomplished" (SCI p. 72). Likewise, to think that others could sacrifice the very one who alone could sacrifice himself was shocking "As we have no priest in the entire human race who is without sin other than Christ alone," Zwingli explained, "then also can no one sacrifice him other than himself. And therefore, whoever calls himself a sacrificer takes Christ's honor away from him and gives it to himself. This is an intolerable abomination" (SCI p. 72). No one has ever offered up the person of Christ to God but Christ himself. "Consequently," wrote Zwingli, "if you want to offer anything to God offer up yourself to him, just as he has done for you" (DRF pp. 97–98).

Since the mass could not possibly be a sacrifice, Zwingli reasoned, then it must be a memorial. "It becomes plain," he wrote, "that the mass is not a sacrifice but a memorial of the sacrifice, and a seal of the redemption, which Christ has manifested to us" (DRF p. 98). "It shall not ever be anything other than a memorial of that which took place once and is to continue as a remembrance of the suffering of Christ and of how wholesome it was and ever shall be. Now, then, if it is a memorial it cannot be a sacrifice, for a sacrifice is not a memorial" (*DRF* p. 110). For Zwingli, the sacrifice differed from the memorial, it would seem, in much the same way that the past tense differed from the present. Christ's sacrifice had taken place in the past as a perfect and unrepeatable event. It was not to be repeated but rather remembered with thanksgiving. That was the point of Christ's commandment: "Do this in remembrance of me." "It means," wrote Zwingli, "'Practice it among you so that you may eat my body and drink my blood in remembrance of me, which is to renew through recollection the good deed which I have shown you'" (*DRF* p. 110). There could be no remembrance without thanksgiving and no thanksgiving without remembrance. For "remembrance is nothing other than a sincere thanksgiving for the great deed and a memorial of his humble suffering by which he has united us with God" (*DRF* p. 110).

Although Zwingli, in line with the apostle Paul, could interpret the eucharist in terms of Passover, "remembrance" remained for him a decidedly spiritual or even mental event. The contrast between things material and things spiritual was fundamental for him. "I try to lift you to the things above," he wrote, "by comparisons and pleasant allegories, but you are always sinking to the depths by the weight of your unbelief. The thing of which I am speaking [the Lord's Supper] is a spiritual thing, and has nothing to do with bodily things" (*TFR* p. 208). As W. P. Stephens has observed of Zwingli, "To say that if the believer eats the body and drinks the blood of Christ, then he has the body and blood present, is not to say any more than that 'the faithful have the body and blood of Christ present in the mind.'"[4] This presence of Christ to the mind supplied the context within which Zwingli compared

---

[4] W. P. Stephens, *The Theology of Huldrych Zwingli* (Oxford: Clarendon Press, 1986), p. 243 (quoting Zwingli).

Passover to the eucharist. What they had in common was that both were commemorations of a sacrifice. "A commemoration is instituted in the one case and in the other" (SCI p. 212). What distinguished them was that the Passover commemorated the deliverance of Israel from Egypt while the eucharist commemorated the world's deliverance from sin and death (SCI pp. 210–11). Zwingli could describe Christ himself as "the true Passover" (SCI p. 210). But he could not conceive of Christ's eucharistic presence except as a spiritual presence to the believer's remembering and thankful mind – just as he could not conceive of the eucharistic bread and wine except as bare memorials of Christ's body and blood.

Although Zwingli seems rather far, in many respects, from any future ecumenical consensus, he nonetheless lifted up at least five points that would seem to be full of promise. He insisted (1) that Christ alone is the acting subject of his own sacrificial act, (2) that Christ himself is the sole and sufficient content of his intercessory death, (3) that Christ's sacrifice took place once for all on the cross and so cannot be repeated, (4) that this sacrifice has eternal validity, and (5) that "remembrance" or "memorial" is somehow essential to the celebration of eucharist. From an ecumenical standpoint, perhaps the main question to Zwingli would be whether "sacrifice" and "memorial" are as mutually exclusive in the eucharist as he supposed. Do they really differ from one another as the past tense differs from the present? After all, as even Zwingli acknowledged, rather suggestively, about the present tense: "As often as we want to go to God we ought to remind him that Christ has suffered for us" (DRF p. 95).

The Reformation critique: Luther

Although Luther largely agreed with Zwingli's critique of the mass, he supplied his own special emphases. On the christological difficulty, however, their views were virtually identical. Like Zwingli, Luther affirmed that only Christ could offer himself as a sacrifice, that his sacrificial death had been final and all-sufficient, and that therefore it could not be repeated. There was only one acting subject in the work of Christ's sacrifice: Christ alone. "Only Christ," wrote Luther, "can make and has made satisfaction for us."[5] He alone "has washed sin away and has died and risen again" (*LW* 36, p. 320). How could Christ's sacrifice be repeated or continued by another? "Has not the sacrifice for the whole world already been made through Christ?" (*LW* 36, p. 315). Christ's unique sacrifice was final and all-sufficient. He alone had "taken away and swallowed up all sins," and he had done it "through his one death and sacrifice" (*LW* 36, p. 320). "There is no sacrifice in the New Testament," Luther insisted, "other than the sacrifice of the cross" (*LW* 36, p. 162). "We know and have no other sacrifice than that which [Christ] made on the cross, on which he died once for all" (*LW* 36, p. 313). "Christ has sacrificed himself once; henceforth he will not be sacrificed by anyone else" (*LW* 36, p. 147).

For Luther as for Zwingli, Christ's sacrifice was inseparable from his person. Christ's benefits and his person were one. As Luther never tired of stating, Christ alone was "our righteousness and our life" (*LW* 26, p. 11). "Christ himself," wrote Luther, "is our Reconciliation, Righteousness, Peace, Life, and Salvation" (*LW* 26, p. 150). The perfect sufficiency of Christ's self-sacrifice meant that "Christ is our entire holiness" (*LW* 26, p. 109) – "our principal, complete, and perfect righteousness" (*LW* 27, p. 71). No other righteousness, Luther affirmed, was either necessary or possible than Christ himself and Christ alone. "Christ is our only righteousness" (*LW* 27, p. 148).

---

[5] Martin Luther, *Luther's Works*, American Edition, 55 vols. (St. Louis: Concordia Publishing House; Philadelphia: Fortress Press, 1955–86), vol. 37, p. 369. (Hereafter cited in the text by volume and page number, e.g., *LW* 37, p. 369).

A repetition of Christ's once-for-all sacrifice in the mass was clearly as inconceivable to Luther as to Zwingli. To Luther the contradiction was self-evident: "The priest offers up once again the Lord Christ, who offered himself only once and cannot die again or be offered up again" (*LW* 36, p. 320). "They deny God and insult the sacrifice that Christ has made and disgrace his blood, because they try to do what only Christ's blood can do" (*LW* 36, p. 313). "They do not thank him. Indeed, they despise and deny his sacrifice and try to come before God with their own sacrifice" (*LW* 36, p. 313). "The good Christ is not pleasing to the Father unless the holy canon comes and makes him pleasing, in that the offering reconciles him with God" (*LW* 36, p. 327). "It is un-Christian to sacrifice Christ daily, who sacrificed himself once and neither can nor will be sacrificed again" (*LW* 37, p. 142). "Christ cannot be sacrificed over and above the one single time he sacrificed himself" (*LW* 37, p. 143).

Consequently, for Luther the idea of the mass as a sacrifice was "by far the most wicked abuse of all" (*LW* 36, p. 35). It was "the greatest of all abominations" (*LW* 37, p. 370), "the height of perversity" (*LW* 36, p. 114), "nothing but a terrible and abominable blasphemy" (*LW* 36, p. 318), and "surely the devil's work" (*LW* 36, p. 154). In other words, Luther heaped his usual quotient of invective on an idea he found it necessary to reject.

Besides the christological problem, the primary reason why Luther reacted with such vehemence was that he thought the theory of the propitiatory mass had turned it into that worst of perversions, a "meritorious" work. This theme is more prominent in Luther than in Zwingli. The eucharist, Luther stressed, was not a work. On the contrary, it was a gift, a promise, a testament, an assurance to the troubled conscience, and an act of thanks and praise.

"There is no opinion more generally held or more firmly believed in the church today," wrote Luther in *The Babylonian Captivity of the Church*, "than this, that the mass is a good work and a sacrifice" (*LW* 36, p. 35). As opposed to a "sacrament," which Luther defined as a divine gift, a "sacrifice" is a human work in which we present something to God in order to allay his wrath and gain his favor (*LW* 36, p. 169). When the mass is turned into a sacrifice, "Christ's office and work" are wrongly given over to the priests (*LW* 38, p. 117). They "imagine that they are offering up Christ ... and performing a good work for all those whom they intend to benefit, for they put their trust in the work which the mass accomplishes" (*LW* 36, p. 50). They regard Christ's body and blood "as a sacrifice of works ... in which they obtain merits for themselves and others and, first and foremost, secure grace" (*LW* 38, p. 117). In this way the meaning of the eucharist was stood on its head. "Thus Christ has not won grace for us, but we want to win grace for ourselves through our works by offering God his Son's body and blood" (*LW* 38, pp. 117–18). Such a view could hardly be more wrong-headed. "All priests today are perversely mistaken who regard the mass as a work by which they may relieve their own needs and those of others, whether dead or alive" (*LW* 36, p. 50). "It is a manifest and wicked error to offer or apply the mass for sins, for satisfactions, for the dead or for any needs whatsoever of one's own or of others" (*LW* 36, p. 48). It was particularly erroneous to hold, as Luther believed his opponents did, that the mass was efficacious *ex opere operato*. How could it be efficacious, automatically, by the very work of performing the mass, if in fact its efficacy depended solely on divine grace and could be received solely by faith? (*LW* 35, pp. 63–4, 102).

For Luther the eucharist had to reflect what Christ accomplished through his unique sacrifice. "Our gospel," he wrote, is "that Christ made us righteous and holy through that sacrifice and has redeemed us from sin, death, and the devil and has brought us into his heavenly kingdom. We have to grasp this and hold it fast through faith alone" (*LW* 36, p. 313). No other saving work is needed than the one already accomplished by Christ. "All our works undertaken to expiate sin and escape from death are necessarily blasphemous. They deny God and insult the sacrifice that Christ has made and disgrace his blood, because they try to do what only Christ's blood can do" (*LW* 36, p. 313). When the mass is offered as a meritorious work, it is as if the cross had not occurred, or as if it were not sufficient. It is as if Christ needed to be crucified repeatedly. "Your sacrifice," charged Luther, "is nothing else than the crucifying of Christ again and again" (*LW* 36, p. 147). God does not need to be propitiated by the mass. "Everything that offers another way or another sacrifice must be false" (*LW* 36, p. 313).

Since Christ's sacrifice is finished, all-sufficient and unrepeatable, it could only be received as a gift. The sacrament, insisted Luther, is a means of grace, not a propitiatory sacrifice (*LW* 36, p. 172). In the sacrament, he wrote, we should seek the forgiveness of sins, receiving it by faith, "as a free gift which Christ procured for us with his body and blood"; we should not seek to earn forgiveness through sacrifices and works (*LW* 36, p. 180). The sacrament is actually a promise that our forgiveness is given gratis (*LW* 36, pp. 176–77). It is not a sacrifice that we offer, but a testament we receive from Christ, for "the same thing cannot be received and offered at the same time" (*LW* 36, p. 52). A sacrifice implies that God still needs to be rendered favorable toward us, but the sacrament assures us of God's mercy and strengthens our faith (*LW* 37, p. 142). The sacrament is a sacrifice not of works but of thanks and praise. It seeks not to propitiate God, but to remember Christ's gracious self-offering. "I am making neither the mass nor the sacrament a sacrifice," wrote Luther; "rather, the sacrifice is the remembrance of Christ which consists of the teaching and faith concerning grace in opposition to our merits and works" (*LW* 38, p. 117). In the sacrament remembrance and thanksgiving were one. "It is a sacrifice of thanksgiving," wrote Luther, "for by this very remembrance we confess and thank God that we have been saved and become righteous and blessed by sheer grace through Christ's suffering" (*LW* 38, p. 117).

However, because Luther went on, as we will see, to develop a concept of eucharistic sacrifice by another name, his understanding of salvation's present tense differed significantly from Zwingli's. For Zwingli, salvation in Christ had taken place almost exclusively in the perfect or the aorist tense (to borrow grammatical terms used of Greek). Salvation's present tense then consisted, for him, almost entirely in remembrance, thanksgiving, and ethics. For Luther, salvation in Christ had much the same contours as for Zwingli, regarding what had taken place for our sakes on the cross. But Luther understood salvation's present tense in a more complex way than Zwingli did. While the Wittenberg Reformer sometimes distinguished drastically between eucharistic sacrifice as a meritorious work and the church's self-offering to God in prayer, at other times his thinking took a surprising turn. Perhaps for Luther, after all, the same thing could be received and offered at the same time.

The Reformation critique: Calvin

In his critique of the mass John Calvin synthesized the concerns of Zwingli and Luther. Like them, he stressed that Christ's sacrifice had been perfect and all-sufficient, and that therefore it could not be repeated. Like Luther but in contrast to Zwingli, he did not regard the sacrament as a bare memorial. Yet where Luther had interpreted the sacrament primarily as a gift not a work, Calvin laid rather more weight on the Lord's Supper as a means of union and communion with Christ. By comparison with his predecessors, he also took greater notice of Roman Catholic rebuttals, though he rejected them out of hand.

While yielding nothing to others at the level of invective – Calvin could describe the mass, for example, as "a most pestilential error"[6] – he had the virtue of being rhetorically forceful and admirably concise. He summarized his objections in five points.

---

[6] John Calvin, *Institutes of the Christian Religion*, 2 vols. (Philadelphia: Westminster Press, 1960), Book IV, ch. 18, section 1. (Hereafter cited in the text according to convention: *Inst.* IV.18.1.)

First, the mass substituted the actions of the priest for Jesus Christ. But Christ had been consecrated as our true High Priest by God. Having risen from the dead to die no more, he needed no replacements. He had been appointed to "an everlasting priesthood" (*Inst.* IV.18.2). "The right and honor of a priesthood among mortal men has ceased," wrote Calvin, "because Christ, who is immortal, is the sole and eternal Priest" (*Inst.* IV.18.2). A continual succession of priests had once been necessary, because of their mortality. But now, "Christ who is not prevented by death, is unique and needs no partners" (*Inst.* IV.18.2). By presuming to sacrifice daily, the Roman priests have usurped the place belonging to Christ. They have robbed him of "the prerogative of that eternal priesthood" whereby he intercedes for us eternally in heaven (*Inst.* IV.18.2). While Calvin acknowledged the rebuttal of his opponents that the priests were regarded not as substitutes, but as assistants of Christ's eternal priesthood, he noted this point only to dismiss it (*Inst.* IV.18.2).

Second, the mass detracted from the perfection of Christ's once-for-all sacrifice. "By his one sacrifice," wrote Calvin, "all that pertained to our salvation has been accomplished and fulfilled" (*Inst.* IV.18.3). But the daily sacrifice of the mass implied that what Christ had done was not enough. "Are we to be allowed," asked Calvin, "to sew innumerable patches upon such a sacrifice, as if it were imperfect, when he has so clearly commended its perfection?" (*Inst.* IV.18.3). Those who required another sacrifice were accusing Christ of "imperfection and weakness" (*Inst.* IV.18.3). "There are no other sacrifices," insisted Calvin, because "this one was offered only once and is never to be repeated" (*Inst.* IV.18.3). "All its force remains for ever" (*Inst.* IV.18.3). Here again, Calvin was aware of a rebuttal. The mass was not a different sacrifice, claimed its defenders, but "the same one often repeated," or, put differently, it was "not a repetition but an application" (*Inst.* IV.18.3). To Calvin these arguments were specious. "For Christ did not once for all offer himself up on condition that his sacrifice should be ratified by new oblations each day" (*Inst.* IV.18.3). On the contrary, Christ's sacrifice was applied and communicated not by repeating it, but by rightly proclaiming the gospel, properly administering the sacraments, and faithfully receiving Christ's sacrifice with thanks and praise.

Third, the mass amended Christ's last will and testament by illicitly adding a codicil to it. Christ's sacrifice was originally instituted as "the testament by which he has given us forgiveness of sins and everlasting righteousness" (*Inst.* IV.18.5). His testament was inviolable, not something anyone could modify or supplement. Yet the mass entailed "a new and wholly different testament" (*Inst.* IV.18.5). "Why so? Do not individual masses promise new forgiveness of sins, and new acquiring of righteousness, so that there are now as many testaments as there are masses?" (*Inst.* IV.18.5). By daily repetition the mass wiped out Christ's sufficient and unrepeatable accomplishment. It undertook to slay him cruelly in a thousand places each day. Calvin acknowledged the plea of opponents who insisted that "we object against them what they never thought, and even now cannot think" (*Inst.* IV.18.5). To which he retorted: "Our purpose is only to show the absurd consequence of their impious and wicked doctrine" (*Inst.* IV.18.5).

Fourth, the mass made us into our own redeemers. It robbed us of Christ's death by making our redemption depend on the performance of a new human work. "And it is no way out," insisted Calvin, "to say that we obtain forgiveness of sins in the mass solely because it has already been purchased by Christ's death" (*Inst.* IV.18.6). Properly understood, the sacrament could not possibly be a work on which the forgiveness of sins depended. On the contrary, it was a remembrance of Christ's unique sacrifice "so that our faith may be made fast to his cross" (*Inst.* IV.18.6).

Finally, the mass destroyed God's free and sovereign grace by making it conditional instead of gratuitous. Like Luther, Calvin saw the ideas of sacrament and sacrifice as mutually exclusive. While a sacrament was a gift of free grace, a sacrifice was a meritorious work. In a sacrament, thanks and praise were given to God; in a sacrifice, God was made to be our debtor. "The sacrifice of the mass," wrote Calvin, "is represented as paying a price to God, which he should receive by way of satisfaction" (*Inst.* IV.18.7). By perverting the sacrament into a sacrifice, he concluded, the way was opened for the notorious abuse of conducting "private masses."

Three points may be noted at this point. First, Calvin went on to define the nature of sacrifice in terms that today could be ecumenically promising. He distinguished four types of sacrifice: those which made satisfaction for sin, those which offered supplication, those which expressed thanks and praise, and those which renewed the covenant from the human side by expressing piety and devotion (*Inst.* IV.18.13). Insofar as the sacrament might be not only a sacrifice of thanks and praise, but also a sacrifice of supplication, renewal, and devotion, a less polarized range of options might emerge for honoring the centrality of Christ's unrepeatable sacrifice.

Second, Calvin defined the sacrament as something more than a gift by which forgiveness was communicated and applied to us. It was primarily a means by which believers were united to Christ and through him to God. Christ was truly present in the sacrament so that we "might enjoy true participation in him" (*Inst.* IV.18.8). In the sacrament, the present Christ who "makes himself common to all, also makes all of us one in himself" (*Inst.* IV.17.38). To receive Christ in the sacrament is to "enjoy true participation in him" (*Inst.* IV.17.11). Through the gift of "his very body and blood," we are made to be "partakers of his substance, that we might sense his power in the communication of all his blessings" (*Inst.* IV.17.11, translation revised). *Participatio Christi* was the sacrament's chief and lively effect. Through the continual giving and receiving of his body and blood in the eucharist, Christ incorporated his people into the body of which he himself was the head, and communicated to them all his benefits.

Finally, for Calvin, Christ's priestly office, which belonged to Christ alone, was not restricted only to the past tense, nor was it incompatible with his people being appointed as priests in him. Christ's priestly work was at once finished and yet also perpetual. Just because Christ had "blotted out our own guilt and made satisfaction for our sins," he was also our "everlasting intercessor" (*Inst.* II.15.6). Through his ongoing intervention we obtained favor with God. "Now, Christ plays the priestly role," wrote Calvin, "not only to render the Father favorable toward us by an eternal law of reconciliation, but also to receive us as his companions in this great office" (*Inst.* II.15.6). In other words, according to Calvin, the community was given a share in the ascended Christ's unique priestly office. "For we who are defiled in ourselves, yet are priests in him" (*Inst.* II.15.6). In and through Christ's priesthood, Calvin continued, we "offer ourselves and all that we are to God" (*Inst.* II.15.6, translation revised). We "freely enter the heavenly sanctuary," so that, in and through the ascended Christ, "the sacrifices of prayer and praise that we offer are acceptable and a sweet-smelling savor before God" (*Inst.* II.15.6, translation revised). Thus, for Calvin, in some important sense, Christ's high-priestly intercession did not preclude an active priestly role for the church within it. The groundwork had been laid for thinking about the eucharist in light of Christ's ascension and eternal priestly intercession.

Conclusion

Zwingli, Luther, and Calvin were all convinced that Christ alone is our salvation. They were convinced that he had accomplished our salvation there and then through his life of obedience to God. His obedience, which had taken place for our sakes and in our stead, was fulfilled in his sacrifical death. The Reformers all interpreted his death as a perfect sacrifice for the sins of the world. The perfection of Christ's sacrifice meant that it was all-sufficient. Nothing else was needed to reconcile us to God, nor could anything ever be added to it. If Christ alone was our salvation, then the decisive locus of salvation was what had taken place for our sakes in him.

If the Reformers were agreed about salvation's perfect tense, they differed from one another about its present tense, especially with respect to the eucharist. (Salvation's future tense, which for now will be bracketed for the sake of convenience, needs to be discussed in due course.) The Reformers all agreed that the proper response to Christ and his saving work was faith. Faith alone corresponded to salvation by grace alone as it had been accomplished by Christ alone. The church could do nothing that contributed to its own salvation. Since salvation in Christ was a sheer gift, no meritorious work was needed to receive it. On the contrary, salvation in Christ was something to be acknowledged, received, and partaken of by faith alone.

The Reformers clearly believed that the mass attempted to repeat Christ's unrepeatable sacrifice. It thereby made God's grace conditional rather than gratuitous. It detracted from the perfection of Christ's accomplishment by adding to it the work of the priest. It gave the church an impossible and illegitimate role in cooperating in, contributing to, and constituting its own salvation. It proceeded as if God still needed to be propitiated by the human work of eucharistic sacrifice. In short, it denied that Christ himself and Christ alone was sufficient for our salvation.

How much of the Reformation critique would survive if the mass were not in fact understood as a repetition of Christ's unique sacrifice is a question to which we will need to return.

A bloodless sacrifice: Aquinas and Trent

When we turn to Thomas Aquinas after having heard from the Protestant Reformers, it is not always easy to see just what accounted for the vehemence of the Reformation critique. Since the Council of Trent allows the issues emerge more clearly, its statement on the sacrifice of the mass will be analyzed and compared with that of Aquinas. Throughout, an implicit question will hover in the background, namely, whether the Reformers might have misplaced their criticisms, at least in part, and whether, on the other hand, they might have failed to emphasize issues that were and remain divisive.

The mass as sacrifice: Thomas Aquinas

What Aquinas taught about eucharistic sacrifice can be summarized under three main points: the nature of Christ's sacrifice, the nature of eucharistic sacrifice, and the different roles in the eucharist allotted to the priest, the community, and Christ himself.

Aquinas affirmed that "Christ's passion was a true sacrifice."[7] "Sacrifice, properly speaking," he explained, "designates what men offer to God in token of the special honor due him, and in order to appease him" (ST 3.48.3). Christ's passion was a sacrifice primarily in the second, propitiatory sense, because "Christ by his suffering made perfect satisfaction for our sins" (ST 3.48.2). No one but Christ offered his sacrifice on the cross (ST 3.48.3). Yet he was also, of course, the one who was offered, being the priest and the victim in one. The efficacy of Christ's sacrifice was grounded in the uniqueness of his person. Since his flesh was indeed "the flesh of God," his sacrifice had been of "infinite value" (ST 3.48.2). His passion was thus "sufficient, and more than sufficient, to satisfy for the sins even of those who crucified him" (ST 3.48.2). "Christ, suffering in a loving and obedient spirit," Aquinas emphasized, "offered more to God than was demanded in recompense for all the sins of mankind"; his passion "was not only sufficient but

---

[7] Thomas Aquinas, *Summa Theologiae* 3.48.3 (Cambridge: Blackfriars; New York: McGraw-Hill, 19). (Hereafter cited in the text.)

superabundant atonement" (*ST* 3.48.2). Whether Aquinas understood the perfection of this sacrifice in the same sense as the Reformers, however, is a question to which we will return.

Aquinas saw no contradiction in claiming that the eucharist was a sacrament and a sacrifice at the same time. "It has the nature of a sacrifice in that it is offered, and of a sacrament in that it is received. Therefore, its effect as a sacrament is in the recipient, its effect as a sacrifice is in the offerer or in those for whom it is offered" (*ST* 3.79.5). A fuller explanation would have been useful at this point, especially regarding how the sacrifice was efficacious in those for whom it was offered, especially for the dead. Was it efficacious for them *ex opere operato*, for example, or only through their devout participation in it? From what Aquinas went on to state, devotion was apparently indispensable. In any case, the idea that the eucharist was both a sacrament and a sacrifice would seem to be no more problematic, in principle, than Calvin's view that through the operation of the Holy Spirit, Christ was at once brought down in the eucharist and made present to us, even as we were lifted up and made present to him in heaven. For Aquinas, the downward movement, from Christ to us, was the sacramental aspect, whereas the sacrificial aspect was the upward movement from us to Christ, or, better, from us through Christ to God. Each movement described the eucharist as a whole under a different aspect.

For Aquinas the eucharist itself was in some sense a "sacrifice of expiation" (*ST* 3.73.6). Here too, however, his remarks remained sketchy, so that beyond a certain point no hard-and-fast conclusions can be drawn. When the eucharist was considered as a sacrifice, Aquinas wrote, it had "the power of rendering satisfaction" (*ST* 3.79.5). In turn, the efficacy of what took place could be considered in two ways. From one standpoint, the offering of the eucharist, in and of itself, was sufficient "to satisfy for all punishment" (*ST* 3.79.5). Yet from another standpoint, the participant's disposition also had to be taken into account. The eucharistic sacrifice, Aquinas wrote, "has no effect save on those who are united to the sacrament through faith and charity" (*ST* 3.79.7). It had no effect, in other words, except on those who were united to Christ in his passion, which meant those in the church (*ST* 3.79.7). From this second standpoint, the efficacy was only relative or proportional. The mass rendered satisfaction for those for whom it was offered, and for those who offered it, "according to the amount of their devotion, and not for the whole penalty" (*ST* 3.79.5). "A person obtains pardon of the penalty of sin," wrote Aquinas, "not indeed all of it, but proportionately to the measure of his devotion and fervor" (*ST* 3.79.5). While the Reformers could (and did) raise fundamental questions about any idea that sacramental efficacy was "proportional" to the degree of devout reception, it is striking that their criticism tended to focus more on the mass itself as a meritorious work *ex opere operato*.

Aquinas emphasized that the eucharist did not offer a different sacrifice than the one offered by Christ on the cross. "There is," he wrote, "but a single sacrifice" (*ST* 3.79.8). "There is one sacrifice" (*ST* 3.83.2). It was never entirely clear, however, just how Christ's unique sacrifice could be one with the eucharist and yet still also be distinguished from it. Aquinas did state that the eucharist was a memorial of Christ's sacrifice while also being a re-presentation of it. As a memorial, he wrote, the sacrament "looks back to the past: in this sense it commemorates the passion of our Lord, which was the true sacrifice" (*ST* 3.73.4). He could also quote Origen to the effect that the sacrifice "is wonderfully offered in memory of Christ" (*ST* 3.82.4). The eucharist was always in some sense meant as "a memorial of the Lord's passion" (*ST* 3.79.7).

That which was commemorated, however, was not absent but present. The eucharist has "the nature of a sacrifice," Aquinas explained, "inasmuch as it makes present Christ's passion" (*ST* 3.79.7). The celebration of the eucharist was "a definite image" through which the true sacrifice of Christ was re-presented here and now (*ST* 3.83.1). It was a "representation of the Lord's passion"

(*ST* 3.83.3). What was intuitively obvious for Aquinas would later be inconceivable to the Reformers, namely, that a once-for-all occurrence in the past could take eucharistic form in the present. Whereas the Reformers condemned this "re-presentation" as an appalling repetition of the unrepeatable, Aquinas was always clear that what took place in eucharist was in no way a repetition of the cross.

The eucharistic sacrifice was rather a way of applying Christ's sacrifice and participating in it. The one sacrifice of Christ assumed form in the eucharist here and now. The eucharistic form was a complex affair of offering, receiving, and participating all in one. Whoever offered the sacrifice, namely, the priest, also had to be a partaker of it. He became a partaker precisely by receiving it (*ST* 3.82.4). In turn, all those who received it through the priest also participated in it. Again, the efficacy of the sacrifice before God was thought to be conditional, not *ex opere operato*. "The priest," wrote Aquinas, "asks that this sacrifice may be accepted by God ... because of the devotion of those who offer it" (*ST* 3.83.4). Ultimately, moreover, participation in the sacrifice depended on union with Christ. "He joins us to himself in this sacrament," wrote Aquinas, "in the reality of his body and blood" (*ST* 3.75.1). Seen from the standpoint of a sacrament, Christ joined the communicants to himself through his body and blood. Seen, in turn, from the standpoint of a sacrifice, Christ offered and was offered through that same body and blood, and the devout with him, to God.

The priest, who mediated between Christ and the faithful, was, in a sense, the central figure in the eucharistic sacrifice. He acted both "in the person of Christ" (*in persona Christi*) as well as "in the person of the church" (*in persona ecclesiae*) (*ST* 3.82.8). In the person of Christ, he consecrated the sacrament. In the person of the church, he offered Christ in prayer to God (*ST* 3.82.8). Whatever the priest did when acting in the person of Christ was taken up in turn by the people (*ST* 3.83.4). The priest's union with Christ, however, was different than it was for the laity. "Devout layfolk are one with Christ by spiritual union through faith and charity," explained Aquinas, but the priest was one with Christ "by sacramental power" (ST, 3.82.1). At his ordination the priest had received a special status, "the power of offering sacrifice in the church for the living and the dead" (ST 3.82.1). The priest was set apart from the people, and above them, by virtue of this sacramental power.

A careful reading of Aquinas suggests that with respect to the eucharistic sacrifice, Christ was present in three distinct roles: he was at once the one who offered the sacrifice, the one who was offered, and the one who mediated the sacrifice to God. As the one who offered, Christ was "the invisible priest" (to cite a term Aquinas borrowed from Eusebius) (ST 3.78.1). The invisible priest operated through the earthly priest; and the earthly priest operated *in persona Christi*. The earthly priest pronounced the words of institution "as if Christ himself were actually amongst us pronouncing them" (ST 3.78.5). The priest thereby consecrated the elements so that they became Christ's body and blood. Christ was also the one who was offered, "the victim sent to us by God" (ST 3.83.5). His one sacrifice became present as he himself became present. "Christ," wrote Aquinas, "is the sacrifice" (ST 3.83.1). Finally, *in persona ecclesiae* the earthly priest "asks that this sacrifice may be accepted by God" (ST 3.83.4). The people offer this prayer through the earthly priest, even as the earthly priest offers it to Christ, or through Christ to God (ST 3.83.5).

To sum up: By a movement, so to speak, from heaven to earth, Christ made his body and blood present through the priest. In turn, by a movement from earth to heaven, Christ mediated himself through the prayers of the priest as the sacrifice pleasing to God. In and with himself as this sacrifice, Christ also offered to God those joined to him by faith and charity. The invisible priest, we might say, was also the invisible sacrifice, hidden under the eucharistic elements. He was also the invisible mediator, who offered himself – through the priest and for the people, who were all one with Christ – to God. "Finally," commented Aquinas, "the whole celebration of the mass ends with the thanksgiving, with the people rejoicing at receiving the mystery, ... and the priest returning thanks in the prayer" (*ST* 3.83.4).

From the standpoint of the Reformation critique, the results of this analysis are mixed. Like the Reformers, Aquinas affirmed that by nature Christ's sacrifice on the cross was of infinite value. As a perfect sacrifice, it was sufficient and more than sufficient for the sins of the whole world. Unlike the Reformers, however, Aquinas insisted that the efficacy of this sacrifice depended, in some strong sense, on the quality of its reception. By making salvation in Christ proportional, from one standpoint, to the devotion of the eucharistic participants, Aquinas had embraced an idea against which the Reformation could only rebel. For the Reformation, the efficacy of grace was in no sense a function of devotion. On the contrary, devotion was a function of efficacy. Whatever might be lacking in anyone's devotion or faith was always more than offset in advance by the gift of unconditional grace.

It is this issue that would seem to be decisive. It is the hidden factor in the Reformation bill of particulars against the mass as a propitiatory sacrifice. The Reformers might fairly have come to accept that the mass was a re-presentation, not a repetition, of Christ's sacrifice. They might have acknowledged that *in optimum partem* it was not a human work alongside the one work of Christ. They might have conceded that, for their opponents, it was not the mass but Christ himself who expiated sin. They might have granted that the mass could be a sacrifice in some non-offending sense as well as being a memorial and a sacrament. They might have allowed the mass to be a relative and derivative renewal of Christ's one atoning sacrifice, not a bogus addition or supplement to it. But they could never allow anything to undermine God's free and sovereign gift of grace. They could not allow grace to become conditional rather than gratuitous. They could not permit the quality of devotion to determine the efficacy of grace. Yet, strangely in light of Aquinas, the direct object of their attack was always the mass itself, as opposed to devotion as the condition of its efficacy. Perhaps the medieval views familiar to them had differed widely from what Aquinas taught. An examination of the Council of Trent will help us to answer this question.

Ambiguities and obscurities existed even in Aquinas. What exactly did he mean, for example, when he wrote that the mass had "the power of rendering satisfaction" (ST 3.79.5)? How was this power related to the satisfaction rendered by Christ on the cross? Did it imply a limitation, as the Reformers furiously raged, on the efficacy of Christ's one perfect sacrifice? Furthermore, just what constituted the priest's so-called sacramental power? Was it really true that in the eucharist the actions of both Christ and the laity revolved almost entirely around power of the priest? What is the true relationship in the sacrament among Christ, the people, and the presiding minister? This question actually persists into the present day, yet the Reformers, in their critique of the mass, did not always bring it into focus.

The mass as sacrifice: the Council of Trent

It is noteworthy that Aquinas had restricted the term "true sacrifice" to Christ's passion (ST 3.48.3; 73.4; 83.1). The mass was then described as an "image" and a "memorial" of the one true sacrifice on the cross (ST 3.83.1; 79.7). By implication (though it remained implicit), the mass was an expiatory sacrifice only in some secondary or derivative sense. Trent, however, applied the term "true sacrifice" to the mass itself. It went so far as to describe the mass not only as "a true and proper sacrifice,"[8] but even as "the true and only sacrifice."[9] While Trent may not have meant anything very different from Aquinas, it was generally more ambiguous in its wording at

---

[8] *The Canons and Decrees of The Council of Trent*, ed. H. J. Schroeder (London: Herder, 1941), Twenty-Second Session, pp. 144–50; Canon 1, p. 149.

[9] Ibid., Preface, p. 144. (Hereafter cited in the text as *CDT*.)

this point and less carefully precise than he had been. It seems fair to say that Trent emphasized the unity of the mass and the cross at the expense of their important distinction.

Aquinas had stated that "Christ by his suffering made perfect satisfaction for our sins" (*ST* 3.48.2). Nothing quite comparable can be found in Trent. The Council affirmed that Christ, who offered himself once upon the cross, had made an "eternal" redemption (*CDT* xxii, ch. 1). His priesthood, however, persisted. In just what sense it did so was never quite explained. Was the apostolic and priestly involvement in Christ's priesthood somehow a continuation or prolongation of it? (Was the church a prolongation of the Incarnation?) Was Christ's priesthood imperfect so that it needed to be supplemented by others after him, or was it something finished and all-sufficient in itself?

The Reformers had, as we know, assumed the worst. They could not see that the medieval view gave proper weight to the perfection of Christ's sacrifice. They insisted on it as something that could not be repeated. They were not impressed by Trent's distinction between a "bloody" and an "unbloody" sacrifice. Not the cross, after all, but the mass, was described by Trent as the "consummation and perfection" of all the Old Testament sacrifices (*CDT* xxii, ch. 1). When Trent spoke, as Aquinas had, about the mass as a "memorial" of Christ's sacrifice and a "representation" of it, when it stated that in the mass Christ's sacrifice was "applied" to the remission of sins, the Reformation saw nothing but an appalling transfer into the present tense of something that had been entirely finished and worked out in the past. The Reformation viewed the unique work of Christ as impossibly supplanted, dishonored, and diminished by the sacrificial work of the priests. It seems fair to say that while the Reformation cannot be given high marks for charity, Trent cannot be praised for having sufficiently removed all obscurities.[10]

---

[10] According to David N. Power: "The first chapter opens with the statement that redemption is solely through the sacrifice of the cross." However, no such

Trent had its own anti-Reformation agenda. It wanted to eliminate the idea that the mass was nothing but a subjective commemoration of Christ's passion. Nor was the mass just a sacrifice of thanks and praise. Nor was it merely an act of obedience on the part of the faithful. It was a visible representation of Christ's one unique sacrifice that added nothing to his merits. It was a fulfillment of the priesthood of Melchizedek. It could not be defiled by any unworthiness on the part of those who offered it. It was in fact a fulfillment of what Christ had instituted at the Last Supper for his apostles. "He instituted," stated Trent, "a new Passover, namely, himself, to be immolated under visible signs by Christ through the priests" (*CDT* xxii, ch. 1). For Trent as for Aquinas, it was Christ who presided in the mass as the invisible priest, and who was also offered, so to speak, as the invisible victim. Although not stating so directly, Trent seemed to allow that those who participated in the eucharist were given a share in Christ's own self-offering, and that Christians have nothing to offer God on their behalf but Christ.[11]

Trent was especially concerned to assert against the Reformers that the mass was propitiatory in nature. If it were not propitiatory, it could not be offered for the living and the dead. It would seem that Trent was more concerned to justify masses for the living and the dead than to clarify the relationship between the mass and the cross. Like Aquinas, Trent asserted that Christ himself was present in the mass as both victim and priest. "The victim is one and the same," stated Trent. The Christ who had offered himself on the cross was the same as the one who now offered himself "by the ministry of priests" (*CDT* xxii, ch. 2).

statement is to be found in the text. What Power writes is a sympathetic inference, but it is not the only possible inference, which is the point. See Power, *The Sacrifice We Offer: The Tridentine Dogma and Its Reinterpretation* (New York: Crossroad, 1987), p. 117. In general I am greatly indebted to Power's book.

[11] Ibid., pp. 4–5. Cf. p. 188.

Whether the mass and the cross were finally two different sacrifices, however, or one single sacrifice in two different modes, remained unclear. (Although Aquinas had not eliminated all uncertainty, he had at least stated explicitly that only one sacrifice was in question.) Did the mass add anything to the cross, or did it simply mediate its fruits into the present? How was the priest's offering in the mass here and now related to Christ's self-sacrifice there and then? Was there one act of offering or finally two? David N. Power, the Roman Catholic liturgical scholar, comments:

> The [Council's] statement is actually open to several interpretations of this relation, or of the sense in which Christ now offers himself through the priest. It is the identity of the principal offerer, Christ, that is pressed, not the identity of the act of offering. One could say that the original act of offering is represented in the mass in a sacramental way, this being the difference in the mode of offering, but one could also say that a new act of offering is posited, and still retain the Council's teaching.[12]

Power suggests that the Council deliberately left the matter unresolved, because of existing disagreements within the ranks. The idea that Christ had endowed the church with the power to make its own separate sacrifice, and that the mass had an efficacy distinct from that of the cross, was advocated by some authorities in the discussions that had led up to the Decree. The Council's final draft did not favor this view, states Power, but neither was it "clearly and unambiguously eliminated as a possible meaning."[13]

---

[12] Ibid., p. 120.

[13] Ibid. If Trent could be read as allowing for a new sacrifice alongside that of the cross, it is hard to see how Power can claim that the Council required everyone to hold that "the sacrifice of the mass is *totally* dependent on the cross" (ibid., emphasis added). Whether the dependence was total or partial is precisely the question of whether or not the mass was *relatively* independent of the cross. A new act of offering would necessarily be relatively independent.

Trent remained ambiguous on the very point of greatest importance to the Reformation.

Insofar as the mass was thought to possess an efficacy of its own relatively (if not totally) independent of the cross, it was vulnerable to the Reformation critique. An independent efficacy would necessarily qualify the perfection of Christ's sacrifice once offered, even if Christ was himself involved in effecting the new sacrifice. If the priest was merely Christ's instrument in effecting this sacrifice, then the mass might escape the charge of being a human work. According to Aquinas, in the work of consecration and sacrifice, the priest played an instrumental role; it was Christ who acted as the principal cause (*ST* 3.78.1, 4). Trent, by contrast, was again less clear. The priesthood of Christ was somehow continued in the priesthood of the church. Whether the church's priests played merely an instrumental role or something more constitutive was not explained. Insofar as the door was not closed to regarding the mass as a new propitiatory sacrifice alongside the cross, the priest could also be seen as a second causal agent alongside Christ. While the Reformers consistently opted to place the medieval view in the worst light rather than the best, it cannot be denied that their critique had some bite, since Trent allowed for a range of viewpoints that were all present to some degree in the church.

Trent anathematized anyone who said that the sacrifice of the mass detracted from that of the cross. A charitable reading would seek to honor this underlying intention. Like Aquinas, Trent affirmed that the sacrifice of the mass was efficacious, if those for whom it was offered were devout. This condition for efficacy meant, as directly stated, that it applied if they were contrite, penitent, sincere, reverent, and faithful (*CDT* xxii, ch. 2). The whole problem of conditional efficacy, as already discussed regarding Aquinas, emerged again at this point. Moreover, it was never entirely clear how the mass could be efficacious for the dead. Were they also to be understood as receiving the sacrifice with devout hearts? Or was it not rather at this point that the whole question of *ex opere operato* entered the picture? Had not the Council decreed in favor of that idea in its earlier canons on the sacraments? "If anyone says that by the sacraments of the New Law grace is not conferred *ex opere operato*, but that faith alone in the divine promise is sufficient to obtain grace, let him be anathema" (*CDT* vii, Can. 8). Again, we are confronted with ambiguities. Power comments:

> At this point, the Council retains a rather standard language and makes no attempt to sort out the mode of application, whether, that is, it is by way of *ex opere operato* efficacy or by way of suffrage and intercession. While noting the conciliar abstinence on points of controversy, one may also suggest that the root of the problem, left unresolved by the council, is not to reconcile the appeal to divine mercy through intercession in remembrance of Christ, which the Conciliar text places in the forefront, with computations of merits, punishments and satisfactions inherited from the medieval penitential system as categories of explanation.[14]

From a Reformational standpoint, the idea of an *ex opere operato* sacramental efficacy would say too much, while making efficacy proportional to devout reception, on the other hand, would be inadmissible. If the efficacy of the mass for the dead, as conceived by medieval theology, did not depend on their devout reception of it, *ex opere operato* efficacy would seem, for the dead, to be inescapable. Yet if the efficacy of the mass were neither automatic nor conditional, might it not be seen as in some sense gratuitous? Efficacy would then be at the disposal neither of the priest nor of the church, but of the God always true to his promises. If Trent and other authorities left this matter indeterminate, might it not be possible to hope that the Catholic Church will reinterpret it some day in a way that moves toward a greater measure of convergence with the Reformation?

[14] Ibid., p. 121.

Trent also made statements about the role of the priest in the eucharistic community. While less clear than Aquinas that Christ mediates to God the sacrifice of himself that he offers here and now through the priest, the Council was clear that "the faithful who are present should communicate" even though masses in which "the priest alone communicates" were not illicit (*CDT* xxii, ch. 6, Can. 8). This language, however, noticeably distinguished between two types of participation in the eucharist. Power comments:

> Here a distinction is made between *sacerdos sacramentaliter communicat* [the priest communicates sacramentally] and *populus spiritualiter communicat* [the people communicate spiritually] which is in the context quite innocuous but which was liable to be used in support of a particularly hierarchical eucharistic theology ... The terms ... can unfortunately be applied to mean a difference between the sacramental act of offering, which pertains to the priest, and spiritual communion in this act which pertains to the people.[15]

Power regrets the way that Trent legitimates the private mass "by reason of a theology of the sacramental role of the priest which separates it from community celebration."[16] He advocates moving toward "a church structure and a practice of ordination that is appropriate to an awareness that the community of faith is the ecclesial subject of celebration, so that the act of the ordained minister is understood in this context."[17] With an eye toward the profoundly divisive ecumenical problem of sacramental ministry, Power even suggests that it can be carried out "in a variety of ways without breaking historical continuity and communion in the one faith and worship."[18] He sees no reason why Trent should be taken as an imperative model for other ecumenical churches.[19] In

[15] Ibid., p. 124. [16] Ibid., p. 125. [17] Ibid., p. 160.
[18] Ibid., p. 142. [19] Ibid., p. 143.

particular, he questions whether the eucharist should be "more the act of the ordained priest than the act of the community."[20]

Finally, as Power keenly observes, the issues at stake between Tridentine Catholicism and the Reformation led to two very different styles of worship. Where Trent with the medieval church saw worship primarily as a matter of propitiation, the Reformation saw it primarily as a matter of giving thanks. Here is Power's observation about medieval worship as ratified by the Council:

> Basic to the position attributed to the priest in this system is the meaning given to worship itself. The order of worship is one in which offering is preferred to thanksgiving ... The only worthy propitiation that can be offered is Christ himself, but this needed to be integrated into a religious system in which the propitiation is continually offered. There were moments in the practice and theology of the church when this seemed to be an offering made by the church, but in their better moments both made it clear that the offering in question was Christ's own sacramental offering, now made available to the church so that it could share in it.[21]

The Reformers, on the other hand, gave the primacy in worship not to offering but to thanksgiving. The order of worship, for them, was determined by the free gift of grace. Power comments:

> [The Reformers] by no means excluded the demand on believers to make of themselves a self-offering, in communion with Christ, but they wished neither the offering of gifts nor the offering of Christ by the church to be at the heart of worship. That heart could be nothing other than the free gift of the divine mercy won by the death of Christ, the once and for all offering or sacrifice of redemption.[22]

Power goes on to suggest that because these two systems of worship are not incompatible, they might be allowed to coexist.

---

[20] Ibid., p. 164. [21] Ibid., pp. 143–44. [22] Ibid., p. 144.

"Perhaps what we need to see today in ecumenical dialogue is that faith in the saving death and resurrection of Christ can be appropriated through and in worship in systematically different ways, and that there is no single absolute order of worship or absolute eucharistic theology."[23] This suggestion is a very attractive one. Nevertheless, the more the two systems can be brought into convergence, the brighter the ecumenical prospects would seem to be. Therefore, an attempt will here be made to integrate a conception of eucharistic sacrifice into a view of worship ordered around the primacy of grace.

Conclusion

Although Aquinas insisted that the eucharist re-presented Christ's sacrifice without repeating it, it was never entirely clear just how this distinction could be maintained. Since Christ's passion was wholly in the past, it would seem that, as Dom Gregory Dix has observed, the church could enter into it in only one of two ways: "either purely *mentally* by remembering or imagining it; or else, if the entering into it [was] to have any objective reality outside the mind, by way of some sort of *repetition* or iteration of the redeeming act of Christ."[24]

In other words, insofar as the late medieval church had separated Christ's work from his person, it had also separated the past occurrence of salvation from the present. "There was no conceptual tool," writes J. M. R. Tillard, "which allowed the radical *ephapax* of the oblation itself to be held together with its perpetual presence in the sacrament."[25] Dix elaborates on this crucial point:

---

[23] Ibid.
[24] Dom Gregory Dix, *The Shape of the Liturgy* (Westminster: Dacre Press, 1945), p. 623.
[25] J. M. R. Tillard, "Sacrificial Terminology and the Eucharist," *One in Christ* 17 (1981), pp. 306–23; on p. 319.

Thus the way was not so much laid open as forced upon the church to that general late medieval notion of some *fresh* sacrifice of Christ, and His immolation again at every eucharist. There was no other way by which the reality of the eucharistic action could be preserved on the medieval understanding of it ... And since the eucharistic action was now viewed as the act of the priest alone – though the liturgy itself continued to state a different view ... there was no escaping the idea that the priest sacrifices Christ afresh at every mass ... However hard they tried to conciliate this view of the matter with the doctrine of the Epistle to the Hebrews of the one oblation for sins, perfect and complete ... on Calvary, the medieval theologians ... never quite got away from the necessity of defending the reality of the eucharistic sacrifice as in some sense the iteration of the sacrifice of Christ at the hands of the priest, even though they insisted that it was not a *new* sacrifice.[26]

The Protestant Reformers, for their part, then embraced the other horn of the dilemma. If it was intolerable to think that the eucharist actually repeated Christ's sacrifice, then the only option was for it to be remembered with thanks and praise. Again, Dix traces the train of thought:

The Reformers, on the other hand, likewise carrying on the medieval insistence on the passion as the whole redeeming act into which the eucharist enters, took the other alternative. Since the passion is wholly in the past, the church now can only enter into it purely mentally, by *remembering* and imagining it. There is for them, therefore, no real sacrifice whatever in the eucharist. The external rite is at the most an acted memorial, *reminding* us of something no longer present.[27]

In short, Dix concludes: "For both parties alike the sacrifice of Christ is irremediably in the remote past. Along this line the

---

[26] Dix, *Shape of the Liturgy*, p. 623.   [27] Ibid.

impasse between entering into His action as mere mental *remembering* and something which has at least the appearance of repetition by the priest is inevitable, even though it is still concealed by the use of the word memory by both sides."[28]

Whether the word "memory" might be susceptible to a more favorable usage is considered in the next chapter.

---

[28] Ibid., p. 643.

4 | Christ our Passover: a proposal

In his work *The Shape of the Liturgy*,[1] Dom Gregory Dix surveys how churches in the post-apostolic period understood the idea of eucharistic sacrifice. Although this once influential work has been subjected to searching critique,[2] Dix's comments at this point seem sound. The writings of Clement, Justin, and Hippolytus make it possible to conclude, Dix states, that already by the last quarter of the first century, the eucharist was generally seen, in some sense, as a sacrifice. The liturgical traditions, as they can now be reconstructed, are somewhat localized, but the existing evidence points in one direction. "All we can say," writes Dix, "is that every one of these local traditions at the earliest point at which extant documents permit us to interrogate it, reveals the same general understanding of the eucharist as an 'oblation' (*prosphora*) or 'sacrifice' (*thusia*) – something offered to God; and that the substance of the sacrifice is in every case in some sense the bread and the cup."[3] Though variations exist within it, the sacrificial idea of the eucharist was the rule. "There is no exception whatever," states

---

[1] Dom Gregory Dix, *The Shape of the Liturgy* (Westminster: Dacre Press, 1945).

[2] See Bryan D. Spinks, "Mis-shapen: Gregory Dix and the Four Action Shape of the Liturgy," *Lutheran Quarterly* 4 (1990), pp. 161–77; Paul F. Bradshaw, *The Search for the Origins of Christian Worship* (New York: Oxford University Press, 2002), pp. 122–26, 140; Kenneth W. Stevenson, *Gregory Dix: Twenty-five Years On* (Bramcote: Grove Books, 1977); Pierre-Marie Gy, "Re-Visiting Dom Gregory Dix After Fifty Years," *Worship* 70 (1996), pp. 2–15.

[3] Dix, *Shape of the Liturgy*, p. 112 (*supra* n. 1).

Dix, "in any Christian tradition in the second century and no hint of an alternative understanding anywhere."[4]

"Just how early the idea of sacrifice was applied to Christian worship, specifically to the eucharist, is the subject of controversy," notes Jaroslav Pelikan. "But by the date of the *Didache* – although that date is itself a controversial issue [from the late first to the third century] – the application of the term 'sacrifice' to the eucharist seems to have been quite natural."[5] While doubts have been raised whether in that treatise the bread and cup were thought of as being offered,[6] Kenneth W. Stevenson has concluded that the *Didache* regards the eucharist as a sacrifice in which the gifts were indeed a communion offering.[7]

By the fourth century the idea was well established that the cross and the eucharist were somehow one.[8] They were related by a pattern of unity-in-distinction and distinction-in-unity. The unity pertained at once to the Christ who was offered as well as to the act of offering. There was but a single victim and a single sacrifice. The distinction, on the other hand, pertained to the different forms that the victim and the sacrifice assumed, first on the cross and then in the eucharist, though even this simple way of putting it was rarely explicit.[9] Lack of analytical clarity here would, of course, vex,

---

[4] Ibid., p. 113. This judgment, which would be heavily qualified by R. P. C. Hanson, is generally supported by Kenneth W. Stevenson. See Hanson, *Eucharistic Offering in the Early Church* (Bramcote: Grove Books, 1979), pp. 6–8; Stevenson, *Eucharist and Offering* (New York: Pueblo, 1986), pp. 17–24. Not to be overlooked, however, is Dix's caveat: "It does not appear that the question of *how* the eucharist is a sacrifice was ever treated of fully and scientifically by any author in the first five centuries." Dix, *Shape of the Liturgy*, p. 241.

[5] Jaroslav Pelikan, *The Christian Tradition*, vol. 1, *The Emergence of the Catholic Tradition* (*100–600*) (Chicago: University of Chicago Press, 1971), p. 146.

[6] Hanson, *Eucharistic Offering*, p. 7 (*supra* n. 4).

[7] Stevenson, *Eucharist and Offering*, pp. 14–16, 37 (*supra* n. 4).

[8] See ibid., pp. 38–83.

[9] See Frances M. Young, *The Use of Sacrificial Ideas in Greek Christian Writers from the New Testament to John Chrysostom* (Cambridge, MA: Philadelphia Patristic Foundation, 1979). Young argues that in the East the eucharist was seen primarily

and eventually divide, the churches. Yet intuitively the essential relation was clear. "What the Body and Blood of Christ were on Calvary," writes Dix, "and *before* and *after* – 'an offering and a sacrifice to God for us' (Eph. 5:2) – that they are now in the eucharist, the *anamnesis* not of his death only, but 'of me' – of the Redeemer in the fullness of his offered self, and work and life and death, perpetually accepted by the Father in the world to come."[10] The fourth-century church, emphasizes Dix, did not isolate Christ's sacrifice on the cross from either his life or his resurrection. His cross was the fulfillment of his life, even as his resurrection had made him manifest in his sacrificial significance – at once to God in eternity and yet also to the church in history. Just as his cross was not to be detached from either his life or his resurrection, so also was his sacrificial work not to be detached from his person. As T. F. Torrance has said somewhere, in the fourth century it was understood that we are saved not by the death of Christ, but by the person of Christ in his death.

This linkage of ideas is evident in a homily on Hebrews by Chrysostom which Dix cites at length:

> What then? Do we not offer daily? Certainly we offer thus, making an *anamnesis* of his death. How is it one and not many? Because it was offered once, like that which was carried [in the Old Testament on the day of Atonement] into the Holy of Holies ... For we ever offer the same person, not today one sheep and the next time a different one, but ever the same offering. Therefore the sacrifice is one. By this argument then, since the offering is made in many places, does it not follow that there are many Christs? Not at all, for Christ is everywhere one, complete here and complete there, a single body. Thus, as when offered in many places he is one body and not many bodies, so also there is one sacrifice. One High Priest

as a thank-offering and a communion-sacrifice while in the West it was mainly a gift-sacrifice.

[10] Dix, *Shape of the Liturgy*, pp. 242–43 (*supra* n. 1).

is he who offered the sacrifice which cleanses us. We offer even now that which was then offered, which cannot be exhausted. This is done for an *anamnesis* of that which was then done, for "Do this," said he, "for the *anamnesis* of me." We do not offer a different sacrifice like the high priest of old, but we ever offer the same. Or rather we offer the *anamnesis* of the sacrifice.[11]

Dix comments:

For [Chrysostom] as for his predecessors in the pre-Nicene church, it is the absolute unity of the church's sacrifice in the eucharist with that of Christ – unity of the offerer (for it is Christ "our High Priest" who offers through the church, his body), unity of the offering (for that which is offered is what he offered, his body and blood), unity of the effects ("which cleanses us") – it is the indissoluble unity of the eucharist with the sacrifice of Christ himself which is the basis of the ancient eucharistic theology.[12]

While the unity is here made clear – clearer than the ongoing distinction – the distinction needs to be made equally clear. Otherwise, it is hard to see how the idea of eucharistic sacrifice can be retrieved for the churches of the Reformation.

Before turning to the task of retrieval, a further point may be made. Following the Epistle to the Hebrews, Chrysostom had associated Christ's sacrifice with the Day of Atonement. Paul, on the other hand, had associated it with Passover: "Christ our Passover is sacrificed" (1 Cor. 5:7, KJV). As Dix points out, these differences were finally a matter of interpretation and illustration. Moreover, "in point of fact the Passover illustration was found to be more strikingly applicable to the Christian feast of the *Pascha* as the annual commemoration of the actual historical events by

---

[11] Chrysostom, *Heb. Hom.* xvii.3, quoted by Dix, *Shape of the Liturgy*, p. 243.
[12] Dix, *Shape of the Liturgy*, p. 244.

which redemption was achieved."[13] A document from Hippolytus in the third century seems to have been the first to connect the eating of the Passover with the reception of Holy Communion.[14] But in the Ethiopic version of the apocryphal *Epistle of the Apostles*, from the mid-second century, the risen Christ addresses his apostles with the words: "And you therefore celebrate the remembrance of my death, i.e. the Passover."[15] Connecting Passover with the eucharist seems to have been both natural and early – and, in principle, dominical.[16]

The mass as sacrifice: Luther and Calvin revisited

In an unexpected about-face Luther once explained the sense in which he thought the mass could be regarded as a sacrifice. First, he observed that the faithful cannot really offer God thanks and praise without also offering themselves. We thank God with our whole heart, stated Luther, for everything promised and given in the sacrament. At the same time, in response we offer "ourselves, and all that we have, with constant prayer" (*LW* 35, p. 98). We can and should offer ourselves to God under any circumstances, but it is most fitting that we should do so in the mass. "It is more precious, more appropriate, more mighty, and also more acceptable," wrote Luther, "when it takes place with the multitude and in the assembly" (*LW* 35, p. 98). We offer ourselves not to obtain some benefit, but simply as a free response to God's free grace.

---

[13] Ibid., pp. 273–74. See Stevenson, "The Ceremonies of Light – Their Shape and Function in the Paschal Vigil Liturgy," *Ephemerides Liturgicae* 99 (1985), pp. 170–85.

[14] Dix, *Shape of the Liturgy*, p. 274n. (*supra* n. 1).

[15] *New Testament Apocrypha*, ed. Edgar Hennecke and W. Schneemelcher (Philadelphia: Westminster Press, 1963), vol. I, p. 199.

[16] The classic case for placing the Last Supper in a Passover context is still Joachim Jeremias, *The Eucharistic Words of Jesus* (New York: Charles Scribner's Sons, 1966), ch. 1.

This self-offering is made not on our own, Luther continued, but only in and through Christ. "To be sure this sacrifice of prayer, praise and thanksgiving, and of ourselves as well, we are not to present to God in our own person, but we are to lay it upon Christ and let him present it for us" (*LW* 35, p. 99). It is only "through Christ" (as it were, *in persona Christi*) that we offer ourselves, because Christ has been appointed as our eternal High Priest. He is present in the midst of the eucharistic assembly that gathers in his name, even as he intercedes for them in heaven (*LW* 35, pp. 98–9). "He receives our prayer and sacrifice, and through himself, as a godly priest, makes them pleasing to God" (*LW* p. 99).

Accordingly, it is not the faithful who offer Christ so much as Christ who offers them. "And in this way," wrote Luther, "it is permissible, yes, profitable, to call the mass a sacrifice; not on its own account, but because we offer ourselves as a sacrifice along with Christ" (*LW* 35, p. 99). The faithful lay themselves on Christ whenever they trust firmly in his promises. It is only "through Christ and his mediation" that they appear before God with their prayer, their praise and their very selves. Christ intercedes before God in heaven. Nothing more is needed than that they should offer themselves by faith. "Such faith, truly, brings it to pass," stated Luther, "that Christ takes up our cause, presents us and our prayer and praise, and also offers himself for us in heaven" (*LW* 35, p. 99). Christ takes up their eucharistic self-offering into his eternal self-offering for their sakes. "If the mass were so understood and for this reason called a sacrifice," concluded Luther, "it would be well. Not that we offer the sacrament, but that by our praise, prayer, and sacrifice we move him and give him occasion to offer himself for us in heaven and ourselves with him" (*LW* 35, p. 99).

With this line of reasoning Luther had transcended some otherwise highly charged contrasts. "Sacrament," for example, was no longer the polar opposite of "sacrifice." Instead, Christ's gift of himself to believers (sacrament) included his eternal offering of himself for their sakes to God (sacrifice). Moreover, not only were believers offered by Christ, but Christ was also offered by them. Luther spoke of Christ in the passive as well as the active voice. The Christ who gave himself to the faithful, and who offered himself for them to God, was also offered by them in the mass. It was not only Christ who offered the faithful in and through himself. "I also offer Christ," wrote Luther, "in that I desire and believe that he accepts me and my prayer and praise and presents it to God in his own person" (*LW* 35, p. 100). The bread and wine of the sacrament were Christ's pledge to faith that he would never cease in his work of intercession.

The relationship on which Luther focused in this discussion of eucharistic sacrifice was that between Christ and the believer. From that point he moved out, so to speak, to include the faithful community, and within the community he accepted a representative role for the priest. The priest symbolized the priesthood of all believers, while possessing no special powers of consecration and sacrifice. Luther stated:

> Thus it becomes clear that it is not the priest alone who offers the sacrifice of the mass; it is the faith which each one has for himself. This is the true priestly office, through which Christ is offered as a sacrifice to God, an office which the priest, with the outward ceremonies of the mass, simply represents. Each and all are, therefore, equally priests before God ... For faith must do everything. Faith alone is the true priestly office. It permits no one to take its place. Therefore all Christian men are priests, all women are priestesses, be they young or old, master or servant, mistress or maid, learned or unlearned. Here there is no difference unless faith be unequal. (*LW* 35, pp. 100–1)[17]

It is important to note just what Luther has and has not accomplished with this long aside. He has interpreted eucharistic sacrifice

---

[17] See Brian A. Gerrish, "Priesthood and Ministry: Luther's Fifth Means of Grace," in *The Old Protestantism and the New* (Chicago: University of Chicago Press, 1982), pp. 90–105.

in such a way that it is not a meritorious work. The gratuitous nature of grace is assumed and sustained throughout. He has upheld the idea of grace alone by combining christological mediation with communal participation. The believer and the community can be said to offer Christ by participating in Christ's own self-offering, which in turn mediates them into eternal life with God. Inclusion in Christ's priestly self-offering is at once the promise and the consequence of grace.

At the same time, the place of the priest in the mass has been radically redefined. Christ the eternal priest does not operate in and through the visible priest, nor does the priest offer Christ as the invisible victim through the bread and the cup. The bread and the cup, for Luther, are the sacramental but not the sacrificial body and blood of Christ. That is, they are not the means of reciprocal self-offering to God by Christ, priest, and people. They are not the eucharistic means by which Christ is offered up. The bread and cup are simply a pledge of Christ's faithfulness to his promises. It is not the priest but the faith of each believer that offers Christ to God. The role of the priest is simply to symbolize by outward ceremonies the one true priestly office, which is faith.

Furthermore, Luther did not address the conceptual dilemma of how past occurrence in Christ was related to present reality. He did not clarify how the sacrifice of the cross was integrated with Christ's ongoing heavenly intercession, nor did he say much about how that intercession might be accessible through the eucharist. He simply assumed the eternal priesthood of Christ and its accessibility to faith. Luther clearly accepted that Christ's once-for-all sacrifice had an eternal and perpetual aspect. Its perpetual aspect did not contradict the complete sufficiency of the cross. For Luther the remembered Christ was clearly the present Christ, and the present Christ was the heavenly intercessor. However, how eucharistic remembrance might be related to eucharistic sacrifice did not emerge as a theme for reflection. How was the cross related to what takes place in the eucharist here and now?

When we turn from Luther to Calvin, other elements emerge from which a Protestant view of eucharistic sacrifice might be constructed. Their perspectives are complementary. Although Calvin did not ask, as Luther did, what an acceptable doctrine of eucharistic sacrifice might look like, he devoted more attention than did the Wittenberg Reformer to Christ's eternal high-priesthood. Whereas Luther focused on the mass and alluded to the ascension, Calvin gave more thought to the ascension in a way that might be adapted to the eucharist, though he avoided making that connection himself, and indeed shunned it whenever it crossed his mind.

Calvin of course endorsed the Reformation's normative separation between "a sacrifice of thanks and praise" and "a sacrifice of expiation" (*Inst.* IV.18.13). Only a sacrifice of thanks and praise, he felt, was fitting for the eucharist, because the sacrifice of expiation had taken place once for all on Calvary. The sacrifice of expiation nevertheless involved two aspects, one finished, the other perpetual. How these aspects were related turned out to be more subtle than might at first meet the eye.

The simplest way to make the point was to distinguish Christ's sacrifice from its efficacy. An expiatory sacrifice had occurred whose efficacy was eternal. "And it was done but once, because the effectiveness and force of that one sacrifice accomplished by Christ are eternal" (*Inst.* IV.18.13). Its efficacy pertained to Christ's priestly office of intercession. "It belongs to a priest to intercede," wrote Calvin, "in order that the people may find favor with God. Christ is continually doing this because he rose from the dead for this purpose. He justifies his rightful name of priest by his continual task of intercession" (*Comm.* on Heb. 7:25).[18] Sometimes the eternal efficacy would be ascribed to Christ's death or to his blood. "The power of his death avails as an everlasting intercession"

---

[18] Calvin, "The Epistle to the Hebrews," in *Calvin's New Testament Commentaries*, vol. XII, ed. D. W. Torrance *et al.* (Grand Rapids: Wm. B. Eerdmans, 1963), p. 101.

(*Inst.* III.20.20). "The blood by which he atoned for our sins . . . is a continual intercession for us" (*Comm.* on Jn. 16:26).[19] At other times, however, the efficacy would be ascribed more nearly to Christ's person. "Christ is a continual sacrifice to atone for the iniquities of the saints" (*Inst.* III.3.23).

The idea of a "continual sacrifice" could sometimes receive remarkable expression. "This is the continual consecration of his life that the blood of Christ is continually being shed before the face of the Father to spread over heaven and earth" (*Comm.* on Heb. 10:19).[20] "God continually reconciles himself to the church when he sets before it the sacrifice of Christ in the gospel" (*Comm.* on Ex. 29:38).[21] Apparently, in Calvin's mind, the idea of Christ's finished work was not necessarily incompatible with some form of continual re-presentation. Despite his finished and unrepeatable work, Christ's blood was continually being shed, in some sense, before the Father, who was himself, in some sense, continually being reconciled to the church. It might be inferred that, for Calvin, the perfect sacrifice of Christ, though always complete in itself, was also, paradoxically, being offered continually anew.

The perpetual efficacy of Christ's blood had important daily implications. Although "sin has been destroyed" by "the one death of Christ," so that the faithful were indeed "reconciled to God," it was also true, wrote Calvin, that "we must daily seek for pardon since we daily provoke God's wrath" (*Comm.* on Heb. 9:26).[22] While sin ought not to reign over the faithful, it is nonetheless true that "we sin daily, and God pardons daily, and the blood of Christ make us clean from our sins" (*Comm.* on 2 Pet. 1:8).[23] "We must

---

[19] Calvin, "The Gospel According to St. John," in ibid., vol. v, p. 130.

[20] Calvin, "Hebrews," p. 141.

[21] Calvin, "On the Four Last Books of Moses: A Harmony," in *Calvin's Commentaries*, vol. II, tr. C. W. Bingham (Grand Rapids: Baker Book House, 1989), p. 297.

[22] Calvin, "Hebrews," p. 130 (translation revised).

[23] Calvin, "The Second Epistle of Peter," in *New Testament Commentaries*, vol. XII, p. 333.

remember everyday our sins," stated Calvin. "The apostle means that our sins are set before us so that the guilt may be removed by the mediation of this present sacrifice" (*Comm.* Heb. 10:3).[24]

Not only did Christ's sacrifice make itself present again and again, so as daily to remove the sins of the faithful, but Christ himself had to be offered in an act of continual intercession. "It is necessary that each of us should offer Christ to the Father," Calvin wrote in an astonishing statement. "For, although he only, and that but once, has offered himself," Calvin explained, "still a daily offering of him, which is effected by faith and prayers, is enjoined to us" (*Comm.* on Num. 19:2).[25] Indeed, Christ's finished work notwithstanding, the faithful still "set Christ before God's face in order to propitiate him" (*Comm.* on Num. 19:3).[26] The Christ who alone could offer himself in expiation had in turn to be offered by the faithful day by day.

It would seem that Christ's sacrifice assumed a daily relevance through his office of continual intercession. Because his sacrifice was finished in its perfection, it was also eternal in its efficacy, and was therefore new every morning. Even Christ's complete propitiation of God's wrath stood in need of constant re-presentation. Consider a prayer written by Calvin for use in weekly worship: "Look, therefore, O Lord, not on us but on the face of Christ, that by his intercession thy anger may be appeased, and thy face may shine forth upon us for our joy and salvation."[27] The propitiatory sacrifice as once offered was constantly to be implored by the faithful and re-presented on a daily basis.

Vital elements for a doctrine of eucharistic sacrifice were clearly not lacking in Calvin's theology. He saw that Christ's expiatory sacrifice was finished in perfection, perpetual in efficacy, and new

---

[24] Calvin, "Hebrews," p. 133.   [25] Calvin, "On the Last Four Books," p. 39.
[26] Ibid.
[27] Calvin, "Forms of Prayer for the Church," in *Tracts and Letters*, vol. II, ed. Henry Beveridge (Grand Rapids: Baker Book House, 1983), pp. 109–10.

in relevance each day. He saw that in offering himself to the Father, Christ offered the faithful along with himself, not only once for all but continually. And he saw that in their sacrifice of thanks and praise, the faithful were offering not just words but themselves, all that they had and were. They offered themselves in thanks and praise to the Father through the Son and in the Spirit. They did not offer their sacrifices otherwise than through the perpetual intercession of the Son, who by his blood had made them his own, and continued to make them his own. They offered Christ daily to the Father. All this was present in Calvin, yet a doctrine of eucharistic sacrifice was spurned. Alasdair Heron comments:

> To put it at its sharpest, is there not a valid sense in which it is always and only *the sacrifice of Christ himself* that we set forth and hold out to the Father, because he has so identified himself with us that we are united with him? This union lies at the heart of Calvin's theology, but when it comes to the controversial matter of the sacrifice of the Mass he is so anxious to avoid any idea of repeating or adding to Christ's sacrifice that he also seems to rule out our *participation* in his self-offering. Our offering becomes simply a response – response *to* him rather than a sharing *with* him in his offering, not only *of himself for us*, but *of us with himself.*[28]

The meaning of Passover: an interpretation

Recall the words of Chrysostom cited earlier: "We do not offer a different sacrifice like the high priest of old, but we ever offer the same. Or rather we offer the *anamnesis* of the sacrifice." In the eucharist, the Patriarch implied, the memorial and the sacrifice were one. The memorial was precisely what was offered, even as

---

[28] Alasdair Heron, *Table and Tradition: Toward an Ecumenical Understanding of the Eucharist* (Edinburgh: Handsel Press, 1983), p. 169.

the offering took the form of a memorial. The memorial or remembrance, the *anamnesis*, was not just an act of mental recollection. The *anamnesis* was indeed the eucharist itself. It was a matter of communal, liturgical enactment. The remembrance of Christ's sacrifice was precisely the liturgy in the form of a symbolic meal.

"Do this in *anamnesis* of me" (Luke 22:19).[29] The imperative of the verb "to do" appears in the second person plural. The *anamnesis* takes place by doing, not merely by meditating, and the doing is a communal event. The remembrance is enacted in the liturgical sacrifice. The community sacrifices by remembering and remembers by partaking in the sacred meal. Through the meal the faithful are made one with the sacrifice, and the sacrifice is Christ himself. The Christ whose sacrifice is remembered re-presents himself under the aspects of his body and blood. The same body and blood, once offered on the cross, are now presented to the faithful as bread and wine. The faithful, in receiving them, become one with the Christ who had made himself one with them in his sacrifice. He had made their sin and death his own so that sin might be removed and death destroyed.

Love had been crucified by sin so that sin might be crucified by love – and that love might prevail. The body and blood offered in love on the cross are the same by which the King of Love joins the community to himself, and himself to the community, in the sacred meal. The community is made one with Christ in his perfect and perpetual sacrifice. The Christ whom the faithful receive through the bread and the wine is the Christ in whose sacrifice they are incorporated by grace. Their participation in his sacrifice and new life is a foretaste of his eternal kingdom. Remembrance, sacrifice, reception, communion, thanksgiving, and promise all come

---

[29] "Was ever another command so obeyed? For century after century, spreading slowly to every continent and country and among every race on earth, this action has been done." Dix, *Shape of the Liturgy*, p. 744 (*supra* n. 1).

together in the eucharist to form a seamless web. They are all one in Christ as he makes himself present by his Spirit in the sacrament of the sacrifice of his body and blood.

The eucharist, when seen in this way, takes up the celebration of Passover and transforms it. The *anamnesis* of Passover is assumed and reconfigured in the eucharistic *anamnesis*. The ancient Jewish Passover involved three main elements: a sacrifice, a sacred meal, and a deliverance. Each is reconfigured in the eucharist. The sacrifice in the Passover was the lamb even as Christ then became the Lamb of God. In each case the lamb was sacrificed in order that the people might be spared. The blood of the Passover lamb was put on the doorposts and the lintels of the houses in which the sacrifice would be eaten. By this blood the people of Israel were protected from the terrible judgment that the Lord would execute upon the sin of Egypt, which was said principally to be the sin of idolatry (Ex. 12:12). Likewise, by the sacrificial blood of Christ as the Lamb of God, the faithful had been cleansed of their sin and delivered from the divine wrath against it. In each case the sacrificial lamb was the divinely appointed means of grace, and in each case the significance of the lamb was arguably that of a vicarious sacrifice.[30]

The death deserved by sin[31] was borne and borne away by the lamb in the people's stead. In the story of the Passover, it is clearly implied that but for the blood of the lamb, Israel itself would not have escaped from the judgment that fell upon Egypt. Only by remaining inside the doors of their houses until morning were the

---

[30] It is an error to suppose that the divine mercy which provides the means of deliverance is incompatible with divine wrath against sin (the divine No), or that this mercy (the divine Yes) somehow precludes the need for "propitiation" (ending the wrath) by the process of "expiation" (vicarious sacrifice as the taking away of sin). Divine mercy, as attested in Scripture, presupposes precisely the need for propitiation and expiation, which the mercy condescends to meet. See Calvin's classic appeal to Augustine (*Inst.* 11.16.4).

[31] By sacrificing an innocent animal, noted Calvin, the sinner acknowledged before God that he was worthy of death (*Comm.* on Heb. 9:15) (cf. Rom. 1:32; 6:23).

people to be spared from destruction (Ex. 12:23). In the case of Christ as the Lamb of God, the one who knew no sin was made to be sin so that sin might be condemned in the flesh and thereby destroyed. In each case there emerges the mysterious biblical pattern of exchange. The innocent one is made to be guilty so that the many who are guilty might be spared and made innocent by an innocence not their own.[32]

The deliverance of Israel from Egypt involved a twofold deliverance from the house of bondage. Israel was delivered not only from the bondage of oppression, but also from the bondage of idolatry. That is why the book of Exodus ends so perplexingly, not with political utopia, but with lengthy and detailed instructions about constructing the Tabernacle. Christ as the Lamb of God, in turn, is said to deliver his people from the disorder at the root of all disorders, namely, the sin whose wages is death. The God who is of purer eyes than to behold evil is seen as delivering his people from evil. He does so by bearing its consequences himself in the Incarnation as it culminates in the cross in order to bear it away.

Just as the paschal sacrifice involved the theme of substitution, so the sacred meal involved that of participation. Whether in the Passover or the eucharist, there was no substitution without participation, and no participation without substitution. The pattern of exchange implied that the guilty were already identified with the lamb sacrificed for their sakes and in their place. The sacred meal then marked the transition, so to speak, from passive to active participation. The lamb whose sacrificial blood had been appointed to avert the judgment of death became, in Christ, the

---

[32] For a different view of sacrifice, see Robert J. Daly, *The Origins of the Christian Doctrine of Sacrifice* (Philadelphia: Fortress Press, 1978); Daly, "Sacrifice: The Way to Enter the Paschal Mystery," *America* 188 (May 12, 2003), pp. 14–17. Daly argues for a view of sacrifice based on fellowship with God without the need for expiation as its premise, but this seems incompatible with Scripture and tradition. See also Kathryn Tanner, "Incarnation, Cross, and Sacrifice: A Feminist-Inspired Reappraisal," *Anglican Theological Review* 86 (2004), pp. 35–56.

lamb of life-giving flesh. By eating the flesh of the lamb the people were actively incorporated into its saving efficacy. "The lamb whose life was poured out as an offering for sin," wrote John Nevin, "must itself be incorporated as it were with the life of the worshippers, to give them a fair and full claim on the value of its vicarious death."[33] The lamb was fulfilled in its atonement for them by really entering into their flesh. In the meal they became one flesh with the lamb, even as in the sacrifice the lamb was made one flesh with them.

The theme of memorial was inseparable from those of substitution and participation. The Passover was to be commemorated every year by re-enacting the sacred meal. "You shall observe the festival of unleavened bread, for on this very day I brought your companies out of the land of Egypt; you shall observe this day throughout your generations as a perpetual ordinance" (Ex. 12:17). The lamb was sacrificed yearly, followed by a feast, whose celebration lasted for seven days (Ex. 12:15). Again, the *anamnesis* of the original Passover was more than just a mental act. It was a ritual re-presentation conducted by the entire community in which every member actively took part in the Exodus. The past was ritually re-enacted in the present, even as the present was made to take part in the saving events of the past.

Because of the institution of Passover, the deliverance of the people from bondage could never be separated in their minds from a simultaneous deliverance from death. Again, the grace of their deliverance had been more than just political. It was also essentially spiritual. The people were delivered, through no merit of their own, not only from bitter oppression, but also from all that Egypt represented in idolatry, judgment, and death. For all succeeding generations, the yearly celebration of Passover served as a living reminder that there was no grace without appointed sacrifice, no

---

[33] John Nevin, *The Mystical Presence: A Vindication of the Reformed or Calvinistic Doctrine of the Holy Eucharist* (Philadelphia: J. B. Lippencott & Co., 1846), p. 235.

sacrifice without vicarious substitution, and no substitution without participation in the sacred meal.

Finally, the theme of promise was involved with those of memorial, substitution, and participation. The promise given with Passover brought an orientation toward the future, even as the memorial had been oriented toward the past, and participation in the paschal meal toward the present. An eternal orientation toward God was also implicit throughout, in the theme of deliverance. Deliverance through vicarious substitution had occurred for the sake of sanctification (Lev. 11:45; 1 Pet. 1:16), which was to be expressed before God in worship and moral responsibility (Ex. 20:1–17). The promise received in Passover was seen by the Rabbis as the promise of an everlasting covenant. Passover was a covenantal promise of divine mercy, guidance, and protection. Though the mercy be severe, the guidance hard and the protection hidden, the God who had supplied the means of deliverance could be trusted to do so again. The hope for a coming salvation in the day of the Messiah would eventually find its place here.[34]

Unlike the Passover lamb, Christ as the Lamb of God had been sacrificed only to be raised to new life. The weekly celebration of the eucharist took up and reconfigured the yearly celebration of Passover. The day of resurrection became the day of weekly celebration (eventually to be placed in the yearly context of Lent, Good Friday, and Easter). The Lamb who had died had become a living presence. His definitive sacrifice on the cross was re-actualized with each *anamnesis*. It was re-presented in sacramental form. His flesh was given and received in the sacred meal. Christ and his sacrifice were inseparably one. As he became present, his sacrifice became present with him. The content of the cross and of the

---

[34] For a discussion of the other main passages in the Old Testament pertaining to Passover, see T. D. Alexander, "The Passover Sacrifice," in *Sacrifice in the Bible*, ed. Roger T. Beckwith and Martin J. Selman (Grand Rapids: Baker Book House, 1995), pp. 1–24.

eucharist was the same, but the forms were very different. Where the sacrifice of the cross was primary, that of the eucharist was secondary; where the one was constitutive, the other was derivative; where the one was complete in itself, the other was its daily memorial (*anamnesis*). The eucharist brought Christ's sacrifice into the present, while the cross remained its dimension of depth. Although the eucharist added nothing to the perfection of Christ's saving work, the perfection of his work was present and effectual in the eucharist, because Christ himself, as the High Priest and Lamb of God in one person, became present and effectual sacramentally under the forms of his body and blood.

The eucharist as paschal meal: Warfield, Torrance, and Thurian

Three examples from the Reformed tradition will help to show how eucharistic sacrifice might be retrieved for the Protestant churches. The one is from B. B. Warfield, the second from T. F. Torrance, and the last from Max Thurian. Each interprets the eucharist as a paschal meal. At the same time each needs to be examined for its limitations. The goal will be to bring a specifically Reformed doctrine into convergence with patristic and contemporary ecumenical understandings of eucharistic worship.

In an essay on "The Fundamental Significance of the Lord's Supper,"[35] Warfield reflected on the central question of how the eucharist is related to Christ's sacrifice on the cross. He began by noting that the Lord's Supper was instituted in the midst of a

---

[35] Benjamin B. Warfield, "The Fundamental Significance of the Lord's Supper," in *Selected Shorter Writings of Benjamin B. Warfield*, ed. John E. Meeter, vol. I (Nuttley: Presbyterian & Reformed, 1970), pp. 332–38. (Hereafter page references cited in the text.) For calling attention to this essay, I am indebted to the fine discussion of Keith A. Mathison, *Reclaiming Calvin's Doctrine of the Lord's Supper* (Phillipsburg: Presbyterian & Reformed, 2002), pp. 167–70.

Passover meal. Nothing can be more certain, he noted, than that Christ "deliberately chose the Passover meal for the institution of the sacrament of his body and blood" (p. 332). Warfield then considered some similarities between the eucharist and the Passover. The central feature of each, he suggested, is the idea of "eating a symbol of Jesus Christ himself" (p. 332). The Passover lamb is the type to which Christ is then the antitype. Warfield commented:

> The lamb that was slain and lay on the table at this feast was just the typical representative of the Lamb that had been slain from the foundation of the world and in whose hands is the Book of Life. The bread and wine of which we partake at the Lord's table are in like manner, according to our Lord's precise declaration, his blood poured out for us. What is done in the two facts is therefore precisely the same thing: Jesus Christ is symbolically fed upon in both.
>
> (p. 333)

The Lord's Supper can therefore be described as "the Christian Passover meal" (p. 333). It is not so much a replacement or substitute for Passover as it is the same Passover in a new form. "It is much rather," wrote Warfield, "only a new form given to the Passover, for the continuance of its essential substance through all time" (p. 333). The symbols are changed and adapted to the new dispensation in Christ, but the Passover lamb had always been an anticipation of Christ's sacrifice on the cross. When Jesus takes the bread and says, "This is my body," he deliberately identifies himself with the paschal lamb. The fundamental significance of the Lord's Supper is therefore that of a sacrificial meal. Again, Warfield:

> The meal which succeeded the sacrifice in any case owed its significance to its relation to the sacrifice. The victim offered was the material of the meal, and the idea of expiation was therefore

fundamental to it – it was a feast of death. But, on the other hand, just because it was a festive meal, it in any case also celebrated rather the effects than the fact of this death – it was a feast of life.

(p. 336)

Warfield approached the idea of eucharistic sacrifice with caution, displaying the usual Protestant scruples. It is therefore all the more astonishing to see the degree to which he accommodated the sacrificial motif. He wrote: "Assuredly . . . the sacrificial feast is not a repetition of the sacrifice; and equally certainly it is something more than a mere commemoration of the sacrifice; it is specifically a part of the sacrifice, and more particularly this part – the application of it" (p. 336). By resorting to the idea of "application," which was standard in the soteriology of the older Reformed orthodoxy, Warfield avoided two ideas that would greatly enhance the possibilities of ecumenical convergence, namely, "re-presentation" and "participation." It is one of Torrance's virtues, as will be suggested, to have shown how Reformed theology might retrieve precisely these ideas for the eucharist.

To continue with Warfield, he did at least approach a conception of participation. "Everyone who partook of the sacrificial feast," he stated, "had 'communion with the altar' . . . Those who ate of the sacrificed victim became thereby participants in the benefits attained by the sacrifice" (p. 336). Unlike Luther, and also unlike Calvin, Warfield restricted the idea of participation to Christ's benefits or effects, as if one could participate in Christ's benefits without at the same time participating in his person. Like Luther and Calvin, however, Warfield saw the priestly activity as primarily a function of the community. "Only one or two of the household, perchance, bore the paschal lamb to the temple and were engaged in its sacrificial slaying: all those who partook of the feast, however, were alike the offerers of the sacrifice and its beneficiaries" (p. 336). The priestly role was a function of the community.

In this context Warfield could explain the sense in which he thought the eucharist gave new form to the Passover:

Precisely what our Lord did, therefore, when at the last Passover he changed the symbols by which he was represented – he, the true Passover, the Lamb of God, that takes away the sin of the world – was to establish a perpetual sacrificial feast, under universal forms, capable of observation everywhere and at all times, and to command it to be celebrated as a proclamation of his death "till he came." All who partake of this bread and wine, the appointed symbols of his body and blood, therefore, are symbolically partaking of the victim offered on the altar of the cross, and are by this act professing themselves offerers of the sacrifice and seeking to become beneficiaries of it. That is the fundamental significance of the Lord's Supper.

(pp. 336–37)

Warfield was careful to stay within the bounds of a purely symbolic interpretation. He made no mention of any real presence of Christ, let alone of his body and blood in sacramental form. Yet he interpreted the eucharist not just as a sacrament, but also as a sacrifice:

Whenever the Lord's Supper is spread before us we are invited to take our place at the sacrificial feast, the substance of which is the flesh and blood of the victim which has been sacrificed once for all at Calvary; and as we eat these in their symbols, we are – certainly not repeating his sacrifice, nor yet prolonging it – but continuing that solemn festival upon it instituted by Christ, by which we testify our "participation in the altar" and claim our part in the benefits bought by the offering immolated on it. The sacrificial feast is not the sacrifice, in the sense of the act of offering: it is, however, the sacrifice, in the sense of the thing offered, that is eaten in it: and therefore it is presuppositive of the sacrifice in the sense of the act of offering and implies that this offering has already been performed.

(p. 337)

CHRIST OUR PASSOVER: A PROPOSAL

Warfield skated to the very edge of a merely symbolic interpretation. The eucharist itself, he stated, is not the act of offering,
because for him that would be restricted to the cross. Yet he went
so far as to say that the eucharist is "the sacrifice in the sense of the
thing offered, that is eaten in it." Within the terms of his presuppositions, however, this eating would have to be "symbolic"
rather than "real," with no way of combining them. Nonetheless,
he almost broke through this sterile contrast. His concluding
thoughts were intriguingly ambiguous:

> The Lord's Supper as a sacrificial feast is accordingly not the
> sacrifice, that is, the act of offering up Christ's body and blood: it
> is, however, the sacrifice, that is the body and blood of Christ that
> were offered, which is eaten in it: and therefore it is presuppositive
> of the sacrifice as an act of offering and implies that this act has
> already been performed once for all.

(p. 337)

The eucharist, Warfield stated, presupposes the cross, and only
in the cross do we have the sacrifice – the act of offering up Christ's
body and blood. Nevertheless, Warfield affirmed that the sacrifice
in another sense – namely, "the body and blood that were offered" –
is eaten in the sacred meal. Undoubtedly, he again meant this
symbolically. But if the antithesis between the symbolic and the
real were overcome so that each included the other, as was shown
to be the case for Eastern Orthodoxy as explained by Harnack and
Schmemann, and as was approximated by the Reformed Vermigli,
then a greater measure of ecumenical convergence would be near.[36]

The contribution of Thomas F. Torrance to the question of
eucharistic sacrifice is at least threefold. He developed an integrated
conception of Christ's person and work, he showed how the cross
and the eucharist can be held together in a pattern of unity-in-
distinction, and he explained how Christ's vicarious humanity

---

[36] See the discussion in chapter 2 above.

149

allows *participatio Christi* to be grounded in grace alone. In addition, he also connected eucharistic sacrifice with Christ's ascension.

First, Torrance developed an integrated conception of Christ's person and work. The person of Christ, he explained, cannot be separated from his work, nor his work from his person, because "his person and his work are one."[37] As the Incarnate Son, Christ "confronts us as he in whom person and word and work are indissolubly one. It is his own person that he communicates in his words and deeds, while his words and deeds do not only derive from his person but inhere in it."[38]

As Christ's person and work are one, so also are his Incarnation and atonement. The two are necessarily inseparable and mutually implicated in each other. For Torrance, as for the great patristic theologians on whom he relies, like Athanasius and Cyril, the Incarnation reaches its fulfillment in the atonement, while the atonement finds its essential premise in the Incarnation. That was the point of Torrance's insight that we are not saved by the death of Christ, but by the person of Christ in his death.

"Atoning reconciliation," Torrance wrote, "takes place within the personal being of the mediator . . . In him the Incarnation and Atonement are one . . . for atoning reconciliation falls within the incarnational constitution of his person as mediator."[39] By virtue of his resurrection from the dead, Christ himself is "the living Atonement," who prevails eternally in his intercession before God, and who avails perpetually for us here and now as the propitiation for our sins."[40] Resurrection means "the real presence of the whole Jesus Christ."[41] His earthly life and passion, including his unique

---

[37] Thomas F. Torrance, *The Mediation of Christ* (Colorado Springs: Helmers & Howard, 1992), p. 63.

[38] Thomas F. Torrance, *Space, Time and Resurrection* (Grand Rapids: Wm. B. Eerdmans, 1976), p. 48.

[39] Torrance, *Mediation*, p. 63.   [40] Torrance, *Space, Time and Resurrection*, p. 55.

[41] Thomas F. Torrance, *Theology in Reconciliation* (Grand Rapids: Wm. B. Eerdmans, 1976), p. 135.

and unrepeatable sacrifice on the cross, "far from being past, persist through the triumph of the resurrection over all corruption and decay."[42] The risen Christ mediates himself to faith as the living atonement in the eucharistic worship of the church. The Lamb who has been slain but is alive for evermore offers us his body and blood that we may participate in his vicarious self-offering to the Father.[43] Christ's expiatory sacrifice is one with his person: "He is the expiation [*hilasmos*] for our sins" (1 Jn. 2:2, RSV).

Torrance's second contribution was to show how the cross and the eucharist are held in a unity that does not violate but reinforces their distinction. The one perfect and indivisible act of atonement in Jesus Christ assumes two different forms. The constitutive form is the cross while the mediating form is the eucharist. The cross is always central, constitutive, and definitive, while the eucharist is always secondary, relative, and derivative. The eucharistic form of the one sacrifice does not repeat the unrepeatable, but it does attest what it mediates and mediate what it attests. What it mediates and attests is the one whole Jesus Christ, who in his body and blood is both the sacrifice and the sacrament in one. As the sacrifice, he is the Offerer and the Offering. As the sacrament, he is the Giver and the Gift. The Son's sacrificial offering of himself to the Father for us on the cross is the ground of the Father's sacramental gift of his Son to the faithful in the eucharist.

The cross was styled by Torrance as the "dimension of depth" in the eucharist.[44] The eucharist has no significance in itself that is not derived from the cross and grounded in it. Therefore the cross alone is the saving "content, reality and power" of the eucharist.[45] It is a matter of one reality, one priestly sacrifice of Christ, in two different temporal forms. The eucharistic form here and now

---

[42] Ibid. [43] Ibid., pp. 120, 111.

[44] See George Hunsinger, "The Dimension of Depth: Thomas F. Torrance on the Sacraments of Baptism and the Lord's Supper," *Scottish Journal of Theology* 54 (2001), pp. 155–76.

[45] Torrance, *Theology in Reconciliation*, p. 82 (*supra* n. 41).

participates in, manifests, and attests the incarnational form of the sacrifice there and then. What took place in the perfect tense is finished, indivisible, and all-sufficient. What takes place in the eucharistic sacrifice is not a matter of repetition but of participation, manifestation, and witness. The real presence of the one Jesus Christ – who is the same yesterday, today, and for ever (Heb. 13:8) – gives the faithful a share here and now in the salvation once accomplished there and then. Christ's real eucharistic presence is the presence of his personal being and atoning self-sacrifice.

Mention may be made, thirdly, of a further contribution, namely, Torrance's idea of Christ's vicarious humanity. Christ himself, Torrance proposed, functions vicariously as our human response to God. It is by grace through faith that the faithful are given to participate in Christ's perfect human offering of himself to God. Eucharistic mediation and participation provide an answer to the question of repetition that so worried the Reformers. These ideas also address the problem of the mass as a meritorious work. In the eucharist the living Christ re-presents himself in his vicarious humanity – that is, in his body and blood – so that the faithful are given an active though secondary and derivative participation in it. Recall Calvin's view that it is in and through the priesthood of Christ that we "offer ourselves and all that we are to God" (*Inst.* II.15.6). Torrance has shown that there is no reason why this, the self-offering of the faithful, should not be given a eucharistic location. The body and blood of Christ's vicarious humanity, by which Christ unites the faithful sacramentally to himself, are the very same body and blood by which he graciously includes them in his own perfect self-offering on their behalf to God.

The event of Passover allowed Torrance to deepen his incarnational view of how the cross and the eucharist were one. He wrote:

The early Christians called [the message of Good Friday and Easter] the *Pascha* in view of the *Passover* which was celebrated in

Israel at that time and in which Christ fulfilled his own *Passion* as the *Paschal Lamb.* Jesus Christ was regarded as constituting in himself the great Passover from death to life, from man-in-death to man-in-the-life-of-God, from damnation to salvation, from destruction to new creation. But that *Pascha* which he accomplished in himself for our sakes is proclaimed as the great *Pascha* which he has accomplished for the Church and for the world. It is, then, in that profound unity and continuity, ontologically structured in and through the Person of Christ as Mediator, that the resurrection was understood as forming with the crucifixion the great Paschal Mystery of our salvation.[46]

The paschal mystery of the eucharist meant that Christ himself was present in sacramental form as the living atonement.

Finally, like Calvin and the general Reformed tradition, Torrance developed the idea of Christ's ascension. Unlike them, however, he applied it to the question of eucharistic sacrifice. Torrance distinguished three aspects of Christ's priestly office in his ascension: his eternal self-offering, his perpetual intercession, and his continual benediction.[47] These will be discussed, briefly, in reverse order. According to Torrance:

(1) The ascended Christ's eternal benediction is his sending of his Spirit. It is this gift that creates union and communion with Christ. Through this benediction the faithful live no longer for themselves but for him who for their sakes died and was raised (2 Cor. 5:15).

(2) The ascended Christ's perpetual intercession, in turn, is his continual prayer before the Father. By his Spirit he takes up the church's prayers into his own continual intercession, where they are purified and perfected. Because Christ's being is in his act, however, his perpetual intercession is finally inseparable

---

[46] Torrance, *Space, Time and Resurrection*, p. 49. [47] Ibid., pp. 115–18.

from his person. His perpetual intercession and his eternal self-offering are one.[48]

(3) Finally, the ascended Christ's eternal self-offering provides a basis for understanding eucharistic sacrifice. Christ's priestly sacrifice and oblation of himself are multifaceted. In one sense they are necessarily over and done with. But "in their once for all completion," noted Torrance, "they are taken up eternally into the life of God and remain prevalent, efficacious, valid, [and] abidingly real."[49] Christ's historical self-offering on Calvary has taken place once for all and needs no repetition. But since the Offerer and the Offering are inherently one, Christ's atoning sacrifice is taken up, through his resurrection and ascension, into the eternal presence of the Father. His self-offering "endures for ever as the one, perfect, sufficient sacrifice for the sins of the world."[50]

The eucharist must be seen to have a twofold aspect. It involves feeding on Christ through the reception of his life-giving flesh

---

[48] A subtle issue arises at this point. One view, represented by Milligan (whom Torrance follows), stresses that the intercession and the offering of Christ in his ascension are inseparable. Another view, as taken by Tait, insists that it is not the atoning sacrifice but only its efficacy which can be eternal, because the sacrifice was finished on Calvary. Over against those who have contended that if the sacrifice is eternal it cannot have been historically completed, Tait is correct. Whether Milligan makes this error is not clear. Torrance, however, avoids it, since he acknowledged that Christ's atoning sacrifice on Calvary is completed, perfect, and sufficient in itself. See William Milligan, *The Ascension and Heavenly Priesthood of our Lord* (London: Macmillan, 1894); Arthur J. Tait, *The Heavenly Session of Our Lord* (London: R. Scott, 1912). For a critique of Torrance that sides with Tait, see Peter Toon, *The Ascension of Our Lord* (Nashville: Thomas Nelson, 1984). Toon fails to grasp that for Torrance Christ's finished historical self-offering is inseparable from his person. On the other hand, for examples of the error that Tait rightly rejects, see R. J. Coates, "The Doctrine of Eucharistic Sacrifice in Modern Times," in *Eucharistic Sacrifice*, ed. J. I. Packer (London: Church Book Room Press, 1962), pp. 127–53.

[49] Torrance, *Space, Time and Resurrection*, p. 115 (*supra* n. 38).

[50] Torrance, *Theology in Reconciliation*, p. 133 (*supra* n. 41).

(communion) while it also means worshipping the Father in the Spirit through the Son, in union with his eternal self-offering (sacrifice). "Eucharistic sacrifice means that we *through the Spirit* are so intimately united to Christ, by his body and blood, that we participate in his self-consecration and self-offering to the Father."[51] We thus "appear with him and in him and through him before the Majesty of God in worship, praise and adoration with no other sacrifice than the sacrifice of Jesus our Mediator and High Priest."[52] "It is his one sufficient and once for all offering of himself for us that is our only sacrifice before God."[53] "What we do as we gather together in Christ's name is to offer Christ to the Father, for he who has united us to himself has gathered up and sanctified all our worship and prayer in himself."[54]

There is therefore one sacrifice common to Christ and his church – that is the highpoint of Torrance's teaching. What he says about the eucharist runs parallel to what he said in another place, following Athanasius, about baptism, namely, that there is "one baptism common to Christ and his church."[55] "Because he is baptized," wrote Athanasius, "it is we who are baptized in him."[56] The baptism of the faithful is not another or separate baptism alongside the baptism of Christ. It is rather a participation in his one vicarious baptism as undergone for their sakes. Just as Christ's baptism is vicarious, encompassing, and inclusive, so the same is also true of his atoning sacrifice on the cross. The sacrifice of thanks and praise that is offered by the faithful in the eucharist is taken up into the one atoning sacrifice of Christ, enacted on their behalf. His completed and perpetual self-offering, as sacramentally

---

[51] Ibid., p. 134. [52] Ibid. [53] Torrance, *Space, Time and Resurrection*, p. 117.

[54] Torrance, *Theology in Reconciliation*, p. 212.

[55] Torrance, "The One Baptism Common to Christ and His Church," in *Theology and Reconciliation*, pp. 82–105.

[56] Athanasius, *Oration Against the Arians* 1.48, in *Athanasius*, ed. Kahled Anatolios (London: Routledge, 2004), p. 106.

re-presented in the eucharist, serves as their means of eternal access to the Father of all mercy and righteousness.

The sacrifice common to Christ and his church is seen as one sacrifice in three modes:

- the once-for-all and historical mode in which the work of expiation was completed,
- the ascended and eternal mode by which its efficacy never ends,
- the daily and eucharistic mode through which the faithful come to dwell in Christ and he in them as his sacrifice continually becomes theirs and theirs his.

While these different modes remain truly distinct, they also form an inseparable unity. It is the unity of a single great sacrifice. It was once accomplished on the cross, then elevated in its efficacy to eternity, on which basis it is re-presented in the Word and by the Spirit for daily participation, reception, and acknowledgment by the church. The sacramental means for this daily participation, reception, and acknowledgment is the eucharist as communion and sacrifice.[57]

Max Thurian, the Swiss Reformed theologian who later became a Roman Catholic priest, also reflected significantly on the meaning of Passover for the eucharist. He was always concerned to guide the Protestant churches toward eucharistic convergence with the high sacramental traditions. *Anamnesis* and *epiclesis* are themes in his writings that call for special comment.

The idea of *anamnesis*, Thurian wrote, "is the link between the Jewish Passover and the Christian Eucharist."[58] The Passover celebration allowed the Jews to "relive mystically, sacramentally, the events of deliverance and Exodus from Egypt." It involved

---

[57] I use the word "daily" here both literally and metaphorically, in conformity with the discourse of Chrysostom.

[58] Max Thurian, *The Eucharistic Memorial*, vol. II (London: Lutterworth Press, 1960), p. 39.

"a kind of telescoping of two periods of history, the present and the Exodus." The redemptive act that had been accomplished once for all was yet also "ever renewed, present and applied" in a kind of sacramental or mystical form. It was a ritual and communal act of memorial, not a mere subjective remembering. It enabled "*the concrete re-living* of the deliverance" of God's people. "The Eucharist, instituted in this tradition and context, presents the same conception of the mystery of history . . . [as] present in the liturgical and sacramental action."[59]

The *anamnesis* of the paschal meal actually involved a "triple memorial." There was "the past deliverance regarded as typical," the "liturgical reliving of the deliverance" in the present, and the promise of a future deliverance of salvation in the day of the Messiah.[60] The Eucharist involves this same threefold horizon. "Like the paschal meal, the Eucharist moves from faith in a deliverance, which has been accomplished and is actualized in the sacrament, to a prayer that the Lord may come for every [human being] and thus hasten the last day."[61]

At the same time a vertical aspect was involved along with this more horizontal aspect. Just as the eucharistic *anamnesis* gave form, within present liturgical experience, to past and future saving events, so it also brought into the present Christ's historical sacrifice and eternal intercession. It makes them available for sacramental participation by the faithful. "The Eucharist is the liturgical presentation of the sacrifice of the Son by the Church to the Father. This is the sense in which we have understood the Eucharist to be a memorial."[62] The eucharist brought about a sacramental convergence, so to speak, not only of past and future (the horizontal), but also of heaven and earth (the vertical).

---

[59] Ibid., p. 19 (italics original).   [60] Ibid., p. 28.   [61] Ibid., p. 29.
[62] Max Thurian, *The Eucharistic Memorial*, vol. II (London: Lutterworth Press, 1961), p. 83.

More precisely, what brings about this convergence is the gift of the Holy Spirit through the prayer of *epiclesis*. "The sacramental presence of the sacrifice of the cross is accomplished by the power of the Holy Spirit and of the Word. No action of the Church can be conceived as taking place outside the work of the Holy Spirit, and no liturgy can omit reference to him."[63] Through the *epiclesis* or invocation of the Holy Spirit, the various elements in the eucharistic liturgy come mystically to converge: *anamnesis* (re-presentation), *prolepsis* (anticipatory realization), *koinonia* (communion), *thusia* (self-offering) and *entugchano* (intercession).[64] By the Spirit and in the Word, the horizontal and the vertical dimensions of the eucharist become one.[65]

Thurian sums up by citing three reasons why the eucharist is a sacrifice.[66]

1. Sacramental presence. The eucharist is "the sacramental presence of the cross, by the power of the Holy Spirit and the Word, and it is the liturgical presentation of the Son's sacrifice by the Church to the Father, in thanksgiving for all his blessings and in intercession that he may grant them afresh."
2. Ecclesial participation. The eucharist is "the participation of the Church in the intercession of the Son before the Father in the Holy Spirit, that salvation may be accorded to all [human beings] and that the Kingdom may come in glory."
3. Priestly self-offering. The eucharist is "the offering which the Church makes of itself to the Father, united to the Son's intercession, as its supreme act of adoration and its perfect consecration in the Holy Spirit."

---

[63] Ibid., pp. 82–83.
[64] Note that I extrapolate here to expand the *epiclesis* beyond what Thurian has said.
[65] Cf. Max Thurian, "The Lima Liturgy: Origin, Intention and Structure," in *Eucharistic Worship in Ecumenical Contexts*, ed. Thomas F. Best and Dagmar Heller (Geneva: WCC Publications, 1998), pp. 14–21.
[66] Thurian, *Eucharistic Memorial*, vol. II, p. 76 (*supra* n. 62).

The eucharistic sacrifice is a sacramental form of the expiatory sacrifice of Christ. Yet in and with the presence of that sacrifice, and based on it, everything is presented to God for the sake of receiving a blessing. "The Church presents the bread and the wine that they may be blessed; it presents the gifts that they may become signs of brotherly [and sisterly] charity; it presents itself that it may be sanctified ... It is the sacrifice of praise, which according to rabbinic tradition, could be offered only in the messianic era."[67]

Re-presentation and participation, two ideas that were not fully available to Warfield, are richly developed by both Torrance and Thurian; and unlike Warfield, both go on to develop the paschal mystery of the eucharist in a context informed by Christ's ascension. At every point Torrance's theological account is more fully elaborated, yet Thurian lifts up the ideas of *anamnesis* and *epiclesis* in a special way that is not to be overlooked. From an ecumenical standpoint, however, both Thurian and Torrance suffer from a common weakness. Neither gives particular attention in these discussions to the office of the ordained presbyter or priest, especially with respect to the question of eucharistic sacrifice.[68] Yet even where a high degree of agreement has been reached about eucharistic sacrifice in bilateral dialogues, the question of ministry has emerged as the point of impasse. The official dialogues, notes Robert W. Jenson, have all tended to falter at the same point, "namely, not *what* is done at the Eucharist, but *who* does it."[69] Although "Eucharist and ministry" is a topic to be addressed in Part III of this book, the specific question of agency – who does what in the eucharist – is tackled in the proposal below. At the same time, an equally large sticking point not yet considered – the Tridentine doctrine of eucharistic sacrifice – is also grappled with.

[67] Ibid., p. 77.
[68] Both dealt with this question elsewhere. See Max Thurian, *Priesthood and Ministry: Ecumenical Research* (London: Mowbray, 1983); Thomas F. Torrance, *Royal Priesthood: A Theology of Ordained Ministry* (Edinburgh: T. & T. Clark, 1993).
[69] Robert W. Jenson, *Unbaptized God* (Minneapolis: Fortress Press, 1992), p. 43.

Cracking the deadlock

According to Erwin Iserloh, medieval views about eucharistic sacrifice fell broadly into two types.[70] The one was "Thomist," the other "Scotist." The first type was represented by a minority of theologians, whereas the latter predominated at the time of the Reformation. Though the first type was espoused by Cardinal Cajetan, he apparently exercised little influence. The more widespread view was expressed by John Eck. Nevertheless, ideas about eucharistic sacrifice were fluid, and prior to the Council of Trent no official doctrine was in existence.[71]

According to the "Thomist" view, Christ and his sacrifice were present in the eucharist in a sacramental way. Christ acted in and through the presiding minister, who for his part was acting *in persona Christi.* There was only one priesthood – the priesthood of Christ – in which the presiding minister participated. Likewise, there was only one sacrifice – that of the cross – which was made present through the minister's mediation. The point at which the minister's mediation became effective – so as to confer grace *ex opere operato* – was the moment of consecration. With the words of consecration Christ became present on the altar as the sacrificial victim. The consecrated elements were at once a sacrifice and a sacrament. As the real, substantial presence of Christ's body and blood for the forgiveness of sins, they were a sacrament. As the means by which Christ offered satisfaction to God, they were a sacrifice. Whether as sacrifice or as sacrament, the effectiveness of the eucharist for the faithful was proportional to

---

[70] Erwin Iserloh, "Das Wert der Messe in der Diskussion der Theologen vom Mittelalter bis zum 16. Jahrhundert," *Zeitschrift für katolische Theologie* 83 (1961), pp. 44–79.

[71] Nicholas Thompson, whose lead is being followed here, describes Iserloh's work as "still definitive." See Thompson, *Eucharistic Sacrifice and Patristic Tradition in the Theology of Martin Bucer, 1534–1546* (Leiden: Brill, 2005), p. 11.

the quality of their devotion. It did not depend on either the holiness of the minister or the efficacy of his sacramental action. The "Scotist" view differed from the first in important ways. The mass was limited, because it merely represented Christ's sacrifice, but was not the sacrifice itself. Its efficacy was inherently restricted, and not only by the dispositions of those who shared in it. Because Christ's sacrifice on Calvary was of infinite value, it was difficult for the "Scotist" view to explain why the mass was not a different sacrifice altogether. The doctrine of limited value also promoted the idea that grace was somehow quantitative and materialistic. A mass celebrated for the benefit of one person was of more value for him than if it were celebrated for others at the same time, because the "fruits" of the mass had to be shared with the other beneficiaries. The idea was thus encouraged that through various religious practices salvation could be earned for oneself and others. Moreover, on this view, the celebrant overshadowed Christ, for it was the celebrant who offered Christ to God after the consecration had made him present. The celebrant's actions were efficacious *ex opere operato*, first in consecrating the elements, then in offering the sacrifice on behalf of a beneficiary. Christ was present as Victim but not an acting subject as Priest.

For the Reformation, two problems were evident in these eucharistic teachings: not only the idea of limited efficacy, regardless of whether by representation or by disposition, but also the idea of the celebrant exercising causal agency in the eucharist alongside the agency of Christ. Both problems pointed in much the same direction, namely, toward what Roman Catholic scholar Nicholas Thompson has called "liturgical Pelagianism."[72] Unfortunately Iserloh was mistaken when he supposed that the Thomist view of the eucharist would have been enough to allay the concerns

---

[72] Ibid. Liturgical Pelagianism also results whenever the idea of Christ's sacrifice as an expiatory sacrifice is dismissed. See Torrance, *Theology in Reconciliation*, pp. 134, 172 (*supra* n. 41).

THE EUCHARIST AND ECUMENISM

of the Reformers. They would still have found it unacceptable to say that Christ is the "principal" offerer of the mass, or that while the offering is "primarily" Christ's work, it is "secondarily" that of the priest as well. To see why takes us into the heart of the Reformation's understanding of *solus Christus*. Only a doctrine of eucharistic sacrifice that did justice to the *solus Christus* could be acceptable to Reformational theology.

The Reformation's concern can be explained by introducing a distinction between an acting subject and a saving agent. According to Catholic theologian Cornelius Ernst, an "agent" is technically an "efficient cause," whose action brings about some modification of being. An efficient cause may be either "principal or secondary." A *principal* efficient cause may be the exclusive cause, or it may be supplemented by a *secondary* efficient cause that acts in virtue of the principal cause. A secondary cause, however, may only be "instrumental." "A secondary cause is instrumental when its causal action is confined to transmitting the action of the principal agent."[73] From the Reformation's standpoint, with respect to the work of salvation, an acting subject might be an instrumental cause in this latter sense, but it could not be either a principal or a supplementary efficient cause.

A related distinction would be between an efficacious work and an accompanying act. For the Reformation there was only one saving agent in the work of salvation, namely, Christ alone. Whether in the perfect tense, the present tense, or the future tense, the work of salvation belonged exclusively to Christ and to no other. The sole efficacy of Christ with respect to salvation did not exclude the involvement, in various ways, of other acting subjects. But it did exclude their contributing essentially, as opposed to extrinsically, to the his saving work.

---

[73] See Cornelius Ernst, "Glossary," in Thomas Aquinas, *Summa Theologiae*, Blackfriars, vol. 30, *The Gospel of Grace* (New York: McGraw-Hill Book Co., 1972), p. 245.

All other acting subjects besides Christ were sinners in need of salvation. Even sinners in a state of grace had no capacity to contribute to Christ's one saving work. When Christ graciously allowed a person to participate in his saving work in some respect – as, say, in the case of the minister who presided at the eucharist – the minister could in no way become a secondary "cause" of salvation, whether for himself or for someone else. Other acting subjects could do many things. They could acknowledge, receive, participate in, mediate, cooperate with, and above all attest Christ's one saving work, and they could do these things in any number of different ways. But they could not possibly contribute to Christ's work materially. They were always the saved, not the Saviour – not even "partially" or "secondarily." The Saviour did not, and could not possibly, divide up his one efficacious work with needy sinners, not even when joined to him by grace through faith.

The appropriation of salvation by faith – regardless of how partial, valid or flawed – did nothing to change this situation. Salvation as accomplished by Christ simply did not admit of degrees. Its gradual appropriation was always the gift of grace, resting on the foundation of faith. The reception of Christ by faith was all that was needed for salvation, where salvation was understood as deliverance from death to eternal life in communion with God. The Christian life was in consequence one of continual prayer, repentance, and gratitude. Devout dispositions and deeds had no saving efficacy in themselves. With no ulterior motive, they were not undertaken as a means of earning salvation. Being removed from the realm of some further "necessity" in obtaining salvation, they were a free response to a gift freely given. As the classic Protestant hymn extolled: "Love so amazing, so divine, demands my soul, my life, my all" (Isaac Watts). Salvation rested not on the works of the faithful, but on the sole sufficiency of Christ's expiatory death. Works were a consequence of salvation, not a cause.

Christ's multifaceted work of salvation – whether *extra nos,* *contra nos, pro nobis,* or *in nobis* – always came to the faithful as a sheer gift. It was not something they could "merit" through their own cooperation, for the simple reason that their cooperation, regardless of how real, had no saving efficacy. It was itself entirely a gift of grace. If "synergism" meant that the faithful "cooperated" with Christ in certain respects as he actualized his finished work of salvation here and now, then the term would not be problematic. But if "synergism" meant that the faithful somehow contributed essentially to the efficacy of Christ's saving work, then, at least for the Reformers, it was completely inadmissible.

There was only one saving agent in the work of salvation. In that sense the Reformation rejected synergism in favor of monergism. Salvation was a pure gift. It was never in any sense, not even partially, a human work. "But if it is by grace, it is no longer on the basis of works, otherwise grace would no longer be grace" (Rom. 11:6). "They are now justified by his grace as a gift, through the redemption that is in Christ Jesus" (Rom. 3:24). "For by grace you have been saved through faith, and this is not your own doing; it is the gift of God – not the result of works" (Eph. 2:8–9). "He saved us, not because of any works of righteousness that we had done, but according to his mercy ... so that, having been justified by his grace, we might become heirs according to the hope of eternal life" (Titus 3:5, 7).

A Reformational affirmation of eucharistic sacrifice would be based on Christ as the sole saving agent. Others might participate in the eucharistic sacrifice as acting subjects in various ways, whether in the mode of accompanying operation (the celebrant) or receptive participation (the congregation). Accompaniment and reception would be forms of *koinonia* with Christ, not forms of causal agency. They would be means by which Christ drew the church into union with himself, not means by which the church contributed to its own salvation or that of others. The sole saving agency of Christ in the eucharist would be the Reformation's answer to liturgical Pelagianism. Only the sole saving agency of the *Christus praesens* could prevent eucharistic sacrifice from becoming in any sense an efficacious human work. But the reverse would also be true. When eucharistic sacrifice was elucidated in terms of Christ's sole saving agency, it could be explained in a way that the Reformation would have no valid reason to deny.

In his book *Eucharistic Sacrifice and the Reformation*, the Jesuit scholar Francis Clark summarized the doctrine of eucharistic sacrifice at the time of the Reformation in ten points. He clearly believed them to be both valid and insuperable. On the grounds stated above – which allow for one saving agent along with many acting subjects – Clark's ten points can be interpreted in accord with the Reformation.[74]

(1) "In the Mass there is offered to God a true and proper sacrifice," the highest act of Christian worship.

From the standpoint of the *solus Christus*, this statement could be interpreted to mean that Christ himself is the sole saving agent who is active not only in the eucharistic sacrifice, but also in its significance as the "highest act" of worship.[75] The highest act of Christian worship is to plead Christ's eternal sacrifice. It is to give God thanks and praise for this salvation, which is inseparable from the giving of ourselves to Christ. For us and our salvation, the incarnate Son offers himself eternally to the Father, under the aspect of his body and blood, on our behalf. "For Christ did not enter a sanctuary made by human hands ... but he entered into

---

[74] See Francis Clark, *Eucharistic Sacrifice and the Reformation* (Oxford: Basil Blackwell, 1967), pp. 93–94. I have abbreviated some of his statements. The phrases in quotation marks are taken from the Council of Trent in its "Decree on the Sacrifice of the Mass."

[75] The point about sole saving agency could also be stated more directly in trinitarian terms. The sole saving agent in the eucharist could be described, for example, as the Father through the Son and in the Spirit, who brings us in the Spirit and through the Son to himself. Similarly, it could be said that in the sacrament Christ offers himself to us in the Word and by the Spirit, or more simply that through the *epiclesis* the Spirit so joins us to Christ. The christological idiom is chosen here only for the sake of convenience.

heaven itself, now to appear in the presence of God on our behalf" (Heb. 9:24; cf. 9:12). In his vicarious self-offering (Heb. 8:1–2), Christ graciously takes up and incorporates our own self-offering to him, for we live no longer for ourselves but for him who for our sakes died and was raised (2 Cor. 5:15). The mass is "a true and proper sacrifice," in that it gives sacramental form here and now to Christ's one indivisible sacrifice on the cross there and then.

> (2) The sacrifice of Christ's redemptive passion is all-sufficient to atone for the sins of all [human beings] ... The eucharistic oblation in no way implies that anything is wanting in the sacrifice of the cross, nor does it in any way detract from that sacrifice.

From a Reformational standpoint, Christ's atoning sacrifice must be understood on the basis that salvation has three tenses. When the Greek New Testament speaks of Christ's saving work in the aorist and perfect tenses, it sets forth his sacrifice in its definitive and constitutive form. When it speaks in the present tense, it sets forth that sacrifice in two further forms, one intermediate, the other eternal. Finally, when it speaks in the future tense, it sets forth that sacrifice in its final and unsurpassable form. The intermediate form – to which the eucharist belongs – looks both backward and forward. It is at once secondary and derivative while yet also being anticipatory and provisional.

The three temporal forms of Christ's one indivisible sacrifice – Calvary, eucharist, and Messianic Banquet – are mutually related. To borrow from Karl Barth on another theme: "Each of them also contains the other two by way of anticipation and recapitulation, so that without losing their individuality or destroying that of the others, they participate and are active and are revealed in them."[76] The three temporal forms of Christ's sacrifice form a complex

---

[76] Karl Barth, *Church Dogmatics*, vol. IV, part 3 (Edinburgh: T. & T. Clark, 1961), p. 296.

differentiated unity. Each form dwells in, and is active in, and is revealed in, the other. Each contains the other two by way of anticipation or recapitulation. They are three temporal forms of one and the same sacrifice.

At the same time there is a double asymmetry. In one respect the aorist or perfect-tense form of Christ's sacrifice – his life of obedience as it culminated in the cross – formally constitutes the fundamental ground in relation to which the other two forms (eucharist and Messianic Banquet) are simply the consequence. (This is essentially what Torrance means when he speaks of Calvary as the "dimension of depth."[77]) In another respect, however, the future-tense form – the Messianic Banquet at the end of all things – formally constitutes the final goal in relation to which the other two forms (Calvary and eucharist) are simply the precondition.[78] As both retrospective and prospective, the eucharist holds an intermediate position between Calvary and the Messianic Banquet. It is in that sense both derivative and provisional.

Insofar as Christ's heavenly intercession is perpetual and eternal, however, the eucharist looks not only backward and forward, but also upward. It participates here and now – in a provisional though real way – in Christ's heavenly intercession on our behalf, even as it also participates in the heavenly worship of the church triumphant.

Finally, the eucharist always mediates that in which it participates.[79] To the church on earth it at once mediates Calvary, the Messianic Banquet, the intercession of Christ, and the worship of the church triumphant. The eucharist stands, as it were, at the crossroads, uniting the past of Jesus Christ with his future, as well

---

[77] See Hunsinger, "Dimension of Depth" (*supra* n. 44).

[78] See the beautiful statement by E. L. Mascall cited below in chapter 7 of this volume, in which he combines imagery of eucharistic sacrifice with that of Messianic Banquet in a vision of the end of all things.

[79] By "mediate," I mean that these other realities are active in the eucharist and are revealed by it or at least in relation to it.

as Christ's heavenly intercession with the church's worship in heaven and on earth.

(3) Christ, "since his priesthood was not to be terminated with his death," established in his church an order of priests, "the Apostles and their succession in the priesthood," through whom he would continue his sacrifice for all time.

Although there is indeed a unity between the priesthood of Christ and that of his church, an ineffaceable distinction also exists between them, and a necessary asymmetry as well. From a Reformational standpoint, the priestly office belongs first to the community and only through the community to its eucharistic ministers (cf. 1 Pet. 2:5, 9). Neither the community nor its eucharistic ministers hold their priestly office in any respect on a par with Christ. His priestly office was not terminated with his death because he himself was not terminated with his death. "He was raised on the third day in accordance with the scriptures" (1 Cor. 15:4). Nor was the exclusive uniqueness of his priestly office terminated.

While he may "continue" his one indivisible sacrifice, he does so only in the sense of supplying it with ever new actualizations and forms, never in the sense of quantitatively or materially adding to it, as if it were somehow imperfect. Least of all does he need to "supplement" it through the work of human priests. Moreover, he "continues" his sacrifice in his own right (Heb. 9:24), without working through the priesthood of the church and its ministers, though in certain respects he does that as well.

The danger must be scrupulously avoided of placing "an order of priests" outside and over against the worshipping community, as if the order of priests were an order of secondary saving agents alongside Christ. Although in various respects Christ draws the community and its eucharistic ministers into his ongoing priestly work (in the Word and by the Spirit), he does so in such a way that they always accompany, receive, participate in, mediate, and attest that priestly work only as acting subjects, never as saving agents.

Accompaniment, reception, participation, mediation, and above all witness – not secondary causal agency – describe the high privilege of the church's priesthood in relation to that of Christ.

(4) The Mass is not an absolute sacrifice, independent of the unique sacrifice by which Christ "wrought our eternal redemption"; but it was instituted at the Last Supper as a relative sacrifice, by which that "sacrifice in blood, accomplished but once on the cross, was to be represented, so that memory thereof should remain till the world's end."

The sacrifice of the mass is not "absolute," because only the cross is constitutive and definitive. Likewise, it is not "independent," because only Christ's prior sacrifice supplies it with content. Because salvation has three tenses, however, the eucharist is not only a memorial but also a real anticipation. It is a liturgically enacted *prolepsis* as well as a liturgically enacted *anamnesis*. It not only memorializes something in the past, but also anticipates something in the future. It becomes a concrete anticipatory actualization here and now of the Messianic Banquet yet to come. In the modes of commemoration and anticipation, it mediates these realities into the present.

(5) Nevertheless, "the sacrifice of the Mass is not a mere commemoration," nor "only a sacrifice of praise and thanks"; in it, really present, "Christ himself is contained," and in very truth "his body and blood are offered to the Father under the appearances of bread and wine."

Just as the being of the worshippers themselves is taken up in their sacrifice of thanks and praise, so is their communal self-offering taken up by Christ and incorporated into his own vicarious offering to the Father (*totus Christus*). The participants are included through Christ's body and blood as offered and received under the forms of bread and wine. The oneness of Christ and his people is proclaimed, mediated, and renewed.

Whether on Calvary, or in the eucharist, or at the Messianic Banquet, Christ always unites himself to us, and us to himself, by means of his body and blood. It is therefore better to say that in his Word and by his Spirit, Christ transforms the consecrated elements, by elevating and incorporating them into his body and blood, so that the elements are contained in and by his body and blood, so that they are all made one, than to say that his body and blood are "contained" in the elements (although both statements are true). It is always a matter of their mutual indwelling in an asymmetrical pattern of differentiated unity. The unqualified precedence belongs always to the living and sovereign Christ. Containment of Christ's body in the consecrated elements (the downward vector) without elevation of those elements into oneness with Christ's spiritual body (the upward vector) tends to reinforce the unhappy view of the priest as a secondary causal agent of salvation, because it makes the priest seem like the agent (or co-agent) of the elements' transformation.

The charism of the priest must not be thought of in causal terms. Christ in his Spirit works *through* the priest but not (causally) *by* the priest. The special vocation of the priest in the prayers of *epiclesis* and consecration is a vocation of participation, not causation. It is Christ alone who sends his Spirit and consecrates the eucharistic gifts. Again, Christ is the sole saving agent and the primary acting subject, whereas the priest is an auxiliary subject with a special vocation – no more, no less. Monergism with respect to saving efficacy that allows for priestly synergism at the level of liturgical performance is the Reformation's solution to the danger of liturgical Pelagianism.[80] Christ acts through the priest, even as the priest acts through Christ, while the effectual agency belongs to Christ alone.

(6) The sacrifice of the altar is in a true sense one with the sacrifice of the cross. "The victim is one and the same, and he who now

---

[80] Again, the pattern of the synergism is of course necessarily asymmetrical.

offers through the ministry of the priests is the selfsame as he who then offered himself on the cross."

This statement leaves nothing to be desired so long as it is remembered that Christ is the sole saving agent, and that the priests through whom he now offers are set apart as auxiliary subjects appointed to a high sacramental (if non-causal) role. In the Word and by the Spirit, Christ himself sees to it that the sacrifice which took place there and then becomes truly present and actual in the sacrament. His person is in his sacrifice, and his sacrifice is in his person – the Offerer is in the Offering and the Offering is in the Offerer – so that the two are always inseparable and neither can be present without the other.

> (7) The newness of the mass-sacrifice, and its difference from the sacrifice of Calvary, "is only in the manner of the offering." For the mass is "an unbloody immolation," a mystical sacrifice, in which "the church through her priests immolates Christ under visible signs." Hence Christ, who offered himself only once by way of death, does not in any way suffer death, pain, or change in the sacrifice of the altar.

It is correct to say that the eucharistic sacrifice is something mystical rather than crudely literal. It is also correct that it differs from the sacrifice of Calvary in form, but not in content. Moreover, it is correct and even commendable to say that it is the community which is acting through the priest, for in a real and mystical though non-causal way, the priest acts *in persona ecclesiae* as well as *in persona Christi.*

It is at best misleading, however, if not worse, to say that under the visible signs Christ is "immolated" by the church through her priests. If this statement were made from the standpoint of saving agency, it would be false. On the other hand, if it were made from a more modest standpoint of acting subjecthood, it could still be true only if the church were somehow a community of unrepentant sinners. The Christ who was "immolated" by his enemies is not subjected to that indignity yet again through the priestly manipulation of the visible signs. Christ himself makes his person and his sacrifice really present without any new or secondary "re-enactment." The signs actualize and attest, but do not "re-enact," his one indivisible sacrifice. Otherwise, the mass would indeed be a repetition of the unrepeatable, and so a new or additional saving work. The unfortunate language of "immolation," if used at all, must be interpreted by the language of attestation, mediation, and real presence – *not* by the language of re-enactment or repetition. Least of all does the church "do" something to Christ through the celebrant in order to "make" Christ into an immolated victim. To suppose otherwise would be to introduce gross and impious confusion with regard to both agency and auxiliary subjecthood.

(8) All the efficacy of the mass flows from the sacrifice of Calvary; "the fruits of the bloody oblation are received in superabundance by means of the unbloody oblation." Through the latter [human beings] are enabled to participate in all the graces and benefits won for them by Christ. It "applies the saving force of the sacrifice of the cross for the remission of the sins which we daily commit"; it is "offered for the sins, penalties, satisfactions and needs of the faithful." Thus "the Mass is in truth a propitiatory sacrifice."

The eucharistic sacrifice is not a new sacrifice alongside that of Calvary. It is the one sacrifice of Christ in sacramental form. The sacrifice of Calvary is not one thing and the efficacy of the eucharist quite another. The sacrifice of Calvary, which is efficacious in all its forms, mediates and actualizes its one indivisible efficacy in the eucharist. Since Christ's sacrifice is of infinite value, it cannot really surpass itself. The language of "superabundance" must therefore be interpreted as the hyperbole of religious devotion.

Moreover, nothing must be sought in Christ other than Christ himself. He is not external to his benefits. On the contrary, all his benefits are in him. Christ and his benefits are one. He is himself the remission of our sins. When he encounters us in the eucharist under the aspect of his body and blood, he assures us of his sufficiency for our forgiveness and for our hope of eternal life. He himself is our righteousness and our life. That is the central message of the Reformation, and these are the chief benefits the faithful receive in union with Christ by grace through faith.

The eucharist actualizes and attests that through his body and blood Christ has made, and continues to make, the faithful one with himself. It therefore actualizes and attests that the sins which they "daily commit" are covered by his blood. It actualizes and attests that "in him we have redemption through his blood, the forgiveness of our trespasses, according to the riches of his grace" (Eph. 1:7). It actualizes and attests that we were "ransomed . . . with the precious blood of Christ, like that of a lamb without defect or blemish" (1 Pet. 1:18–19). It actualizes and attests that even now "the blood of Jesus his Son cleanses us from all sin" (1 Jn. 1:7). The blood shed for our sakes on the cross is the same blood that comes to us in sacramental form "to cover the needs of the faithful" here and now.

The sacrifice of the eucharist is indeed "propitiatory," but only because the sacrifice of the cross is propitiatory. God's wrath is the form taken by God's love when God's love is contradicted and opposed. God's love will not tolerate anything contrary to itself. It does not compromise with evil, or ignore evil, or call evil good. It enters into the realm of evil and destroys it. The wrath of God is propitiated when the disorder of sin is expiated. It would be an error to suppose that "propitiation" and "expiation" must be pitted against each other as though they were mutually exclusive. The wrath of God is removed (propitiation) when the sin that provokes it is abolished (expiation). Moreover, the love of God that takes the form of wrath when provoked by sin is the very same love that provides the efficacious means of expiation (vicarious sacrifice) and therefore of propitiation.[81]

The eternal Son becomes incarnate in order that sin might be overcome and abolished from within. "Here is the Lamb of God who takes away the sin of the world!" (Jn. 1:29). In the sacrifice of the cross, the divine judgment is born and borne away. "And he is the propitiation for our sins: and not for ours only, but also for the sins of the whole world" (1 Jn. 2:2, KJV). The eucharist is the sacramental form of this one propitiatory sacrifice. It does not repeat the propitiation, or re-enact it. But under the gracious forms of bread and wine, it sacramentally actualizes, mediates, and attests it.

(9) This propitiatory application of Christ's sacrifice through its liturgical re-enactment is not to be understood in the sense that the mass justifies the wicked without their repenting; but rather, "appeased by this offering, the Lord, granting grace and the gift of repentance, forgives sins and even the greatest crimes."

In the eucharist the meaning of Christ's propitiatory sacrifice is attested in an unsurpassed way. Just as the eucharist exhibits the cost by which the ungodly are justified, so it also presupposes the faith by which their justification is received. "And to the [ones] who [do] not work but trust him who justifies the ungodly, [their] faith is counted as righteousness" (Rom. 4:5, ESV). It is this faith that brings them into union and communion with Christ. In the eucharist their communion with Christ is continually deepened and renewed, even as their justification before God is reconfirmed.

There is no justification without repentance, because the gift of repentance is included in the grace of justification. This repentance,

---

[81] Propitiation as here defined has nothing to do with "appeasement" or with "placating" God. God's wrath is satisfied not by inflicting punishment but by removing the cause of the offense.

as noted, is a life-long task. Just as no sin is too small for contrition, confession, and restitution, so none is too great to be forgiven. The eucharist ever and again reconfirms that there is more grace in God than sin in us.

> (10) The effects of the mass-sacrifice do not extend to the welfare of the living alone; "but it is also offered for the faithful departed in Christ who are not yet fully cleansed."

Like Eastern Orthodoxy, Protestantism rejects the traditional idea of purgatory and the doctrine of indulgences. Both traditions reject the notion of purgatory as a place distinct from heaven and hell. At the same time, both affirm, along with Roman Catholicism, the scriptural teaching that all will pass through the divine judgment as through fire. "For all of us must appear before the judgement seat of Christ, so that each may receive recompense for what has been done in the body, whether good or evil" (2 Cor. 5:10). "If the work is burned, the builder will suffer loss; the builder will be saved, but only as through fire" (1 Cor. 3:15). No one withstands this judgment apart from the infinite mercy of Christ. "From now on there is reserved for me the crown of righteousness, which the Lord, the righteous judge, will give to me on that day, and not only to me but also to all who have longed for his appearing" (2 Tim. 4:8).

The intermediate efficacy of the eucharistic sacrifice must not be confused with that of the sacrifice on Calvary. The efficacy of the latter applies to the living and the dead; that of the former, only to the living who are assembled to partake of the sacrament. The efficacy of the eucharist mediates the efficacy of Christ, but there is more to Christ's efficacy than is mediated by the eucharist, or more precisely, his efficacy has other ways of being mediated. Christ's efficacy extends to the welfare of all things. "For in him all the fullness of God was pleased to dwell, and through him God was pleased to reconcile to himself all things, whether on earth or in heaven, by making peace through the blood of his cross"

(Col. 1:19–20). When special efficacy is ascribed to the eucharist for persons not present in the gathered assembly, it is difficult to see how the implication can be avoided that the eucharist is an independent work that treats the cross as a resource at its disposal.

Conclusion

Four themes have been developed to affirm eucharistic sacrifice in a way that accords with the Reformation.

First, eucharistic sacrifice must be seen in connection with Passover. The paschal mystery is a mystery of substitution, participation, and exchange. The innocent dies for the guilty in order that the guilty may live and be sanctified for God. The Lamb takes the place of sinners in death, bearing for their sakes the just judgment of God upon sin. It is by the mystery of the Lamb's blood that sin, death, and the devil are defeated and destroyed (Rev. 7:14; 12:11; 17:14). The redeemed, with whom the Lamb has been made one, are then made one with the Lamb through the sacramental meal. In the paschal meal, the sacrifice becomes a sacrament, even as the sacrament actualizes the sacrifice. The sacrifice is received and actualized in memory, communion, and hope. Eucharistic sacrifice cannot be rejected without jeopardizing Christian worship by severing it from its Judaic roots.

Second, the real presence of Christ is inseparable from his benefits and his work. His eucharistic presence, under the aspects of his body and blood, includes the real presence of his expiatory sacrifice. As he makes himself present in the Spirit, under the forms of bread and wine, the one sacrifice of Calvary is made present in its saving efficacy. It is present in its finished, perfect, and perpetual significance before God. It is not repeated but re-presented, not continued but memorialized, not supplemented but made available. It is not something the church manipulates but something in which it participates.

The means of eucharistic participation are the body and blood of Christ. Through them he offers himself daily to the faithful, even as he once offered himself on Calvary, and now offers himself perpetually, to the Father in the Spirit for their sakes. Through them, in turn, the faithful enter into union and communion with him. Through them, they offer themselves, with all that they have and are, in thanks and praise to God. In the sacramental forms of his body and blood, Christ offers himself to God through the faithful, even as they offer themselves to God through him. His sacrifice is made theirs, as theirs is made his, so that the two are one. The faithful have no sacrifice to offer other than Christ himself, whom they offer only by consenting to be offered by him.[82]

Third, eucharistic sacrifice involves three tenses of salvation. It is not another sacrifice than the sacrifice of the cross. It is rather the same sacrifice in sacramental form. It is the form that occurs in the time between the times – in the time between Calvary and the Messianic Banquet. The eucharistic sacrifice is therefore at once provisional and anticipatory, a matter of *anamnesis* but also of *prolepsis*. It is salvation's occurrence in the present tense. It actualizes, mediates, and attests the *Christus praesens* in the past and future forms of his royal and priestly offices. The table is also an altar. The Messianic Banquet is also the marriage feast of the Lamb. The High Priest is also the Victim, and the King of Glory reigns through the cross. The paschal mystery is the sacrament of the kingdom.

Anamnesis, intercession, and *prolepsis* all converge in the eucharistic sacrifice. They converge through the prayer of *epiclesis*. The invocation of the Holy Spirit brings the past and future into the present. Eternity is made present to time, and time to eternity, as well. The invocation of the Spirit unites the vertical and horizontal dimensions. The multifaceted dimensions of Christ's one

---

[82] For a similar view, see Rowan Williams, *Eucharistic Sacrifice: The Roots of a Metaphor* (Bramcote: Grove Books, 1982).

intercession are made present in the eucharist through the Spirit. They are made present as a memorial of the Last Supper, a fore-taste of the coming kingdom, a sharing in the heavenly worship of the saints above, and a pleading of Christ's eternal sacrifice. These convergences in the present tense of the eucharist occur through the mystery of the *epiclesis*.

Finally, Jesus Christ as the sole saving agent must be distinguished from other acting subjects. He alone effects the work of salvation, whether in the perfect tense, the future tense, or the present tense. Therefore, he alone effects salvation in the eucharist. No inferior causes can exist alongside him in this work. In the Word and by the Spirit, he alone makes himself present, he alone effects the eucharistic conversion, and he alone imparts himself to the faithful. He alone re-presents himself in the efficacy of his one multifaceted expiatory sacrifice. Any other acting subjects, notably the ordained ministers and the faithful, are allotted another role. They receive the grace of participating in Christ's one saving work, in various ways, without in any sense effecting it.

The Lord acts in and through his people, even as they act in and through him. Christ acts, for example, through the priest in consecration and intercession, even as the priest acts through him, but the priest is a servant and a steward, an instrument and a means, not a secondary agent, in the efficacy of Christ's self-offering. The people, for their part, are not burdened with a task they could not possibly bear. Acknowledgment, reception, mediation, and witness are a high enough calling in their own right, but with challenges not exceeding the capacities of the faithful.

On the basis of these four points – the paschal mystery, Christ's person as one with his work, the invocation of the Spirit as the secret of horizontal and vertical convergence, and the sole saving agency of Christ – the Reformed tradition should be able to espouse a doctrine of eucharistic sacrifice and incorporate it into its liturgies. The tradition would not be compromised on any essential point of doctrine. It would stretch to accept something it has long thought it had to reject, and in the process would be immensely enriched. Its celebration of the eucharist would be spiritually deepened. Above all, it would embrace a doctrine of eucharistic sacrifice that promised to be not church-dividing but potentially church-enriching. It would thereby help the churches move closer to that desideratum of eucharistic sharing in which the scandal of division would be significantly overcome.

Ecumenical implications

It would seem that the proposal developed here goes some distance toward meeting the concerns about eucharistic sacrifice expressed in recent Roman Catholic statements. In the official Vatican response, issued in 1991, to the Final Report of the Anglican–Roman Catholic International Commission (ARCIC), two regrets were stated.

First, the Vatican agreed with the Final Report that in the eucharist Christ's sacrifice is neither repeated nor supplemented. The Vatican did not find it to be explicitly affirmed, however, "that in the Eucharist, the Church, doing what Christ commanded His Apostles to do at the Last Supper, makes present the sacrifice of Calvary."[83] The proposal developed here meets this shortcoming. No doubt has been left that the sacrifice of Calvary is made present in the eucharist. The sacrifice becomes present in the eucharist in sacramental form.

It has been stressed, on the other hand, that it is not the church *per se* that makes the sacrifice present, but Christ who makes it present through the church. The church can also be said, on this basis, to make the sacrifice present through Christ. It needs to be

---

[83] "The Official Roman Catholic Response to the Final Report of ARCIC (1991)," in *Anglicans and Catholics: The Search for Unity*, ed. Christopher Hill and E. J. Yarnold (London: SPCK/CTS, 1994), p. 162.

explicitly affirmed, however, that while the church is an acting subject in this occurrence, it exercises no "causal" powers, because Christ alone is the agent who effects this presence. The church possesses no capacity, in itself, to make the sacrifice present, but always relies, implicitly, on the faithfulness of Christ to his promises.

Second, the Vatican called for an explicit statement that "the sacrifice of Christ is made present with all its effects." The nature of these effects was said to be twofold. On the one hand, it needed to be made clear that the eucharistic sacrifice is propitiatory in character. On the other hand, it needed to be said in consequence that the mass "may be offered for the living and the dead, including a particular dead person."[84]

As to the first point, it has been made clear that the presence of the sacrifice of Calvary is necessarily expiatory, and therefore propitiatory, in its efficacy. It has also been made clear that the presence of Christ's sacrifice cannot be reduced to a general form of "intercession."[85] The efficacy of the sacrifice of Calvary, as present in the eucharist, is once-for-all, perpetual, and continually made new.

As to the second point, however, reservations were expressed in the proposal. Neither Eastern Orthodoxy nor Protestantism is in accord with the Roman Catholic Church in its practice of offering the eucharist as a propitiation for the dead, including a particular dead person. It would again need to be made clear here why unwarranted causal powers are not being ascribed to the church. In any case it is not clear why the Vatican would impose this condition on the Anglicans when it does not seem to do so with

---

[84] Ibid.

[85] The oversimple conflation of sacrifice with intercession at the expense of propitiation as a necessary aspect of intercession was a concern in the official Vatican response to the Lima document. See "Roman Catholic Church," in *Churches Respond to BEM*, vol. VI, ed. Max Thurian (Geneva: World Council of Churches, 1988), pp. 1–40; on pp. 20–21.

respect to the Eastern Orthodox. Further discussion at this point would seem to be needed.

The two major points, however, would seem to have been addressed. For the sacrifice of Calvary has been affirmed as present in the eucharist, as well as its being propitiatory in character.

According to Geoffrey Wainwright, eucharistic sacrifice "is likely to be the area of greatest difficulty for classical Protestants on the way to an ecumenical Eucharist."[86] Protestants, he notes, "are still likely to balk at the idea from Vatican II that the Church or the faithful 'offer the divine victim to God.'"[87] "Clearly," he continues, "there is still theological work to be done towards an ecumenical Eucharist in so far as its sacrificial nature is at stake."[88] Wainwright even states that eucharistic sacrifice may be a more difficult problem to solve than that of eucharistic ministry: "I would suggest that settlement of the meaning of eucharistic sacrifice is logically prior to the question of the disabling 'defectus' which Vatican II's Decree on Ecumenism alleges in the ministry of those who preside at the Lord's Table in the Protestant churches."[89]

Wainwright does not elaborate on the barriers to a settlement with classical Protestantism. Obviously, as discussed at length above, they are mainly two: first, that the sacrifice of Calvary is unrepeatable; and second, that the eucharist is not a meritorious work. In turn, the proposal developed here has been, first, that the unrepeatable sacrifice becomes sacramentally present, in the power of the Holy Spirit, as a memorial; and second, that the meritorious work of the eucharist belongs entirely to the agency of Christ while not excluding a role of active participation, again in the power of the Holy Spirit, for the church, in pleading Christ's eternal sacrifice.

---

[86] Geoffrey Wainwright, "*Ecclesia de Eucharistia vivit*: An Ecumenical Reading," *Ecumenical Trends* 33 (October 2004), pp. 129–37; on p. 132.

[87] Ibid., p. 133. [88] Ibid.

[89] Ibid., p. 134. The problem of *defectus* is dealt with in Part III of this book.

Liturgical postlude

Are there any precedents for the Reformed churches in particular, and the Protestant churches in general, that could be drawn upon for guidance in incorporating the theme of eucharistic sacrifice into their liturgies? A few prayers and hymns may be noted.

A liturgy from the Church of Scotland (1957) includes this eucharistic prayer:

> We bless you for his continual intercession and rule at your right hand ... and pleading his eternal sacrifice, we your servants set forth this memorial which he has commanded us to make.[90]

In a prayer from the Scottish Episcopal Church (1982), the theme of union with Christ is brought out more directly:

> Made one with him, we offer you these gifts and with them our-selves, a single, holy, living sacrifice.[91]

Christ's once-for-all sacrifice, its perpetual efficacy, and its eucharistic availability through the Holy Spirit, all receive fine expression in this prayer from the Church of England Liturgical Commission (c. 1985):

> Father, as we plead his sacrifice made once for all on the cross, we remember his dying and rising to glory, and rejoice that he prays for us at your right hand: pour out your Holy Spirit over us and these gifts, which we bring before you from your own creation; show them to be for us the body and blood of your dear Son; unite

---

[90] Cited by Thurian, *Eucharistic Memorial*, vol. II, p. 106 (*supra* n. 62). Here lightly edited.

[91] Cited in Kenneth Stevenson, "Eucharistic Sacrifice: What Can We Learn from Christian Antiquity?," in *Essays on Eucharistic Sacrifice in the Early Church*, ed. Colin Buchanan (Bramcote: Grove Books, 1984), pp. 26–33; on p. 32n.

in his eternal sacrifice all who share the food and drink of his new and unending life.[92]

Turning from prayers to hymns, an astonishing number by Charles Wesley have been collected by J. Ernest Rattenbury.[93] For Victorian beauty and the keen spirit of the Reformation, however, William Bright's great hymn of 1874 is unsurpassed and provides a fitting note on which to end:

And now, O Father, mindful of the love
that bought us, once for all, on Calvary's Tree,
and having with us him that pleads above,
we here present, we spread forth to thee
that only Offering perfect in thine eyes,
the one, true, pure, immortal Sacrifice.

Look, Father, look on his anointed face,
and only look on us as found in him;
look not on our misusings of thy grace,
our prayer so languid, and our faith so dim:
for lo, between our sins and their reward
we set the Passion of thy Son our Lord.

And so we come: O draw us to thy feet,
most patient Savior, who canst love us still;
and by this food, so aweful and so sweet,
deliver us from every touch of ill:
in thine own service make us glad and free,
and grant us never more to part with thee.

---

[92] Cited in Bryan D. Spinks, "The Ascension and Vicarious Humanity of Christ," in *Time and Community*, ed. J. Neil Alexander (Washington, DC: Pastoral Press, 1990), pp. 185–201; on p. 201 n. 83.
[93] J. Ernest Rattenbury, *The Eucharistic Hymns of John and Charles Wesley* (Cleveland: Order of St. Luke Publications, 1990).

ADDENDUM: EUCHARISTIC VECTORS
The eucharist (fig. 1)

Comment. Each of these vectors may be seen as describing the liturgical action of the eucharist as a whole. At differing points, any one of them may be more to the forefront than another. It is a matter of shifting configurations in the course of the liturgy. The diagram suggests how the eucharist looks simultaneously backward, forward, downward, and upward. Memorial (*anamnesis*) involves the backward look, while "anticipatory realization" (*prolepsis*) involves the forward look. Both are matters of communal participation in the liturgy (as opposed to merely mental events). From another perspective, the eucharist can be seen as one long invocation of the Holy Spirit (*epiclesis*), the downward vector; as well as one continuous act in which the sacrifice of the church is taken up sacramentally into the eternal intercession of Christ's sacrifice (*thusia/entugchano*), the upward vector.

Christ as acting subject: Word and Sacrament (fig. 2)

Comment. As the sole saving agent, Christ is always the central acting subject in both Word and Sacrament. Called into being by proclamation, and ruled by the authority of scripture, the church is a creature of God's Word (*creatura verbum dei*). Founded in baptism and nourished by the eucharist, the church is also a creature of the sacraments (*creatura sacramenti*). While the Word is the normative vehicle of Christ's self-witness, it is also the vehicle of his self-impartation to faith. In turn, while the sacraments are more nearly vehicles of his self-mediation, they are also vehicles of his self-witness at the same time. The eucharist uniquely manifests the downward and upward vectors of Christ's presence in his office as the Mediator, for it is both a vehicle of his self-impartation (*koinonia*) and most especially of his eternal self-offering on the basis of his finished saving work (intercession). Here and now, whether by Word or Sacrament, Christ always attests and mediates himself in the Spirit by way of self-anticipation as the firstfruits of his final return in glory (*arrabon/aparche*).

Time/eternity axis (fig. 3)

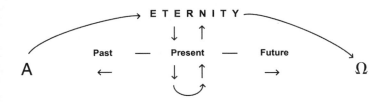

Comment. Whether through Word or Sacrament, Christ's presence can be seen in two basic ways. Insofar as his atoning death is the ground while his return is the consequence, his saving presence here and now is always a secondary form of his once-for-all finished work as accomplished by his obedience there and then. Yet insofar as his glorious return is the fulfillment of his resurrection, for which his death is the necessary precondition, his kerygmatic and eucharistic presence anticipates the future of all things in the promised kingdom. Either way, he is always present as the only Mediator between heaven and earth, who joins himself to us, and us to himself, in communion, elevating us provisionally to eternal life in communion with God, until the day of his coming, which will inaugurate the long-expected Messianic Banquet, the ultimate eucharist as the marriage feast of the Lamb.

PART III

Eucharist and ministry

5 | Eucharistic ministry: controversies

"Church ministry and authority" would not be an item that ranks high in the hierarchy of truths. Barriers to eucharistic sharing would initially seem more formidable elsewhere. The real presence of Christ in the eucharist, for example, as well as whether, or in what sense, the Lord's Supper is a sacrifice, are questions that loomed large for the Reformation and continue to loom large today. Greater progress has now been made among Lutherans, Anglicans, and Roman Catholics on those matters than has yet to occur with the Reformed churches.[1] Although promising resources for ecumenical

---

[1] Reformed–Roman Catholic dialogue has remained at a rather high level of generality regarding real presence, eucharistic sacrifice, and ordained ministry. See United States Conference of Catholic Bishops, "Journey in Faith: Forty Years of Reformed–Catholic Dialogue: 1965–2005," www.usccb.org/seia/journey.shtml; The Council of Churches of the Netherlands, *Intercommunion: The Asymmetrical Discussion Between Protestants and Catholics* (Zoetermeer: Boekencentrum, 1999); "Reformed–Roman Catholic Dialogue: Toward a Common Understanding of the Church, Second Phase, 1984–1990," in *Growth in Agreement II*, ed. Jeffrey Gros, Harding Meyer, and William G. Rusch (Grand Rapids: Wm. B. Eerdmans, 2000), pp. 780–818. Discussions with the Anglicans have been only marginally better. See "Anglican–Reformed Dialogue: God's Reign and Our Unity (1984)," in *Growth in Agreement II*, pp. 113–54. More progress has been made with the Lutherans, though not notably through doctrinal precision. See "A Formula of Agreement: Official Text," www.elca.org/ecumenical/fullcommunion/formula/official_text.html; LWF/WARC, *Towards Church Fellowship*, Report of the Joint Commission between the Lutheran World Federation and the World Alliance of Reformed Churches, Geneva, 1990; Lukas Vischer, "A History of the Leuenberg Agreement," in *Rowing in One Boat*, John Knox Series No. 11 (Geneva: JKIRC, 1999), pp. 9–23.

convergence are available to the Reformed on real presence and eucharistic sacrifice, they remain largely untapped. Yet even if difficulties could be resolved at the conceptual level, entrenched habits of mind would still remain. As long as Zwingli remains our liturgical master, it will be hard for us in the Reformed tradition to benefit from the ecumenical progress occurring elsewhere.

The Reformed tradition has special problems to confront, both doctrinal and attitudinal, regarding eucharistic ministry. In recent decades the ministry issue has moved to the forefront of ecumenical discussion. It involves enormous perplexities. Although some of these are shared by Lutherans and Reformed alike, Lutherans may again find it easier than the Reformed to achieve convergence with historic traditions of ministry as found in Anglicanism, Roman Catholicism, and Eastern Orthodoxy. Throughout the ecumenical movement, it has become increasingly, and even painfully, clear that without significant agreement about eucharistic ministry, the unity that we seek will elude us.

In what follows these perplexities are taken up from a Reformed perspective. First, the issue is focused by turning to the concept of *defectus*. This is a term used in official Roman Catholic documents to characterize the relative invalidity of eucharistic ministry in the Protestant churches. Second, five formal questions are explored. How they are answered differently by the Reformed and Roman Catholic churches is discussed, with occasional reference to Lutheran positions. Next it is suggested that tacitly underlying Reformational/Roman Catholic disagreements are different theological imaginations. One is called a verbal imagination, the other a sacramental imagination. Insofar as each type can be enriched by the other, renewed progress may be possible on the question of ministry. The discussion concludes with a series of ecumenical admonitions directed toward the high sacramental churches from a broadly Reformational standpoint.

The concept of *defectus*

The word *defectus*, being ambiguous, has been used in two different ways. The one is more severe, the other more moderate. Although official Roman Catholic statements can sometimes sound rather harsh, interpretations of remarkable generosity have also been expressed in high places. Nonetheless, because recent papal documents have tended to be cautious, many ecumenical observers see the Catholic assessment of eucharistic ministry in the Protestant churches as still unsettled while perhaps leaning on the whole toward the negative.

Vatican II's *Decree on Ecumenism* (*Unitatis Redintegratio*) from 1964 seemed, at least in some parts, to mince no words: "[We] believe that especially because of the lack [*defectus*] of the sacrament of orders ... [the ecclesial communities] have not preserved the genuine and total reality of the eucharistic mystery."[2] Here the word *defectus*, translated as "lack," apparently asserts that a valid ministry in the Protestant churches is absent. In those churches, we are told, "the sacrament of order" is lacking. Therefore these churches have not preserved the "eucharistic mystery" in a full and genuine way. Since Protestant churches have a defective ministry with a defective sacrament, they are not really churches at all, but merely "ecclesial communities."

This understanding of *defectus*, undoubtedly shared by many traditional Catholics, reappeared in 2000 when the document *Dominus Iesus* was released by the Congregation for the Doctrine of the Faith under the leadership of Joseph Cardinal Ratzinger

[2] Quoted by Harry J. McSorley, "The Roman Catholic Doctrine of the Competent Minister of the Eucharist in Ecumenical Perspective," in *Eucharist and Ministry: Lutherans and Catholics in Dialogue*, vol. IV, published jointly by the US Conference of Catholic Bishops and the Lutheran World Federation (Washington, DC, and New York, 1970), pp. 120–37; on pp. 120–21. See "Decree on Ecumenism" (*Unitatis Redintegratio*), No. 22, in *The Documents of Vatican II*, ed. Walter Abbott (New York: Guild Press, America Press, Association Press, 1966), p. 364.

(now Pope Benedict XVI).[3] "Ecclesial communities" are again regarded as defective. For they "have not preserved the valid Episcopate and the genuine and integral substance of the Eucharistic mystery." It follows that these communities "are not Churches in the proper sense" (*DI* IV.17). Only the Roman Catholic Church meets the requirements without qualification. "Only in the Catholic Church," we read, does the one church truly "subsist." Admittedly, valid elements can be found in ecclesial communities and churches outside Catholicism. "But with respect to these [elements], it needs to be stated that 'they derive their efficacy from the very fullness of grace and truth entrusted to the Catholic Church'" (*DI* IV.16). The only non-defective church, it would seem, is the Roman Catholic one.

Despite this apparent severity, more charitable estimates should not be overlooked. According to Jared Wicks, the distinguished Catholic scholar and ecumenist, the use of the term *defectus* – understood as "flaw," not as "absence" – refers primarily to means as opposed to ends. *Defectus* pertains more to structures than to full salvation.[4] The sacramental means in ecclesial communities, states Wicks, though flawed, "do *not* mediate to them a *defective* justification and salvation." He continues: "Using sacramental terminology, the *res tantum* is given whole and entire, namely, union with Christ, life in the Spirit, and access to the Father." *Res tantum*, a technical term, refers to the reality of grace taken in and of itself, as received by faith with devotion, regardless of how defective the objective mediation may have been. A defective means of grace can still deliver the whole *res tantum* of salvation.

The way Wicks interprets *defectus* has been confirmed by no less an authority than Walter Cardinal Kasper, secretary of the

---

[3] Congregation for the Doctrine of the Faith, "*Dominus Iesus*: On the Unicity and Salvific Universality of Jesus Christ and the Church," *Origins* 30 (September 14, 2000), pp. 208, 211–19. Hereafter cited in the text as *DI*.

[4] Jared Wicks, "The Significance of the 'Ecclesial Communities' of the Reformation," *Ecumenical Trends* 30 (December 2001), pp. 10–13.

Pontifical Council for Promoting Christian Unity. In 2001, in the aftermath of *Dominus Iesus*, Kasper wrote:

> Only in this sacramental and institutional respect can the Council find a lack (*defectus*) in the churches and ecclesial communities of the Reformation. Both Catholic fullness and the *defectus* of the others are therefore sacramental and institutional, and not existential or even moral in nature; they are on the level of the signs and instruments of grace, not on the level of the *res*, the grace of salvation itself.[5]

Much the same idea that salutary outcomes can come through flawed means was once expressed by Cardinal Ratzinger himself. In 1993 he wrote to Johannes Hanselmann, a Lutheran bishop in Germany:

> I count among the most important results of the ecumenical dialogues the insight that the issue of the eucharist cannot be narrowed to the problem of "validity." Even a theology oriented to the concept of succession, such as that which holds in the Catholic and in the Orthodox church, need not in any way deny the salvation-granting presence of the Lord [*Heilschaffende Gegenwart des Herrn*] in a Lutheran [*evangelische*] Lord's Supper.[6]

Most recently, a common statement, *The Church as Koinonia of Salvation*,[7] issued by the US Lutheran–Catholic Dialogue in 2004, concludes that *defectus* as applied to Lutheran ministries should be

---

[5] Walter Cardinal Kasper, "Present Situation and Future of the Ecumenical Movement," *Information Service* (Pontifical Council for Promoting Christian Unity) 109 (2002), pp. 11–20.

[6] "Briefwechsel von Landesbischof Johannes Hanselmann und Joseph Kardinal Ratzinger über das Communio-Schreiben der Römischen Glaubenskongregation," *Una Sancta* 48 (1993), p. 348. Cited in *The Church as Koinonia of Salvation: Its Structures and Ministries*, ed. Randall Lee and Jeffrey Gros (Washington, DC: United States Conference of Catholic Bishops, 2005), at n. 166.

[7] Lee and Gros, *Church as Koinonia*, n. 166.

translated not as "lack," but instead as "deficiency" (*Church as Koinonia*, no. 109). Both Kasper and Ratzinger are cited in support. On this somewhat more generous note, *defectus* seems to imply that while, for ecclesial communities, Christ may be mediated under a sacramentally defective form, he is nonetheless present in a truly saving way.

The evident caution of the papacy, as seen for example in *Ecclesia de Eucharistia*, the Pope's encyclical letter of 2003, has done little to dispel the uncertainty generated by *Dominus Iesus*.[8] The encyclical letter does not assert, as *Dominus Iesus* did, that the fullness of salvation subsists "only in the Catholic church." Yet neither does the letter affirm, along with Wicks and apparently with Kasper, that in ecclesial communities the entire *res tantum* is present and effectual. The official Roman Catholic position, it seems, has yet to dispel the clouds of ambiguity. Do ecclesial communities lack the fullness of salvation as such, since it subsists only in the Roman church, or may they indeed receive the whole *res tantum*, even though in a defective way?

Three observations may be ventured at this point. First, the concept of "fullness" is essentially an eschatological and a christological affirmation. For Reformed theology, fullness subsists only in Jesus Christ. By the same token, until the end of all things, the church's fullness subsists only in the future of Jesus Christ. No church on earth is in a position to claim that Christ's fullness (and thus the fullness of grace and truth) now subsists, without qualification, in itself (to say nothing of subsisting only in itself). "We are more perfectly in Christ," wrote Peter Martyr Vermigli, "than he is in us."[9] While Christ is indeed present in all his fullness to the church, the church's representation of that fullness, even at its best,

[8] John Paul II, "Ecclesia de Eucharistia," *Origins* 32 (May 1, 2003), pp. 753, 755–68.
[9] Quoted in Joseph C. McLelland, *The Visible Words of God: An Exposition of the Sacramental Theology of Peter Martyr Vermigli* (Edinburgh: Oliver & Boyd, 1957), p. 148.

remains flawed until the end.[10] Christ makes himself present to the church, and through the church to the world, despite the church's ongoing imperfections, which he does not remove fully in this life. Though the church's ongoing *defectus* may speak against it, Christ is always greater than the church. Every ecclesial mediation of his fullness only reveals how far the church has yet to go. Its present imperfection holds true *de iure* and not only *de facto*. Any church that wants to claim more for itself is in danger of courting divine judgment.[11]

Second, it will not do for Protestant churches to reject the perception of their *defectus* out of hand. How do they know that this charge does not apply to them? How can they be sure that it does not say something valid which they need to hear? How do they know they do not have something essential to learn from it, despite what we might call its complacent and defective form? Ecumenical discussion either involves admonition as well as affirmation – or it is not ecumenical discussion at all. Truth is truth, as Luther once observed, whether spoken by Jesus or Balaam's ass. In what follows I will assume that the Reformed churches in particular have something crucial to learn, and something difficult to hear, about its eucharistic ministry from the Roman Catholic admonition of *defectus*. I will also assume that

---

[10] Until then, as Luther and Calvin were wont to say, even our best works need to be justified by grace and "all our righteousnesses are as filthy rags" (Isa. 64:6, KJV; cf. Luke 5:8, 1 Tim. 1:15).

[11] This is not the place to explore the Roman Catholic Church's official difficulty in affirming that the church is sinful. Vatican II's "Dogmatic Constitution on the Church" (*Lumen Gentium*), however, does declare: "The church ... clasping sinners to its bosom, at once holy and always in need of purification, follows constantly the path of penance and renewal" (No. 8). (See *Documents of Vatican II*, p. 24.) Catholic theologian Richard P. McBrien comments: "The conciliar text clearly states that the church as such ... is 'always in need of purification' ... because it is indeed a sinful church, not just in its members, but corporately and institutionally." See McBrien, "A Repenting Church," *Commonweal* 126 (November 19, 1999), pp. 12, 14.

the Reformed tradition has admonitions of its own to contribute as well.

Finally, a further complication may be mentioned regarding the loaded term "subsist."[12] Not only is the one church of Christ said by *Dominus Iesus* to "subsist" only in the Roman Catholic Church. The negative corollary is also spelled out: "The interpretation of those who would derive from the formula *subsistit in* the thesis that the one church of Christ could subsist also in non-Catholic churches and ecclesial communities is . . . contrary to the authentic meaning of *Lumen gentium*" (*DI* fn. 56). This statement would seem to correlate with the definition of *defectus* as "absence" rather than merely "flaw." What ecclesial communities are thought gravely to lack is episcopal succession. But since that particular defect does not apply to Eastern Orthodox churches, why could not the one church of Christ "subsist" also in them despite their being "non-Catholic"? Perhaps a clue may be found in an earlier document produced by Cardinal Ratzinger, the 1992 "Letter to the Bishops of the Catholic Church on Some Aspects of the Church Understood as Communion."[13] As Theodor Dieter observes, this Letter contains at least two points of interest. First, it claims that the "universal church" is prior to all "particular churches" so that they themselves are "derived" from it; and second, it claims that "papal superiority" belongs by definition to the term "universal church." Whenever the universal church of Christ is present in any particular

---

[12] For these observations I am indebted to Theodor Dieter, "The Lutheran/Roman Catholic Dialogue: Achievements and Challenges" (June 2007), unpublished. For further remarks on the issue of universal "priority" as conceived by Cardinal Ratzinger, see G. R. Evans, *The Church and the Churches* (Cambridge: Cambridge University Press, 1993), pp. 37n., 41, 104, 106–9, 113, 118. Comprehensive, judicious, and historically sensitive, this is still perhaps the best book written in English on the most difficult problem facing the ecumenical movement today – namely, conflicting views of church and ministry.

[13] Joseph Cardinal Ratzinger / Congregation for Doctrine of the Faith, "Letter to the Bishops of the Catholic Church on Some Aspects of the Church Understood as Communion," *One in Christ* 28 (1992), pp. 282–93.

church, papal superiority is necessarily present along with it. The implication would seem to be that without the presence of papal superiority in an immediate, constitutive, and jurisdictional sense, no church can have the full church subsisting in it.

The question of *defectus* and subsistence has profound implications for the future of ecumenism. A tension exists between the hard-line and the more moderate formulations. Neither the Eastern Orthodox nor the Protestant churches could possibly accede to a non-conciliar view of the papacy, nor to accepting an unqualified jurisdictional primacy of the "universal" church, as centered in Rome, over all "particular" churches elsewhere. The tendency of such ideas is not toward mutual learning, reciprocity, and conversion, but merely toward an impossible "return ecumenism." While the door on these matters is not yet officially closed, neither does it seem widely open at the present time. Nevertheless, the most recent document to emerge from Lutheran–Catholic dialogue, called *The Apostolicity of the Church* (2006), would seem to point in a more hopeful direction.[14] It suggests that different degrees of fellowship should be pursued among the divided churches and that ways should be sought to acknowledge one another's apostolicity and ministry. It would seem that with the resolution of these tensions one way or another, the ecumenical movement hangs in the balance.

Five questions about ministry

At least five formal questions are in dispute about ordained ministry in the church. They concern (1) the authority to ordain, (2) the eligibility to be ordained, (3) the nature of being ordained, (4) the offices of ordained ministry, and (5) the functions of ordained ministry. Since these are very large topics, only a survey

---

[14] *The Apostolicity of the Church: Study Document of the Lutheran–Roman Catholic Commission on Unity* (Minneapolis: Lutheran University Press, 2006).

is possible here. At the same time, however, the outlines of a constructive proposal will be attempted.

Ordained ministry cannot be understood apart from its christological basis. Ministry arguably takes place only in the context of a Christ-centered eschatology of active relations. These relations are essentially relations of participation. The church's active participation in the ministry of Christ presupposes Christ's active participation in the ministries of the church. The living Jesus Christ is the one acting subject in all forms of ecclesial ministry, and all forms of ecclesial ministry have a share in his one active ministry, which, though it takes many forms, is undivided in itself. The church does not have Christ's ministry, but Christ's ministry has a church. Ecclesial ministry finds its ontological ground, its practical basis, and its sure point of departure in the active Lordship of the *Christus praesens*. This thesis may be nothing new. But if worked out carefully, it could still be useful.

Who has the authority to ordain?

The question of authority to ordain involves the question of apostolic succession. Apostolic succession has two aspects. One, we might say, is the question of "who," while the other is the question of "what." That is, the one concerns the official person, while the other involves the substance of the apostolic faith. Everyone agrees that the office held by the original apostles was unique and non-transferable. The disputed question is: who are the apostles' successors, and what do they represent?

In the Roman Catholic Church, apostolic succession means episcopal succession. Only the bishop has the authority to ordain, because only the bishop stands in the unbroken line of ordination, conferred by the laying on of hands, that stretches all the way back to those whom the apostles themselves first ordained. While Catholic theology recognizes that the first ordinands were not bishops in the diocesan sense that later became normative, it holds that the diocesan bishop emerged as their successors. The Catholic church also recognizes that apostolic succession must be evangelical as well as episcopal, since bishops are particularly responsible for teaching the apostolic faith.

In the Reformed tradition apostolic succession means substantive evangelical succession, but not necessarily episcopal succession. Apostolic succession ordinarily devolves on the presbytery, a regional council of presbyters, not on a bishop. It is therefore the presbytery that has the authority to ordain. Ordination is carried out by designated presbyters, not by a bishop, though the presbytery's elected moderator must usually be present. While the question of legitimate office in apostolic succession is not unimportant, the emphasis falls much more fully on its substantive aspect. The presbytery's authority to ordain involves its successful probation of any particular ordinand. The ordinand has been examined for suitability to serve a local congregation, above all with respect to teaching the substance of the faith.

When considering the authority to ordain, Christ as the acting subject is usually left more or less in the background. But if only Christ himself holds this authority, then the church officials representing him, whoever they may rightly be, are at once dignified and yet also relativized. Any church officials acting to ordain are no more, but also no less, than instruments in the hands of the living Christ operating by the Holy Spirit. They are granted to participate in Christ's ordaining activity, even as he operates in and through theirs. Today there is an increasing recognition in ecumenical circles that the highest importance must be attached to apostolic succession in the substantive, evangelical sense. Recognition is also increasing that this succession is being reasonably met by those churches in the various traditions which affirm Nicaea and Chalcedon. If so, then particular questions arise for both the Reformed and the Catholic churches.

The question that arises for the Reformed church is one that we will meet again as we move on. If Christ has acted through bishops to mediate apostolic succession in the substantive sense, and if episcopal ordination has been predominant in the church's history, are historic Reformed objections still weighty enough to prevent the Reformed from acceding, under carefully specified conditions, to some form of episcopal polity and ordination? In obedience to Christ and love for the church, can the Reformed any longer afford to hinder eucharistic sharing on such grounds?

The question for the Catholics is much the same. If Christ has sometimes acted through presbyters to mediate substantive apostolic succession, and if Catholics recognize that historically significant instances have now been unearthed of ordination conducted by presbyters, then can Catholic objections to presbyterial ordination be sufficiently weighty today not to recognize a high degree of validity in Protestant ordinations? Must not the historic objections on both sides, whether Catholic or Reformed, now yield before the wise counsel of Gamaliel (Acts 5:39)? Can either side still presume, given the fruits long since evident in both traditions, that the ordinations of the other are not of God?[15]

Who is qualified to be ordained?

The Reformed and the Catholic churches both recognize formal training as a prerequisite to ordination. Without formal training, presbyters responsible for evangelical teaching and for presiding at sacramental celebrations are not qualified. (The matter of deacons and of presbyters assigned with different duties will be touched upon later.) At the time of the Reformation, the question arose in the West about whether ordinands must take a vow of celibacy. (With certain restrictions Eastern Orthodoxy allows for married

---

[15] For examples of ordinations by presbyters prior to the Reformation, see L. N. Crumb, "Presbyterial Ordination and the See of Rome," *Church Quarterly Review* 164 (1963), pp. 19–31. Though not large in number, these examples could serve as a partial basis for a charitable Roman Catholic construal of ordination in the Protestant churches. Further conditions are discussed in the next chapter.

clergy.) More recently, the question has arisen about whether ordination must be restricted to males. And most recently still, some Protestant churches have struggled with whether ordination can be extended to practicing gays and lesbians.

The Roman Catholic position on these questions is well known. Ordination is restricted to males who have taken a vow of celibacy.[16] Along with other Protestant churches, the Reformed hold that a vow of celibacy is not required, and that, for ministers of Word and Sacrament, marriage is appropriate. Moreover, while some Reformed churches still restrict ordination to males, many have now changed so that in their presbyteries and congregations, female ministers of Word and Sacrament have become common. Extending ordination to non-celibate gays and lesbians is a vexing question that is passionately contested today in the Reformed churches and elsewhere, but one that has yet to be resolved.

If the ordained ministry of the church is always a participation in the one ministry of Jesus Christ, then as Christ alone is qualified to ordain, so also he alone is qualified to be ordained. His ordination, so to speak, was his being sent into the world by the Father. This sending was determined in eternity, actualized in his birth, manifested in his baptism, and fulfilled in his cross. It was then validated in his glorious resurrection. His being sent marked him out as a friend of sinners and social outcasts. He included all in his mission by including the least, and precisely by including the least he included all. Having overcome all vertical separation between God and humankind in himself for the sake of the world, he also overcame in himself all horizontal or social divisions as well. "For in Christ Jesus you are all children of God through faith . . . There is no longer Jew or Greek, there is no longer slave or free, there is no longer male and female; for all of you are one in Christ Jesus" (Gal. 3:26, 28).

---

[16] More precisely, a vow of celibacy is required for Latin Rite Catholic priests, but not for those of the Eastern Rite.

When viewed in this light, *participatio Christi* would seem to point in the direction of inclusiveness when considering who can be admitted to ordination. If all who participate in Christ participate in his mission, they must all have a share in his one ordination, each in a particular and appropriate way. It would seem difficult to exclude any of the faithful from service through ecclesial ordination merely on the basis of categories like ethnicity, social status, gender or sexual orientation.

These matters of course are not simple, and they can hardly be resolved here. Certainly the Reformed and the Catholics would agree, however, that holiness of life is required for all Christians, and especially for those who would be ordained to the offices of presbyter or bishop. Holiness of life is rightly central to current disputes in the Protestant churches about gay and lesbian ordination. Let me comment on this latter question briefly from a Reformed perspective. In another place I have argued that the standard which all Christians must meet in their sexuality is chastity. This standard, which rules out every form of casual, promiscuous, and abusive sexuality, applies across the board. Chastity, I have argued, applies to all Christians whether they are single or married, male or female, straight or gay. It applies especially to ordained ministers: bishops, presbyters, and deacons. I have further proposed that gays and lesbians who have committed themselves to fidelity within a life-long partnership should be regarded as meeting the chastity-standard. Therefore they should not automatically be excluded from eligibility for ordained ministry.[17]

This is of course a very Protestant argument that not even all Protestants would accept. At a minimum many would object that

[17] See George Hunsinger, "There is a Third Way," *Presbyterian Outlook* (November 26, 2001); "Thinking Outside the Box," parts 1–4, *Presbyterian Outlook* (March 4, 11, 18, 25, 2002); "On Chastity," *Presbyterian Outlook* (June 3, 2002). In these articles I chart a course that avoids the polarized extremes of celebration and prohibition. Seeking to defuse this highly charged issue (and so disappointing nearly everyone), I argue for non-approval, sober discretion, and principled accommodation.

my proposal flies in the face of Holy Scripture in its *sensus literalis.* Here I would only note that this kind of scriptural objection, while it might also be made by Eastern Orthodox and Roman Catholics, is not only broadly Protestant but also distinctively Reformed. An appeal to Scripture is the kind of warrant that the Reformed typically bring to the question of ministry. Catholics, however, operate with another kind of warrant that the Reformed do not share. Not only is ordination seen by Catholics as a sacrament, but the bishop, the presbyter, and the deacon are also, as it were, profoundly sacramental in their official persons. "Representation" plays a key role in Catholic conceptions of who is qualified to be ordained, a role it has not played for the Reformed. Because especially the presbyter and the bishop are seen *in their consecrated persons* as sacramental representations of Christ, ordination cannot easily be extended by the Catholic church to include those who are non-celibate and non-male. Only celibate males are qualified to serve as representations of Christ. We have here an initial indication of how eucharistic ministry is determined for Roman Catholics by a distinctively sacramental imagination.

What is the nature of ordination?

It is often thought that views on the nature of ordination fall into two types. Some believe its nature is ontological while others say it is merely functional. Roman Catholic thinking is associated with the first type; Reformed thinking with the second.

Upon closer analysis, however, the ontological/functional distinction does not seem easy to sustain. Catholics and Reformed would both agree that ordained ministers stand over against the faithful community as well as within it. They would both agree that this being set apart occurs so that essential functions can be carried out for the good of all. They would also agree that anyone set apart by ordination receives the special charism needed for the office to be fulfilled. If the nature of ordination is such that there is no charism apart from a function, and no function that does not require being set apart within the community, then it would seem that ontological and functional elements are so closely intertwined as almost to be inextricable.

If the church's ministry is a participation in the one ministry of Jesus Christ, and if Christ himself is the principal acting subject in all its forms, then the charism needed for ministry inheres principally in Christ himself. It belongs to the church, and to ordained ministers within the church, only as it is granted via *participatio Christi*. Since no form of ministry is without the promise of its charism, Christ grants to those ordained the charism they need by giving it to them as a special form of participation in himself and his ministerial action.

According to traditional Catholic dogma, the nature of ordination is such that it imparts a charism or sacramental character on the ordinand's soul. Since this gift is indelible for the rest of the minister's life (*character indelebilis*), it is received only once.

From a Reformed standpoint, this teaching would be more acceptable if the *character indelebilis* could be interpreted dynamically rather than statically. Might not the *character indelebilis* be seen more nearly as a gift than as a simple possession, or better, as something possessed only as it is given? Is not the ministerial charism once given, promised to be given constantly again (*character donatus et semper donandus*)? And once received, is it not expected to be received ever anew (*character receptus et semper recipiendus*)? Is not the charism constantly renewed in the context of ministry, worship, and daily prayer? Is it not actualized again and again in the liturgy through proclaiming the Word, celebrating the eucharist, and announcing the forgiveness of sins? The charism of ordination would be seen as an irrevocable gift that stands under the promise of continual renewal. It would be seen within a larger christocentric context of active participation and ongoing reception. It would not be a static possession, but would be marked by the lively relations of giving and receiving in equipment for ministry.

What are the offices of ministry?

The offices of ministry, seen both in themselves and in their mutual relations, are undoubtedly a problem of major proportions when it comes to hopes for ecumenical convergence. According to the 1982 Lima document, *Baptism, Eucharist and Ministry*, "the threefold ministry of bishop, presbyter, and deacon may serve today as an expression of the unity we seek" (III.22).[18] This threefold pattern applies readily to Roman Catholic and Eastern Orthodox churches as well as to Protestant churches like the Anglican and the Lutheran. It does not apply to the Reformed churches as they now stand. Whether Reformed churches can and should adapt themselves to this ministerial pattern is a difficult question for them to face.

Although Catholic teaching emphasizes the common priesthood of the faithful, it identifies the church by means of the bishop who presides over it. The relationships of bishop to priest, and of priest to the community, are expressly hierarchical. The bishop signifies the unity of the church, and the priest represents the bishop to the people. According to Vatican II's "Dogmatic Constitution on the Church" (*Lumen Gentium*, 1964), the common priesthood of the faithful and the ministerial or hierarchical priesthood "differ from one another in essence and not only in degree" (Constitution, 10).[19] Similar statements are made to distinguish the bishop from the priest. The bishop is not simply a priest with special powers. He is a priest of a higher order. The fullness of priesthood resides only in him. The same logic then applies to the pope. He is not merely a bishop with special powers, but a bishop of a higher order. What it

---

[18] Faith and Order Commission, *Baptism, Eucharist and Ministry* (Geneva: World Council of Churches, 1982). (Hereafter cited in the text as *BEM*.)

[19] "Dogmatic Constitution of the Church" (*Lumen Gentium*), *Documents of Vatican II*, pp. 14–101 (*supra* n. 2).

means to see these distinctions as a matter of essence rather than degree, however, is neither fully defined nor always easy to see. Questions of ontology can elide, as we have seen, into questions of function. Nevertheless, the hierarchical spirit is clear.

Besides not usually having bishops, the Reformed tradition holds a distinctive view of both presbyters and deacons. Since a fair amount of variation exists within the tradition, these offices are not always defined in the same way from one Reformed body to the next. Local congregations are usually governed by a council, consistory or session, and sometimes this council consists of "presbyters." The minister of Word and Sacrament is usually the moderator of this council, but at least in the presybterian churches there can also be two kinds of presbyters or elders. The minister of Word and Sacrament is called a "teaching elder," while the others are called "ruling elders." Both are ordained. Only the minister of Word and Sacrament corresponds with the term "presbyter" as used in the Lima document. Ruling elders fall outside the rubric. Moreover, the teaching elder is just that. All priestly connotations have been stripped from the office (in the cultic or intercessory sense). In the high sacramental traditions, the presbyter is essentially a priest who also teaches. In the Reformed tradition, the presbyter is essentially a teacher with no official priestly role.[20] Meanwhile, the priesthood of all believers, while roundly acclaimed, is often little more than a slogan. Practically speaking, the congregation is a priesthood without portfolio.

Where Lima's threefold pattern would locate the bishop, the Reformed tradition institutes a regional council, which the Presbyterians call a presbytery. The presbytery elects its own moderator, usually on a revolving basis, conducts the ordination process, and oversees a variety of presbytery-wide business. If the

---

[20] The office of priest in Israel was mainly cultic but included a teaching role. In the Reformed tradition teaching has usually been associated more with the prophetic office.

spirit of Catholicism is hierarchical, the spirit of Reformed polity unites democratic with aristocratic elements. The one moves essentially from the top down, with a strong intermediate role for the bishop; the other moves in several directions at once, with the *episcope* assigned to the presbytery. From the standpoint of ecumenical convergence, the problems of mutual recognition are obvious.

If Jesus Christ is present in the eucharist as the High Priest who sacrificed himself once for all, and if the eucharist is a new form of Passover determined by the Lamb of God who takes away the world's sin, then is it hard to see how the eucharist can be divested of all sacrifical elements. Nor can the presiding minister be divested of all priestly functions. From the standpoint of *participatio Christi*, the presiding minister would celebrate the sacrament *in persona Christi*, as the Catholic Church rightly teaches, but only as the living Christ himself celebrates it *in persona ministri* or *ministrae*, in and on behalf of both the minister and the congregation, as the Reformed would need to add. Whether the Reformed tradition can overcome its aversion to eucharistic sacrifice, however, and whether Catholic teaching can reinvigorate the common priesthood of the faithful (as is also incumbent upon the Reformed), and whether both can recapture a more vivid sense of Christ's centrality in the sacrament as the principal acting subject – these are some of the great questions on which any future united church will depend.

Nevertheless, it seems fair to suggest that for the sake of ecumenical unity and rectification, the Reformed churches would do well conscientiously to embrace the threefold pattern of ministry as indicated by *BEM*. The Reformed will not only need to overcome a historic aversion to hierarchy and the episcopate. They will also need to accept a central role for the bishop of Rome, along conciliar lines as suggested below. Like the Protestant movement in general, the Reformed have not been notable for avoiding splits and schisms within their own ranks. It is astonishing to realize that there are currently 746 different Reformed churches worldwide.[21] Visible unity cannot be said to have been well maintained in churches lacking the historic episcopate.[22] The Reformed will need to seek creative new ways to preserve the values they rightly cherish in their confessions, their form of polity, and their congregational ethos, with its unique blend of democratic and aristocratic elements. But some day, one may hope, they will need to do so within the structures of a reunited Orthodox, Catholic, and Evangelical Church.[23] As Francis A. Sullivan has noted: "The unity which is the goal of the ecumenical movement may have to be different from the unity that exists in any present church."[24]

Two recent developments would seem to be promising. First are some recommendations of the Anglican–Reformed International Commission.

> If our two communions are to become one, Reformed churches will have to face the question of bishops, Anglican churches will have to reconsider the diaconate and take into account the Reformed experience of the eldership, and both communions will

---

[21] See *The Reformed Family Worldwide: A Survey of Reformed Churches, Theological Schools, and International Organizations*, ed. Jean-Jacques Bauswein and Lukas Vischer (Grand Rapids: Wm. B. Eerdmans, 1999); Edmund Doogue, "746 Reformed Churches Worldwide: Reformed International Handbook Identifies Startling 746 Churches," *Ecumenical News International* (February 5, 1999).

[22] For a Reformed discussion, see Max Thurian, *Visible Unity and Tradition* (Baltimore: Helicon Press, 1962).

[23] Albert Outler has suggested that Protestant denominations might retain their distinctive identities as something like "religious orders" within a future united church. Visible unity, on this account, would indeed mean structural unity, but neither organic (homogenized) unity on the one hand nor a loose federated association on the other. Cf. Albert C. Outler, "Do Methodists Have a Doctrine of the Church?," in *The Doctrine of the Church*, ed. Dow Kirkpatrick (Nashville: Abingdon, 1964), pp. 11–28.

[24] Francis A. Sullivan, "Faith and Order: *The Nature and Purpose of the Church*," *Ecumenical Trends* 32 (2003), pp. 145–52, on p. 149.

have to take more seriously the role of the whole membership in the governance of the Church.[25]

The Reformed are invited to consider what practical changes would be involved if the moderator of presbytery were to be reconceived as "bishop-in-presbytery." Anglicans, in turn, are asked to consider how the office of deacon might be reconfigured were the role of elder to be incorporated into it.[26] These steps would bring the churches closer to the goal of visible unity.

A more radical but ecumenically more far-reaching measure is indicated by the "Porvoo Common Statement" (1993).[27] Full, visible unity is understood to require the historic episcopate. Regardless of how unpleasant this recognition may be for the Reformed, it is hard to see how any church rejecting it can be regarded as ecumenically serious. Visible unity will never be achieved without a mutual recognition of ministries and a rectification of the formal defect subsisting in those churches where the historic episcopate is lacking.

The genius of Porvoo is that it looks forward rather than backward. The past is accepted for what it is while the future is shaped by the need for visible unity. Historic episcopal succession is set forth as a sign of apostolic continuity. It is to be recognized without requiring complete agreement about its value and significance. Obviously the ordained ministers in churches aligned with the Porvoo statement would, over time, all be formally folded into the historic episcopal succession.[28]

---

[25] Anglican–Reformed International Commission, *God's Reign and Our Unity: Report of the Anglican–Reformed International Commission, 1981–1984* (London: SPCK; Edinburgh: Saint Andrew Press, 1984), No. 112. Reprinted in *Growth in Agreement II*, pp. 114–54 (*supra* n. 1).

[26] Ibid., No. 96.

[27] "The Porvoo Common Statement: Conversations Between the British and Irish Anglican Churches and the Nordic and Baltic Lutheran Churches" (London: Council for Christian Unity of the General Synod of the Church of England, 1993). (Hereafter cited as "Porvoo" in the text, by numbered paragraph.)

[28] See *Apostolicity and Unity: Essays on the Porvoo Common Statement*, ed. Ola Tjorhom (Grand Rapids: Wm. B. Eerdmans, 2002).

"Those churches in which the sign has at some time not been used are free to recognize the value of the sign and should embrace it without denying their own apostolic continuity."

(Porvoo No. 52)

"Resumption of the use of the sign does not imply an adverse judgment on the ministries of those churches which did not previously make use of the sign. It is rather a means of making more visible the unity and continuity of the Church at all times and in all places."

(Porvoo No. 53)

To put Porvoo-type provisions into practice, the Evangelical Lutheran Church in America entered into formal agreement with the Episcopal Church. In "Called to Common Mission" (1999),[29] the Lutherans agreed to conduct all future ordinations within historic episcopal succession.

Both churches ... promise to include regularly one or more bishops of the other church to participate in the laying-on-of-hands at the ordinations [or] installations of their own bishops ... We agree that when persons duly called and elected are ordained [or] installed in this way, they are understood to join bishops already in this succession and thus to enter the historic episcopate.

(CCM No. 12)

The Episcopalians acknowledge that the historic episcopate is not "necessary for salvation or for the recognition of another church as a church." The Lutherans, in turn, "maintain that this same episcopate, although pastorally desirable when exercised in personal, collegial, and communal ways, is nonetheless not necessary for the relationship of full communion."

(CCM No. 13)

---

[29] Evangelical Lutheran Church in America, *Called to Common Mission* (Evangelical Lutheran Church in America, 1998). (Hereafter cited as *CCM* in the text, by numbered paragraph.)

Despite some initial resistance, the *CCM* agreement is proceeding apace.[30] "Since 2000, all bishops in the Evangelical Lutheran Church in America have entered office through the laying on of hands by three bishops themselves in succession."[31]

For their part the Reformed are even farther from consenting to a Porvoo-style ordination process, since of course they usually lack an episcopate to begin with. Nevertheless, without alignment into the historic episcopate, there would seem to be little hope of an ecumenical future. The criteria for visible unity are well known: "unity in the same faith, unity in the same sacraments and unity in church ministry, i.e., in episcopal ministry, in apostolic succession."[32] If the Reformed are to take the imperative for visible unity seriously, they must struggle at this point, as all churches must struggle at some point, with the need for their own ecclesial conversion. They must find a way to stretch, without theological compromise, into the need for ordination by bishops who themselves have been ordained in the historic succession of bishops. They must find a way to combine episcopal succession with other values that they rightly cherish, like relative local autonomy and permanent openness to continuing reformation under the Word of God by the guidance of the Holy Spirit:[33] *Ecclesia reformata et semper reformanda secundum verbum dei.* Today *semper reformanda* involves openness to episcopal succession.

[30] For a favorable assessment of *CCM*, see William G. Rusch, "Structures of Unity: The Next Ecumenical Challenge – A Possible Way Forward," *Ecclesiology* 2 (2005), pp. 107–22, on pp. 119–21. For an unsympathetic account, see Meg Madson, "The Episcopal No Spin Zone," *Dialog* 39 (2000), pp. 293–95.

[31] Michael Root, "Bishops, Ministry, and the Unity of the Church in Ecumenical Dialogue: Deadlock, Breakthrough, or Both?," *Catholic Theological Society of America Proceedings* 62 (2007), pp. 19–35.

[32] Walter Kasper, "May They All Be One? But How? A Vision of Christian Unity for the Next Generation," *The Tablet* (May 24, 2003).

[33] For a Reformed attempt to think about visible unity along these lines, see Horace T. Allen. "One Visibly Catholic Church," *Theology Today* 18 (1961), pp. 321–29.

As Robert McAfee Brown has observed:

> It is patently clear that episcopacy will be one of the features of a reunited church. Those who cannot accept this as a premise will have to settle for a permanently divided Christendom and content themselves with patching up denominational family quarrels.[34]

A rule once expressed by Calvin would also seem to be relevant here:

> We ought to make mutual concessions in all ceremonies that do not involve any prejudice to the confession of our faith, and for this end, that the unity of the church be not destroyed by our excessive rigor or moroseness.[35]

The definitions and procedures of the Porvoo Common Statement would seem to honor the spirit of both Brown's observation and Calvin's rule. It is hard to see how ecclesial conversion for the Reformed would not entail adopting the traditional threefold pattern: bishops, presbyters, and deacons.[36] The fissiparous Reformed family has much to gain by submitting to the discipline of this polity.[37]

---

[34] Robert McAfee Brown, *The Ecumenical Revolution* (Garden City: Doubleday, 1967), p. 149.

[35] John Calvin, Letter 346 (To the brethren at Wezel in 1554), in *Selected Works of John Calvin*, vol. VI, *Letters*, part 3, ed. Jules Bonnet (Grand Rapids: Baker Book House, 1983), pp. 29–32; on p. 31.

[36] The possible alternatives to adopting the threefold pattern are carefully explored by Evans and found wanting. See Evans, *The Church and the Churches*, pp. 212–90 (*supra* n. 12).

[37] The resistance is of course formidable. Reunion efforts begun in 1937 between Presbyterians and Episcopalians in the USA fizzled largely because of disagreements about the historic episcopate. See Cyril Richardson, "The Presbyterian–Episcopalian Concordat," *Christendom* (1939), pp. 252–59; George Stewart, "Union from a Presbyterian Point of View," *Anglican Theological Review* (1940), pp. 291–98. Nearly seventy years later the same sticking point has prevented the mutual recognition of ministries in the newly formed Churches Uniting in Christ (CUIC), inaugurated in 2002. In Canada decades-long efforts beginning in 1943

What are the functions of ordained ministry?

Witness, worship and service – *marturia, leiturgia* and *diakonia* – are terms that orient the church's ministry as a whole, and its ordained ministry in particular. If the one ministry of Jesus Christ can be said to consist in his actions of self-witness, self-mediation, and self-anticipation, then these are, in a secondary and dependent way, also the actions of the *totus Christus*. Because they are the actions of Christ in and through his people, they are also the contingent actions of Christ's people in and through him. Witness gives us the identity of Jesus Christ, mediation gives us his presence, and anticipation gives us his future.

- By pointing to his unique identity as Lord and Savior, witness preserves the *irreducible distinction* between Christ and his people. This distinction is safeguarded in the community most especially through the of proclamation and teaching of Scripture.
- By communicating his saving presence, mediation expresses the *inseparable union* between Christ and his people. This union is centered most especially in eucharistic worship.
- Finally, by foreshadowing his return in glory, anticipation gives us a preview of Christ as the great *Pantokrator* (Ruler of the cosmos), and so of the *promised fulfillment* of all things. This cosmic fulfillment is prefigured most especially in the work of service and mission.

reached the advanced stage of drawing up a *Plan of Union and By-Laws: Anglican, Christian and United Church of Canada* (Toronto: General Commission on Church Union, 1973). Everything unraveled at the end. See John Webster Grant, "Leading a Horse to Water: Reflections on Church Union Conversations in Canada," in *Studies of the Church in History*, ed. Horton Davies (Allison Park: Pickwick Publications, 1983); Douglas F. Campbell, "The Anglican and United Churches in Church Union Dialogue, 1943–75," *Studies in Religion / Sciences Religieuses* 17 (1988), pp. 303–14. A US Presbyterian–Episcopal Bilateral Dialogue, which began in 2000, held eight meetings between 2002 and 2006. Its special concerns are the role of the historic episcopate and the practice of "corporate *episkope*." No reports are yet released. Dialogue in Canada has also resumed.

For the sake of his self-witness, self-mediation, and self-anticipation, Christ incorporates his people into himself. They become the body of which he makes himself the Head. Through their ministry of witness, mediation, and anticipation, Christ attests his identity and communicates his presence and promise to the world. All Christians are ordained to some form of participation in Christ's ministry through their baptism.

We might say that witness is prophetic, that worship is priestly, and that service is royal, but this would be to oversimplify. We can say, however, that Word and Sacrament are the special vehicles of Christ's ministry in his living self-witness, self-mediation, and self-anticipation. Word and Sacrament are also the special vehicles entrusted uniquely to the ordained ministry. The unique function of the ordained ministry is to attest Christ and to mediate him, authoritatively, by means of Word and Sacrament, and so to equip the community for mission. The ordained ministry represents an authoritative, unique, and indispensable form of the one ministry entrusted to the whole community.

It is important to see that the Word is a vehicle of mediation and not just of witness. It is equally important to see that the eucharist is a vehicle of witness and not just of mediation. A certain one-sidedness can be discerned in both the Reformed and the Roman Catholic traditions. Historically, the predominant categories for the Reformed have been Word, witness, and teaching. The eucharist has been seen in this context, and the reality of mediation has been left to some extent in the shadows. For the Catholic tradition, the situation is much the reverse. Sacrament, mediation, and representation have been in the foreground. Preaching has been de-emphasized, and the reality of witness has been relegated to some extent to the margins. If this analysis is reasonably correct, then certain admonitions and affirmations necessary from each side to the other should be relatively clear.

In short, ordained ministry, like the ministry of the entire community, needs to be seen in light of Christ's threefold office as prophet, priest, and king. Christ was sent to fulfill these roles, but in fulfilling them he transformed them at the same time. Like the prophets of Israel, he announced the Word of God, but unlike them he was identical with the Word he proclaimed. "The Word became flesh and lived among us ... full of grace and truth" (Jn. 1:14). Like Israel's priests he was called to offer sacrifice that the people might be cleansed of their sin, but unlike them he was himself the sacrifice to be offered. "Here is the Lamb of God who takes away the sin of the world!" (Jn. 1:29). "We have a great high priest who has passed through the heavens, Jesus, the Son of God" (Heb. 4:14). Finally, like Israel's kings, he was called to rule justly in the fear of God, uphold the poor and needy, and defend the people from their enemies. But unlike them he was the Lord who took the form of a servant, perfecting his royal power in weakness. "And being found in human form, he humbled himself and became obedient to the point of death – even death on a cross (Phil. 2:8). [My] power is made perfect in weakness" (2 Cor. 12:9).[38]

While the entire community is called to attest and worship Christ in his uniqueness as the one in whom this threefold office was perfected, and to serve in mediating him to the world, the ordained ministry is called to perform these tasks in a unique and authoritative way. Consider the following official summary of Vatican II on the essence of ministerial priesthood:

> Among the various charisms and service, the priestly ministry of
> the New Testament, which continues Christs function as mediator,
> and which in essence and not merely in degree is distinct from the
> common priesthood of all the faithful (*Lumen Gentium*, no. 10),
> alone perpetuates the essential work of the Apostles: By effectively
> proclaiming the gospel, by gathering together and leading the

---

[38] See Presbyterian Church (USA), *The Study Catechism, Full Version* (Louisville: Witherspoon Press, 2003), Questions 36–41. (I served on the committee which wrote this document. It can be accessed online at www.pcusa.org/catech/studycat. htm.)

community, by remitting sins, and especially by celebrating the Eucharist, *it makes* Christ, the head of the community, present in the exercise of his work of redeeming humanity and glorifying God perfectly.[39]

From a Reformed perspective, this statement nicely brings out the cultic, prophetic, and governing aspects of ordained ministry. Preaching, leadership, and sacramental presidency all receive their due. What distinguishes ordained ministry from that of the community is also carefully set forth. At the same time, however, the continuity between Christ and those ordained is arguably overstated so that necessary distinctions get blurred. The following questions might be posed:

• Is not Christ himself the only one who can continue his unique mediatorial work? Would it not be better to say that he himself continues this work through the minister rather than that the minister is the one who continues it? Does not the priestly minister simply serve Christ without encroaching upon his undivided work?

• Moreover, is it really proper to assert that the priestly minister "perpetuates" the work of the apostles? Is there not something unique and non-transferable about their work? Are not priestly ministers appointed as servants and stewards, rather than as perpetuators, of the apostolate?

• Finally, is it not again Christ himself rather than the presiding minister who makes himself present in the eucharist? Does not Christ make himself present by the Spirit and in the Word? Is he not himself the sole saving agent, with the minister acting as his servant and his instrument, in this sacrament? Does not the

---

[39] From Documents of the Synod of Bishops: I. "The Ministerial Priesthood," part one, 5, AAS 63 (1971). Translated in *The Catholic Mind* (March, 1972), pp. 33–51; on p. 39 n. 4. As cited by Benedict M. Ashley, "Gender and the Priesthood of Christ: A Theological Reflection," *The Thomist* 57 (1993), pp. 343–79; on p. 354.

efficacy of the ministerial office belong entirely to Christ himself so that the priest functions strictly as his servant, steward, and witness? Why is so much emphasis placed on mediation here and so little on bearing witness?

No reason would seem to exist in principle for the Roman Catholic Church to reject what has just been suggested about the unique efficacy of Christ in relation to the ministerial priesthood. As Benedict M. Ashley, the Dominican theologian, has written:

> Presiding at the Eucharist or reconciling the sinner are [sic] not an exercise of power by the priest in his own right but by Christ and the Church through him. A priest acting in the name of Christ and the Church is gravely obliged to act simply as their servant.[40]

Nevertheless, it seems clear that when it comes to ministerial priesthood, the formulas of Roman Catholic teaching often tend to emphasize unities at the expense of necessary distinctions, and that this one-sidedness has something to do with an equally one-sided emphasis on the idea of Sacrament at the expense of the Word.
Cardinal Kasper is encouraging here:

> From Reformation theology [Catholic theology] has learnt that the proclamation of the Word of God also has the function of establishing church and *communio*. Conversely, the Catholic Church is convinced that its institutional "elements", such as episcopacy and the Petrine ministry, are gifts of the Spirit for all Christians.[41]

When the Lordship of the living Christ is taken adequately into account, a conception of the historic episcopate should be possible that would not divide the sacramental and the presbyterial churches, though it would require significant changes from each. The differentiated unity obtaining among ecclesial ministries and

---

[40] Ashley, "Gender and the Priesthood of Christ," p. 369.
[41] See Kasper, "Present Situation and Future of the Ecumenical Movement," p. 18.

ministerial offices would be clarified and respected. The priesthood proper to the faithful would be seen in its unity with the bishop's ministerial priesthood and the presbyter's ministerial priesthood, while the necessary distinctions among them would also find their proper place. Governing them all, however, would be the centrality and the supremacy of the one indivisible priesthood of Christ himself, in which all ministries and offices would participate, finding their properly ordered and distinctive places.[42]

Types of theological imagination

The Roman Catholic imagination is a sacramental imagination. Representation and mediation are the categories it associates with the sacraments. These categories emphasize the unity between Christ and the church. When they are not balanced by categories of witness, however, the church is tempted to identify itself, its institutions, and its hierarchy with the presence of Christ. The dangers here are the dangers of triumphalism and sacralization. These dangers arguably attend the Catholic understanding of eucharist and ministry.

The Reformed imagination, by contrast, is a verbal imagination. Witness and teaching are the categories it associates with God's Word. These categories serve to bring out the distinction between Christ and the church. When they are not balanced by categories of sacramentality, however, the church is tempted to separate itself, its congregations, its presbyters and its presbyteries, from the presence

---

[42] Although the decades-long bilateral conversations of the Anglican–Roman Catholic International Commission (ARCIC) have set the ecumenical standard in working through questions of ministerial office, much work remains to be done. The respective roles of the pope, bishops, presbyters, and the faithful still need to be defined more precisely with regard to teaching and to decision-making, if divisions are to be overcome. See Mark Santer, "Communion, Unity and Primacy: An Anglican Response to *Ut Unum Sint*," *Ecclesiology* 3 (2007), pp. 283–95, on pp. 292–93. (Santer served as Anglican co-chair of ARCIC.) See also Michael Root, "The Gift of Authority," *The Ecumenical Review* 52 (2000), pp. 57–71; on p. 64.

of Christ. The dangers here are the dangers of intellectualism and secularization. These dangers arguably attend the Reformed understanding of eucharist and ministry.

There is perhaps a third type of theological imagination that can retain the strengths of the other two while avoiding their weaknesses. We might call it the Chalcedonian imagination. This type can appreciate the sacramentality of the Word and the witnessing function of the eucharist, because it sees the activity of the living Christ in his self-witness, self-mediation, and self-anticipation as involving both Word and Sacrament alike in the power of the Holy Spirit.[43] The ministry of the entire church, and of the ordained ministry within it, are given a share, in various degrees and ways, in the one ministry of Christ himself to the world. In this ministry Christ is related to the church, and the church to him, through an ordered pattern of active participation. Between Christ and the church there subsists a unity, a distinction, and an asymmetry in which Christ is always present as the Head of his ecclesial body. Ministry takes place within a christocentric ecclesiology of participation. In his one undivided ministry of self-witness, self-mediation, and self-anticipation, Christ is related to the active ministry of his church without separation or division, and without confusion or change, but he alone remains Savior and Lord.

---

[43] Although the argument of this chapter has been couched in christological terms, it could be transposed into explicitly trinitarian terms as well. For example, it could be said that the incarnate Son bears witness to the Father, who in turn bears witness to the incarnate Son, and that both acts of witness always occur in and through the Holy Spirit (cf. Matt. 11:27). Or again, it could be said that the incarnate Son mediates the Father to us, and us to the Father, by mediating himself, in and through the operation of the Holy Spirit (cf. Jn. 14:10–11). As Thomas Aquinas observed, properly speaking, it is impossible to be christocentric without also being trinitarian, and vice versa. See Aquinas, *ST* 2/2.2.8. The basic grammar is that matters like revelation and reconciliation proceed from the Father, through the Son, and in the Spirit, and then back again in the Spirit, through the Son, to the Father. The christological idiom has been chosen in this chapter for the sake of convenience.

6 | Eucharistic ministry: an impending impasse?

What follows is a series of pointed questions about eucharist, ministry, and related church-dividing matters. The questions are rooted in the Reformational traditions and directed mainly to churches in the high sacramental traditions (Roman Catholic and Eastern Orthodox). They are intended as questions of ecumenical admonition. At every point they enter a plea for developing less rigid, more differentiated, and more reasonable judgments "in order that we may all be one."

Questions of ecumenical admonition

Apostolic succession: doctrine and defect

(1) Is it the case that the episcopate of the high sacramental churches suffers from no defect at all comparable to that which the Vatican finds (not entirely without justice) in the ministries of the Protestant churches?

    (1.1) If the high sacramental churches are not prepared to subject their own episcopates to fundamental self-examination, such as they require of the ministries in other traditions, does that not suggest a defect in itself?

    (1.2) Does not this reluctance threaten to quench the ecumenical imperative of the Holy Spirit? Does it not thwart the Spirit's movement to overcome divisions in the church?

(2) From a theological as well as a historical standpoint, is it really true that the high sacramental churches are bearers of the holy tradition in all its fullness – creedal, doxological, ethical – with no serious shortcomings or defects?

    (2.1) Given the great schism between East and West, how can any tradition possibly be without doctrinal defect?

    (2.2) In a sundered church, how can any tradition claim to be without serious deficiency in its understanding of the Trinity, christology, ecclesiology, and salvation?

    (2.3) In a divided church, does not every tradition, East or West, "breathe with one lung" (Congar)?[1]

(3) If Eastern Orthodoxy and Roman Catholicism need each other in fundamental respects, in order to attain and recover a once and future doctrinal fullness, does that not also relativize any imperious suppositions, insofar as they may exist, that Protestant and other traditions have nothing indispensable to bring the *oikumene* with respect to attaining a higher degree of doctrinal fullness in the common apostolic succession?

    (3.1) Why are high sacramental churches so slow to acknowledge that there is truth in other traditions which they themselves may need and from which they might benefit?

(4) Why have they been so ready to subordinate the supremacy of Christ to the authority of councils and post-apostolic developments?

    (4.1) Why have the standard-bearers of "apostolic succession" allowed the presence of Holy Scripture – the supreme repository of the apostolic witness – to be subordinated too often to other factors?

---

[1] See Yves Congar, "The Human Person and Human Liberty in Oriental Anthropology," in *Dialogue Between Christians* (London: Geoffrey Chapman, 1966), pp. 232–45; on p. 244. Congar's striking image was later picked up by John Paul II, "Reflection on the Visit to Romania" (1999) (No. 3): www.vatican.va/holy_father/john_paul_ii/audiences/1999/documents/hf_jp-ii_aud_12051999_en.html.

(4.2) Why have they historically (with honorable exceptions) been so long on celebrating sacraments and so short on proclaiming the Word of God?

(4.3) Why hasn't Holy Scripture enjoyed the same preeminence for them as has the holy eucharist?

(5) How could they have allowed such a central apostolic doctrine as the justification of the sinner by grace through faith to fall for so long into eclipse?

(5.1) Why should not this lapse be sufficient in itself to alert them to the possibility of their own relative deficiencies?

(5.2) Is this the only apostolic doctrine to have suffered at their hands?

The future of the papacy

(6) Is it not necessary for all traditions, including the Roman Catholic, to rethink the status of the papacy?[2]

(6.1) Does not the bishop of Rome occupy a unique and special place among all other bishops in the world?

(6.2) Is he not called to preside among all other bishops in love?[3]

(6.3) Is he not the *de facto* leader of all Christianity in the modern world?

---

[2] In 1995 the Pope issued an astonishing invitation to the leaders and theologians of other churches to engage in "a patient and fraternal dialogue" with him about the doctrinal and jurisdictional aspects of the papacy. See John Paul II, *That They May Be One: On Commitment to Ecumenism* (Washington, DC: United States Catholic Conference, 1995). For discussion, see *The Petrine Ministry: Catholics and Orthodox in Dialogue*, ed. Walter Cardinal Kasper (New York: Newman Press, 2006); Adriano Garuti, *The Primacy of the Bishop of Rome and Ecumenical Dialogue* (San Francisco: Ignatius Press, 2004); *Church Unity and the Papal Office*, ed. Carl E. Braaten and Robert W. Jenson (Grand Rapids: Wm. B. Eerdmans, 2001); *Petrine Ministry and the Unity of the Church*, ed. James F. Puglisi (Collegeville: Liturgical Press, 1999).

[3] For an eloquent plea along these lines, see Rowan Williams, "The Future of the Papacy: An Anglican View" (The Pelican Trust, 1997), published by Catholics for a Changing Church, 14 West Halkin Street, London SW1X 8JS.

(6.4)   Should he not be upheld in prayer by all congregations and all Christians everywhere?

(7)   Is he not more nearly the servant of God's servants, who should lead primarily by example, than a supreme pontiff whose jurisdiction is universal?[4]

(7.1)   Should he really be authorized to appoint and depose bishops in all other churches?

(7.2)   Should he not rather be the first among equals in an episcopal college?

(7.3)   Should he not himself be chosen by the church in Rome and affirmed by patriarchs, archbishops, and others of comparable authority throughout the worldwide church?

(8)   Similarly, should not other bishops be chosen by their own churches and be affirmed by the pope?

(8.1)   Should not each bishop govern his own church and be accountable, in the first instance, to his regional synod of bishops rather than to a global college directed by the pope?

(8.2)   Should not the supervision of bishops in cases of heresy and other disorders be more nearly collegial than papal, and dealt with synodally in the first instance, according to the principle of subsidiarity?

(9)   Should not matters of doctrine that are undecided be resolved collegially under the leadership of the pope through an open process of discussion marked by freedom, respect, and love?

(10)   Would not a fundamental move in this direction be necessary if there is ever to be a rapprochement between the Roman

---

[4] William G. Rusch points to a 1976 lecture by Joseph Cardinal Ratzinger (now Pope Benedict XVI) which was reprinted without change in 1982. "The Cardinal's position was that Rome must not require from the Eastern churches in terms of primacy any more than was formulated and lived in the first thousand years of the Church's history." Rusch, "Structures of Unity: The Next Ecumenical Challenge – A Possible Way Forward," *Ecclesiology* 2 (2005), pp. 107–22; on p. 121.

Catholic and Eastern Orthodox churches (to say nothing of all others)?[5]

(10.1) Would not other churches need to accommodate their polities to some form of electoral and collegial episcopacy under the spiritual leadership of the bishop of Rome?[6]

(10.2) Has not the abuse of hierarchical authority by means of domination been the "primordial evil" in the church's history (Louis Bouyer)?[7]

(10.3) Would not any future united church need to allot a significant place in policy-making, beyond mere consultation, to the voice of those not bearing holy orders?[8]

The filioque

(11) Does not Eastern Orthodoxy need to strive against entrenched pockets of enclave mentality in its leadership and communities?[9]

(11.1) In light of recent agreed statements on the *filioque* – not only between Orthodoxy and Catholicism, but also

---

[5] The papal "ministry of unity," as conceived by Rome, has in fact proven historically to be divisive.

[6] For an unofficial Reformed acceptance of a "ministry of unity," though not one centered in the bishop of Rome, see "The Successor to Peter," A Paper for Discussion from the Presbyterian Church (USA) (Louisville: December 6–7, 2000). The paper, which must be said to make little progress, is well intentioned. www.pcusa.org/ecumenicalrelations/images/peter.pdf.

[7] Louis Bouyer, *Church of God, Body of Christ, Temple of the Holy Spirit* (Chicago: Franciscan Herald Press, 1982), pp. 504–5.

[8] See Karl Rahner, *Theological Investigations*, vol. 20 (New York: Crossroad, 1986), pp. 123–26. Rahner called for allotting church people a significant role, beyond mere consultation, in ecclesiastical decision-making, including the selection of bishops.

[9] "Orthodoxy's great demonstrated disability is churchly immobility, a simple incapacity to acknowledge past historical change or to consider the possible necessity of future historical change." Robert Jenson, *Unbaptized God* (Minneapolis: Fortress Press, 1992), p. 142.

between Orthodoxy and other ecumenical traditions, like the Reformed – why should this barrier any longer be allowed to stand in the way of eucharistic sharing?[10]

(11.2) Why should not all Orthodox churches set an example worthy of their stature by relinquishing ancient resentments on this score?

(11.3) Why should they not now more widely acknowledge that the *filioque* is susceptible of a charitable interpretation, even as Western traditions have come to acknowledge not only the unacceptable procedural irregularities that brought it into being, but also the valid theological arguments that the Orthodox have urged for their views?

(12) Why must a resolution of this controversy mean that all churches should abandon the *filioque* clause?

(12.1) Why should there not rather be repentance all around for the divisiveness that has prolonged this bitter and unnecessary controversy?

(12.2) As a gesture of good will, would it not be better to set aside a mutually determined season of penitence in which for an appointed period of time (say, five years) the Eastern churches agreed to say the creed with the *filioque* clause while the Western churches agreed to say it without it?[11]

---

[10] See "The *Filioque*: A Church-Dividing Issue?" An Agreed Statement of the North American Orthodox-Catholic Theological Consultation (2003), www.usccb.org/seia/filioque.shtml; "Agreed Statement on the Holy Trinity," in *Theological Dialogue Between Orthodox and Reformed Churches*, vol. 11, ed. Thomas F. Torrance (Edinburgh: Scottish Academic Press, 1993), pp. 219–26; *Anglican–Orthodox Dialogue: The Dublin Agreed Statement, 1984* (Crestwood: St. Vladimir's Seminary Press, 1985). Also reprinted in *Growth in Agreement II*, ed. Jeffrey Gros, Harding Meyer, and William G. Rusch (Grand Rapids: Wm. B. Eerdmans, 2000), pp. 81–104.

[11] It is obvious that this suggestion could not be implemented without careful institutional preparations.

(12.3) Would it not be better after that to allow the *filioque* clause to become adiaphora – as major eleventh-century theologians on both sides, like Theophylact and Anselm, thought it should be?[12]

A tendency toward indifference?

(13) Why have the Eastern churches (again with honorable exceptions) been so long on ethnicity and so short on apostolic mission?[13]

(13.1) Why have they generally been so hesitant to spread the gospel among the nations while overlooking injustices against groups not their own?

(13.2) Why has their official condemnation of "ethnophyletism" not been to greater effect? (The identification of Orthodoxy with any particular ethnic group was condemned as a heresy by an ecclesiastical council in Constantinople in 1872.[14])

(13.3) How can the Eastern Orthodox expect others to turn a blind eye to deficiencies such as these when large claims are incessantly made by them about their supposed superiority?

(14) Why has there never been a direct official response to Vatican II[15] when it decreed that no obstacles stood in the way, in

---

[12] Steven Runciman, *The Eastern Schism* (Oxford: Clarendon Press, 1955), pp. 72–77.

[13] For a candid and balanced discussion of mission in the Eastern Orthodox tradition, see Timothy Ware, *The Orthodox Church*, 2nd edn. (London: Penguin Books, 1997), pp. 187–91.

[14] See G. R. Evans, *The Church and the Churches* (Cambridge: Cambridge University Press, 1993), p. 72. Cf. Vigen Guroian, "The Crisis of Orthodox Ecclesiology," in *The Ecumenical Future*, ed. Carl E. Braaten and Robert W. Jenson (Grand Rapids: Wm. B. Eerdmans, 2004), pp. 162–75.

[15] There have of course been indirect responses. These would include the mutual lifting of the anathemas of 1054 by Pope Paul VI and the Patriarch Athanagoras I in 1965 as well as the launching of the Joint Catholic–Orthodox Commission for Theological Dialogue by Pope Paul II and Patriarch Dimitrios I in 1979.

principle, from the Catholic side to eucharistic sharing with the Orthodox?[16]

(14.1) How could this positive historic gesture be met with silence as though it had never occurred?[17]

(14.2) How could it suffice merely to say that other issues need to be resolved first (as well they may)?[18]

(15) Why is lack of reciprocity such a conspicuous feature of Orthodox participation in ecumenical relations?[19]

(15.1) Why is there not more evidence of symbolic gestures showing that resentment, rancor, and grievance are not

---

[16] See "Decree on Eastern Catholic Churches," Nos. 26–29, in *The Documents of Vatican II*, ed. Walter Abbott (New York: America Press, 1966), pp. 383–85; see also "Decree on Ecumenism" (*Unitatis Redintegratio*), Nos. 14–18, in ibid., pp. 357–61. Worthy of note is Hilaire Marot, "Decrees of Vatican II: First Orthodox Reactions," in *Do We Know the Others?*, ed. Hans Küng (New York: Paulist Press, 1966), pp. 134–54. According to Marot, who could produce no official document on which to comment, the unofficial reactions ran the gamut from unenthusiastic to negative (pp. 150–54).

[17] A short-lived exception transpired in 1969 when Patriarch Alexy II and the Holy Synod of the Russian Orthodox Church decided to allow Orthodox clergy to administer Holy Communion to Old Believers and Catholics, with the unstated possibility that the Orthodox might receive from their clergy as well. Had it been allowed to stand (instead of being met with outrage and alarm), this decision might have marked an important step toward healing the split between Eastern and Western Christianity. See Timothy Kallistos Ware, "News and Comment: Russia," *Eastern Churches Review* 3 (1970), pp. 91–92; Keith A. Nonemaker, "Metropolitan Nikodim and the Russians," *Brethren Life and Thought* 26 (Winter 1981), pp. 45–58; on pp. 53–54.

[18] For a complete overview, see M. Paracleta Amrich, "Catholicism and Orthodoxy: The 'Struggle' for 'Reunion' from the Second Vatican Council to the Holy Year 2000," (unpublished dissertation, Duquesne University, 2006), pp. 353–83.

[19] The efforts of John Paul II are a case in point. Despite his being subjected to much unpleasantness at the hands of the Orthodox, including rebuff, insult, and public humiliation (for example, in Greece), he remained undeterred. In November 2004, in a solemn Vatican ceremony, he publicly returned the relics of Ss. John Chrysostom and Gregory Nazianzen to Patriarch Bartholomew of Constantinople. This was, by any standard, a great and magnanimous exercise in practical ecumenism. What comparable gesture in return has been forthcoming from the Orthodox side?

unmitigated factors in Orthodoxy's attitude toward Rome?[20]

(15.2) Is non-communion with Rome really a defining characteristic of what it means to be "Orthodox"?

(15.3) Does Orthodoxy have any proposal for attaining visible unity besides the dead end of "return ecumenism"?[21]

Apostolic succession: continuity of office

(16) Can the high sacramental churches acknowledge that change has long since belonged to their histories?[22]

(16.1) Can they further acknowledge that in their histories significant complexities and even irregularities can sometimes be found?[23]

(16.2) Could they not put a charitable construction on the procedural and other irregularities that entered into the

---

[20] Evans points to "fear of domination" as a contributing reason, a fear that she thinks is not entirely without cause. See Evans, *The Church and the Churches*, pp. 70, 88, 95–98 (*supra* n. 14).

[21] "We find Orthodoxy envisaging a united Church which will result from the coming over of others to Orthodoxy." G. R. Evans, *Method in Ecumenical Theology* (Cambridge: Cambridge University Press, 1996), p. 227.

[22] "There can be no real *rapprochement* unless a community which is closed to change can come to see itself differently in its relation to other churches." Evans, *The Church and the Churches*, pp. 169–70 (*supra* n. 14).

[23] See for example Francis A. Sullivan, *From Apostles to Bishops: The Development of the Episcopacy in the Early Church* (New York: Newman Press, 2001). Sullivan follows the broad scholarly consensus "that the historical episcopate developed in the post-New Testament period, from the local leadership of a college of presbyters, who were sometimes also called *episkopoi*, to the leadership of a single bishop" (p. 217). He also accepts "that the church of Rome was led by a group of presbyters for at least part of the second century" (p. 217). He believes that the development of the episcopal office in the church was divinely guided by the Holy Spirit in much the same way as was the development of the New Testament canon (p. 230).

Protestant churches regarding the episcopal, presbyterial, and diaconal offices?[24]

(16.3) Could they not stretch to the point of allowing that these irregularities (in combination with other factors) do not necessarily consign the Protestant churches to a merely second-class status *vis-à-vis* the high sacramental churches?[25]

(16.4) Could they not allow that, all things considered, there are enough defects to go around, so that in differing ways and in varying respects, no church can finally rise above the status of claiming to be an "ecclesial community"?

(16.5) Conversely, could they not stretch to the point of allowing not only that all churches are ecclesial communities (in the technical sense), but also that all ecclesial communities have a rightful claim, each in its own way, to being churches?

(17) Is it absolutely necessary to regard a minister of the eucharist as illegitimate (defective) unless that person has been episcopally ordained?

(17.1) Are there no historical precedents upon which the Roman Catholic and Eastern Orthodox churches could draw in order to acknowledge the relative validity of the ministerial office in the Protestant churches?

(17.2) Have there not been historical cases where canon-law prescriptions for ordination were ignored (including the

---

[24] For the tension in official Catholicism between narrow and generous standards for agreement about ministerial office, see Francis A. Sullivan, "The Vatican Response to ARCIC I (1992)," in *Anglicans and Roman Catholics: The Search for Unity*, ed. Christopher Hill and E. J. Yarnold (London: SPCK/CTS, 1994), pp. 298–308.

[25] "Must not the question of mutual recognition of ministries be tackled with much more theological energy and confidence, while aiming at a generous (and possible) solution, than it has been hitherto when there was too much fear and (if we may say so) too little theological imagination?" Karl Rahner, *Theological Investigations*, vol. 20 (New York: Seabury Press, 1976), p. 127.

case of Ambrose) without a declaration of nullity that would have necessitated re-ordination?[26]

(17.3) Have there not in fact been important instances historically where ordination was conducted not by bishops but by presbyters?

(17.4) Would it not be possible, according to recent precedent, to rule that the ordination of ministers in Protestant churches proceeds in a way that is "virtually" if not "literally" valid?[27]

(18) Would it not be salutary, especially under current circumstances, for the Roman Catholic Church to permit its priests to be married – as is already the case for the Eastern Orthodox, whose ministry it accepts as valid, to say nothing of Eastern Rite Catholics?

(18.1) Would not this change exemplify how the Roman Catholic Church is ready to learn from other communions?

(18.2) Indeed, would it not go some way toward resolving the acute and alarming shortage of Roman Catholic priests in Europe, Latin America, and other parts of the world?

---

[26] See the article by K. Mörsdorf, "Die Entwicklung der Zweigliedrigkeit der kirchlichen Hierarchie," cited by Harry J. McSorley, "The Roman Catholic Doctrine of the Competent Minister of the Eucharist in Ecumenical Perspective," in *Eucharist and Ministry: Lutherans and Catholics in Dialogue*, vol. IV, published jointly by the US Conference of Catholic Bishops and the Lutheran World Federation (Washington, DC, and New York, 1970), pp. 120–37; on p. 124.

[27] Consider the recent Roman Catholic decision to accept the "Addai and Mari Anaphora" (Eucharistic Prayer) of the Assyrian Church of the East, even though it does not include the all-important words of consecration. See Robert F. Taft, "Mass Without the Consecration?," *America* 188 (May 12, 2003), pp. 7–11. Taft, who introduces the distinction between the literal and the virtual, notes that there may sometimes be "parallel but divergent expressions of the same basic realities in a different historico-ecclesial milieu." About the decision, he adds: "I consider it to be the most important magisterial teaching since Vatican II."

(19) Does not the refusal of the sacramental churches to admit women into holy orders rest very largely on a theologically misguided theory of imagistic or iconic "representation"?

(19.1) Do they not, in effect, elevate this theory over the eucharistic minister's apostolic role of being a sign and "witness" to Christ in his ineffable uniqueness as fully God and fully human (something arguably far more important)?

(19.2) Can any church seriously teach that when the eternal Word of God became flesh, the maleness of that flesh (as opposed, say, to its Jewishness) entailed any saving significance whatsoever?

(19.3) Under modern circumstances is it not a grievous wound to the body of Christ (a grave defect) for women to be excluded from holy orders?

To sum up, the point of this exercise in ecumenical admonition has not been to make any one tradition look good by making others look bad. It has only been to suggest that there are more than enough warts (*defectus*) to go around. No existing church can reasonably claim to be free of them in non-trivial respects. It is perhaps the special vocation of Reformational churches, formed as they are by the great and liberating doctrine of *simul iustus et peccator*, to press the point. They need not reject the charge that in important respects they are simply "ecclesial communities." They need merely insist on a level playing field in which the term is applied, in appropriate ways, not just to some but to all. The divided churches as we know them are not mutually self-sufficient but mutually (though differently) defective. Learning to heed the admonitions of other churches, in a spirit of chastened humility, can only serve to advance the day when we shall all be one at the great table of the one Lord.

A word on women's ordination

It seems fitting to conclude with a word on women's ordination. Unlike the divisive question of whether practicing gays and lesbians may be ordained, women's ordination has become official policy in a significant number of Protestant denominations. Indeed, in Anglican, Lutheran, and Methodist churches, women have been ordained not only to the presbyteriate but also to the episcopate. Meanwhile, the Roman Catholic and Eastern Orthodox churches have vehemently indicated that the ordination of women could never be made acceptable to them. The ecumenical movement threatens to founder on the shoals of this impasse. What follows is a survey of Catholic statements and Orthodox attitudes along with rejoinders from Protestants and others.

Recent official Roman Catholic thinking about women's ordination can be charted by referring to five important documents.[28]

(1) "Report of the Pontifical Biblical Commission" (1976).[29] The Vatican's own Pontifical Biblical Commission concluded that the biblical evidence was insufficient for deciding whether women should be ordained. "It does not seem that the New Testament by itself alone will permit us to settle in a clear way and once for all the problem of the possible accession of woman to the presbyteriate" (No. 66). This report casts a long shadow over subsequent developments.

(2) "Declaration on the Admission of Women to the Ministerial Priesthood" (*Inter Insigniores*) (1976).[30] Promulgated by the Congregation for the Doctrine of the Faith, this declaration stated that "Jesus did not entrust the apostolic charge to women" (p. 29), that his example was normative, and that it had been followed without exception through the centuries. Also stated was that "the incarnation of the Word took place according to the male sex" (p. 43).

---

[28] Several of these documents have been collected in From "Inter Insigniores" to "Ordinatio Sacerdotalis", ed. Congregation for the Doctrine of the Faith (Washington, DC: United States Catholic Conference, 1998). This edition is bilingual, with the Latin text on one page facing the English translation on the next.

[29] "Report of the Pontifical Biblical Commission," Origins 6 (July 1, 1976), pp. 92–96.

[30] From "Inter Insigniores" to "Ordinatio Sacerdotalis", pp. 21–53. (Hereafter page references cited in the text.)

This fact was said to be significant because it entailed that only males could properly "represent" Christ by a "natural resemblance" in celebrating the eucharist (p. 43). Likewise, only males could properly represent the "nuptial mystery" of Christ as the bridegroom joined mystically to the church (p. 43). "Christ himself was and remains a man" (p. 43). Therefore "in actions which demand the character of ordination," and so above all in the case of the eucharist, the role of Christ "must be taken by a man" (p. 45).

(3) John Paul II, "On Reserving Priestly Ordination to Men Alone" (*Ordinatio Sacerdotalis*), Apostolic Letter (1994).[31] In this intervention the Pope argued less from Christ's example and more nearly from papal authority. Attempting to bring debate on women's ordination to an end within the church, he declared:

> In order that all doubt may be removed regarding a matter of great importance ... I declare that the Church has no authority whatsoever to confer priestly ordination on women and that this judgment is to be definitively held by all the Church's faithful.
>
> (p. 191)

The language about a judgment that must be "definitively held" by all immediately raised questions about whether the Pope understood himself to be speaking infallibly.

(4) "*Responsum ad Dubium* Concerning the Teaching Contained in *Ordinatio Sacerdotalis*" (1995).[32] In this brief document the Congregation for the Doctrine of the Faith declared that, in some sense, *Ordinatio Sacerdotalis* had the status of infallible teaching.

> *Dubium*: Whether the teaching that the Church has no authority whatsoever to confer priestly ordination on women ... is to be understood as belonging to the deposit of faith.
>
> *Responsum*: In the affirmative.

---

[31] Ibid., pp. 184–91. (Hereafter page references cited in the text.)
[32] Ibid., pp. 196–97.

This teaching was said to require "definitive assent," since it had been set forth "infallibly" by the "ordinary and universal Magisterium." New questions immediately arose about this appeal to the "ordinary magisterium." What conditions must be met in order for it to promulgate infallible teaching?

(5) Walter Cardinal Kasper, "Mission of Bishops in the Mystery of the Church: Reflections on the Question of Ordaining Women to Episcopal Office in the Church of England" (2006).[33] Cardinal Kasper's 2006 address to the Anglican House of Bishops included these words:

> A resolution in favour of the ordination of women to the episco-pate within the Church of England would certainly lower the temperature once more; in terms of the possible recognition of Anglican Orders, it would lead not only to a short-lived cold, but to a serious and long-lasting chill . . .
>
> Ecumenical dialogue in the true sense of the word has as its goal the restoration of full church communion. That has been the presupposition of our dialogue until now. That presupposition would realistically no longer exist following the introduction of the ordination of women to episcopal office . . .
>
> Above all – and this is the most painful aspect – the shared partaking of the one Lord's table, which we long for so earnestly, would disappear into the far and ultimately unreachable distance. Instead of moving towards one another we would co-exist along-side one another.

Kasper's sober words seem to suggest that ordaining women would bring an end to the quest for visible unity. The hopes of the modern ecumenical movement would grind to a halt.

Before turning to rebuttals of the Vatican statements, Eastern Orthodox views along the same lines may be noted. The words of

---

[33] www.vatican.va/roman_curia/pontifical_councils/chrstuni/card-kasper-docs/
rc_pc_chrstuni_doc_20060605_ kasper-bishops_en.html.

Alexander Schmemann have been selected for inclusion, both because they are representative and also because of his great prestige. In "A Letter to an [Episcopalian] Friend," he writes:

> The Orthodox Church is *against* women's priesthood ... [It] is alien to the Orthodox mind. For the Orthodox Church has never faced this question; it is for us totally extrinsic, a *casus irrealis* for which we find no basis ... The ordination of women to priesthood for us is tantamount to a radical and irreparable mutilation of the entire faith, the rejection of the whole Scripture – and needless to say, the end of all "dialogues" ... [It presents] the threat of an irreversible and irreparable act which, if it becomes reality, will produce a new, and this time I am convinced final, division among Christians, [and] will signify at least for the Orthodox the end of all dialogues.[34]

Like the Vatican, Schmemann rests his case on three points: the example of Jesus, the practice of the church through the ages in not ordaining women, and the need for the priest to serve as an icon of the male Jesus. He also sees women's ordination as effectively bringing an end not only to efforts for visible unity but also even to ecumenical dialogue.

Serious rebuttals have not been lacking. Roman Catholic scholars have meticulously dismantled the Vatican's shaky argumentation, Eastern Orthodox women have started to find their voice, and Reformational theologians have made a strong theological case for women's ordination that Catholic and Orthodox authorities have yet to take seriously.

---

[34] Alexander Schmemann, "Concerning Women's Ordination: A Letter to an [Episcopalian] Friend," *St. Vladimir's Theological Quarterly* 17 (1973), pp. 239–41. (Note that "Episcopal" describes a church; "Episcopalian," a member of that church. Schmemann makes a common error here.) See also Michael Azkoul, *Order of Creation, Order of Redemption: The Ordination of Women in the Orthodox Church* (Rollinsford: Orthodox Research Institute, 2007).

- A conclusive scholarly case has been made that Junia, whom Paul called an "apostle" (Rom. 16:7), was a woman (not, as traditionally assumed, a man).[35] Nympha in Col. 4:15 shared the same fate as Junia, in that the spelling of her name, too, was altered in the texts to take on a masculine form.
- Of the thirteen women referred to by Paul, seven stand out as leaders. By virtue of their leadership roles, they experienced a "countercultural equality" with men in the church.[36]
- Other documentary evidence has been unearthed suggesting that women's "ordination" was not entirely absent from primitive Christianity.[37]
- The patristic texts cited in *Inter Insigniores* have been challenged on the grounds that some of them involve a belief in women's inferiority, in contradiction to current church teaching, while the rest are inconclusive, because they do not directly touch the point at issue.[38]
- Intriguing evidence exists that some women may have enjoyed "ordination" until the early thirteenth century, though this was clearly a minority option.[39]

---

[35] Eldon Jay Epp, *Junia: The First Woman Apostle* (Minneapolis: Fortress Press, 2005); Richard Bauckham, *Gospel Women: Studies of the Named Women in the Gospels* (Grand Rapids: Wm. B. Eerdmans, 2002); Linda L. Belleville, "Woman Leaders in the Bible," in *Discovering Biblical Equality: Complementarity Without Hierarchy*, ed. Ronald W. Pierce and Rebecca Merrill Groothuis (Downers Grove: InterVarsity Press, 2004), pp. 118–20.

[36] Wendy Cotter, "Women's Authority Roles in Paul's Churches: Countercultural or Conventional?," *Novum Testamentum* 36 (1994), pp. 350–72; on p. 372.

[37] *Ordained Women in the Early Church: A Documentary History*, ed. Kevin Madigan and Carolyn Osiek (Baltimore: Johns Hopkins University Press, 2005); Ute E. Eisen, *Women Officeholders in Early Christianity: Epigraphical and Literary Studies* (Collegeville: Michael Glazier Books, 2000).

[38] John H. Wright, "Patristic Testimony on Women's Ordination in *Inter Insigniores*," *Theological Studies* 58 (1997), pp. 516–26.

[39] Gary Macy, "The Ordination of Women in the Early Middle Ages," *Theological Studies* 61 (2000), pp. 481–507.

• The claim that *Ordinatio Sacerdotalis* satisfies the necessary conditions for being "infallible" according to the "ordinary universal magisterium" is open to serious challenge on procedural grounds.[40]

Contrary to a prominent strand of Vatican argumentation, the question of women's ordination cannot be decided on historical grounds. Appeals to an "unbroken tradition" of not ordaining women, from apostolic times to the present, go well beyond the evidence.[41] "Ordination" in early centuries, of course, would not necessarily have meant the same thing as it came to mean after the thirteenth century. Nevertheless, enough precedent can be found, including suggestions of women presiding at the eucharist, to block automatically disallowing women's ordination by an appeal to history, if the case can be made on other grounds.

Among the Eastern Orthodox, perhaps the most vigorous voice in favor of women's ordination has been that of Elisabeth Behr-Sigel. In her 2003 Florovsky Lecture, delivered at St. Vladimir's Seminary, she affirmed:

> It is in the Church's name – *in persona Ecclesiae* – that the ordained minister, facing East, meaning toward the coming Christ, begs the Father to send the Spirit upon us and upon these gifts here offered, that they may be for us communion in the Body and Blood of Christ "offered up once and for all," as the Epistle to the Hebrews insists. And St. John Chrysostom proclaims that "it is Christ, made present by the Holy Spirit, who is the true minister of the mystery."

---

[40] Richard R. Galliardetz, "The Ordinary Universal Magisterium: Unresolved Questions," *Theological Studies* 63 (2002), pp. 147–71; Galliardetz, "Infallibility and the Ordination of Women," *Louvain Studies* 21 (1996), pp. 3–24; Charles Donahue, Jr., "Theology, Law and Women's Ordination," *Commonweal* 122 (June 2, 1995), pp. 11–16.

[41] See Karl Rahner, "Women in the Priesthood," in *Theological Investigations*, vol. 20, pp. 35–47 (*supra* n. 8). Rahner expresses serious reservations about the argumentation in *Inter Insigniores*.

Removing himself as individual, the priest – minister, meaning servant – turns his hands and his tongue over to Christ. Why could these hands and this tongue not be those of a Christian woman, baptized and chrismated, called by virtue of her personal gifts to a ministry of pastoral guidance, which implies presiding over the eucharist? As the Fathers – with the Gospel as their foundation – have always claimed, the hierarchy of spiritual gifts granted to persons has nothing to do with gender.[42]

Although still a minority position within Orthodoxy, this view is gaining respected adherents. "Such prominent Orthodox as the late Metropolitan Anthony of Sourozh (Anthony Bloom) and Bishop Kallistos of Diokeleia (Kallistos Ware) have said in recent years that Orthodox must face this question seriously, and Metropolitan Anthony made it clear that he was in favor of women's ordination."[43] The second edition of Ware's influential book *The Orthodox Church* displays decided sympathies in this direction.[44]

If the biblical evidence – including Jesus' choice of only males to be among the Twelve – is inconclusive (as the Pontifical Report itself implied), and if the historical record is not unmixed (as scholars have carefully documented), then much would seem to hang on the argument from iconic representation. Yet as Richard A. Norris has pointed out, despite the Vatican's stalwart appeal to tradition, ironically, this argument is "genuinely novel, untraditional," for Jesus' maleness was of no interest to patristic

---

[42] Elisabeth Behr-Sigel, "The Ordination of Women: A Point of Contention in Ecumenical Dialogue," unpublished lecture. Available online: Part 1: http://orthodoxwomensnetwork.org/storydetail.cfm?ArticleID=39; Part 2: http://orthodoxwomensnetwork.org/storydetail.cfm?ArticleID=40. See also Elisabeth Behr-Sigel and Kallistos Ware, *The Ordination of Women in the Orthodox Church* (Geneva: World Council of Churches, 2000).

[43] John Garvey, "The New Pope: An Orthodox View," *Commonweal* 132 (May 20, 2005), pp. 7–8.

[44] Timothy Ware, *The Orthodox Church*, 2nd edn. (London: Penguin Books, 1997), pp. 293–94.

christology. To make maleness essential to the Incarnation would introduce false and dangerous ideas into the mystery of redemption.[45]

The idea that only a male can represent Christ at the eucharist has been condemned with special force by T. F. Torrance. This teaching is false, because it contradicts basic elements in the doctrines of

- the incarnation and the new order of creation,
- the virgin birth, which sets aside male sovereignty and judges it as sinful,
- the hypostatic union of divine and human nature in the one Person of Jesus Christ who is of the same uncreated genderless Being as God the Father and God the Holy Spirit,
- the redemptive and healing assumption of complete human nature in Christ,
- the atoning sacrifice of Christ which he has offered once for all on our behalf, in our place, in our stead.
- And therefore it conflicts also with the essential nature of the Holy Eucharist and the communion in the body and blood of Christ given to us by him.[46]

Each of these points is elaborated in a pithy argument. A few excerpts will have to suffice:

> The idea that only a male can represent the Lord Jesus Christ at the Eucharist is a serious theological error.
>
> (p. 6)

---

[45] Richard A. Norris, Jr., "The Ordination of Women and the 'Maleness' of Christ,'" *Anglican Theological Review* 6 (1976), pp. 69–80; on p. 70.

[46] T. F. Torrance, *The Ministry of Women* (Edinburgh: Handsel Press, 1992), pp. 1–13; on pp. 12–13. (Hereafter cited by page number in the text.) See also Stanley J. Grenz and Denise Muir Kjesb, *Women in the Church: A Biblical Theology of Women in Ministry* (Downers Grove: InterVarsity Press, 1995); Paul K. Jewett, *The Ordination of Woman* (Grand Rapids: Wm. B. Eerdmans, 1980).

When used theologically, creaturely images in language about God have a referential, not a mimetic, relation to the divine realities.

(p. 8)

It is utterly unthinkable that the body and blood given to us by the Lord Jesus in our communion with him is to be regarded as restricted to male body and blood, for it was the body and blood of *the Son of Man*, the bread which came down from heaven.

(p. 9)

At the Eucharist the minister or priest does not act in his own name or in respect of his own status as a male human being, but only in the name of Jesus Christ and in virtue of his incarnate significance as the one Mediator between God and human being ... If the notion of image is used at all here at the Eucharist, it must be image, not in its picturing or mimetic sense, but in its referential sense in which the image points beyond itself altogether and in so doing retreats entirely out of the picture.

(p. 10)

It is upon Christ our ascended High Priest that the Father looks and only on the celebrating priest on earth as found in him. Thus, however we look at it, to insist that man, precisely as man or male, alone is able to represent Christ, would amount to a serious intrusion of male self-consciousness and assumed preeminence into our understanding of the priestly office of Christ, and would be tantamount to some psychological sacerdotalism and eucharistic Pelagianism.

(p. 12)

Through the incarnation, death and resurrection of the Lord Jesus Christ, humanity has thus been set upon an entirely new basis of divine grace, in which there is no respect of persons, and women share equally with men in all the grace-gifts or *charismata* of the Holy Spirit, including gifts for ministry in the church.

(p. 13)

The saving significance of the Incarnation is not that Christ entered male humanity, but that he assumed the flesh of all human beings, male and female, that all might be set free and made one. The presiding minister at the eucharist does not mimic Christ's maleness, but attests, receives, and distributes his saving flesh, *in persona Christi* and by the power of the Holy Spirit – a role of which no one is worthy, but for which any may be equipped, whether male or female, by that disruptive grace which breaks down every wall of division in order to make all things new.

Conclusion

To conclude: All churches need conversion in some ways, and each church needs conversion in its own way. I have argued that churches in the Reformed tradition (my own) need to embrace new ideas of real presence, eucharistic sacrifice, and ministerial office – ideas they thought they had to reject. I have urged them to take seriously the admonitions of other traditions, and especially of the high sacramental traditions. I have tried to show how this can be done without theological compromise, and I have cited precedents in the Reformers themselves. I have no illusion that these proposals will gain ready acceptance, yet without them (or something like them) the churches will never be made one.

At the same time I have ventured to make admonitions to the high sacramental churches. I have sided with the Orthodox against the Roman Catholics, and with the Catholics against the Eastern Orthodox, while always speaking only for myself, and therefore as one without authority. I have argued that the papacy must become more conciliar, more symbolic, and altogether more modest.

I have suggested that the problems surrounding apostolic succession could be rectified if adjustments were made from all sides. I have urged the Orthodox, who can be as exhilarating as they are exasperating, to be more flexible, less insular, and above all more self-critical. I have sided with the Protestants, against the Catholics and the Orthodox, in urging that the views of the faithful need to be given due weight in decision-making through clear structures of accountability in any future united church.

Above all, I have taken a stand on the question that most threatens to wreck the ecumenical movement. I have admonished the high sacramental churches to rethink their reactionary opposition to women's ordination. The stakes are high but the course is set. It makes no sense for the Roman Catholic Church to pretend that women's ordination in the Protestant churches, including the ordination of women bishops, can be reversed. As the Anglican Bishops of Durham and Salisbury have noted in their reply to Cardinal Kasper's 2006 address:

> The Lambeth Conference has already given the green light to ordaining women to the episcopate; all we are being asked now is whether we, in our Province, want to adopt for ourselves something to which worldwide Anglicanism has already given approval, and which can therefore not be seen within our own inter-provincial polity as communion-breaking.[47]

When the Cardinal threatens to withdraw, Durham and Salisbury rightly push back:

> Anglicans will naturally ask by what criteria Rome claims the right to introduce potentially divisive innovations in some areas, while advising Anglicans against developing in practice, rather than

---

[47] Tom Wright and David Stancliffe, "Women Bishops: A Response to Cardinal Kasper" (July 2006), unpublished. (Wright is the Biishop of Durham, and Stancliffe the Bishop of Salisbury.) www.fulcrum-anglican.org.uk/news/2006/20060721kasper.cfm?doc=126.

altering, the doctrine of the church, in others. In what sense would ordaining women to the episcopate alter the doctrine of the church?[48]

The Lutheran World Federation speaks for all of ecumenical Protestantism when it writes:

> The Lutheran World Federation is committed to the ordination of women. The LWF Eighth Assembly stated: "We thank God for the great and enriching gift to the church discovered by many of our member churches in the ordination of women to the pastoral office, and we pray that all members of the LWF, as well as others throughout the ecumenical family, will come to recognize and embrace God's gift of women in the ordained ministry and in other leadership responsibilities in Christ's church."[49]

Conversion in the churches, while perhaps appearing to bring loss, will always, when warranted, effect a boon.

Ut Unum Sint (1995) signaled an impressive recommitment of the Roman Catholic Church to the goal of visible unity. The widespread perception of an "ecumenical winter" is belied by astonishing breakthroughs achieved since that encyclical, and largely because of it. These have occurred most especially, for the Catholics, with the Anglicans and the Lutherans – both of which churches, along with others, have now ordained women bishops. As Kasper intimates, the Roman Catholic Church stands at a crossroads. It can either stay the course and move forward, or else pull back. If it chooses to do the latter, it could still work for unity with the Orthodox. Meanwhile, the Protestants could strive not only for a universal acceptance of the traditional threefold office,

---

[48] Ibid.

[49] "Episcopal Ministry within the Apostolicity of the Church," The Lund Statement of the Lutheran World Federation: A Communion of Churches (Lund, Sweden, March 26, 2007), unpublished ms., p. 8. www.lutheranworld.org/ LWF_Documents/LWF_The_Lund_Statement_2007.pdf.

but also for practical rectification in the formal aspects of episcopal succession. Success achieved independently on both these fronts – Catholic/Orthodox on the one hand, inter-Protestant on the other – might one day set the stage for greater renewal. But why should the Roman Catholic Church not choose instead to move forward, since even then the question of women's ordination will still remain?

Years ago Raymond E. Brown, the distinguished Roman Catholic New Testament scholar, proposed a better context for deciding this question in the Catholic Church. He envisioned giving women public roles in celebrating the eucharist: "allowing younger girls to serve at the altar, having women lectors, incorporating women into dialogue sermons, and having women distribute the eucharist." He also hoped women would be encouraged to receive theological training so that they could eventually assume teaching posts in Catholic seminaries. "When all of these things are done," he mused, "we may be in a better position to discuss intelligently the ordination of women priests."[50] It must be admitted, however, that thirty years later, while progress has been made, not enough along these lines has been achieved.

Brown saw a margin of hope in *Mysterium Ecclesiae* (1973), a declaration of the Congregation for the Doctrine of the Faith. "This document," he noted, "goes farther than the Catholic Church has ever gone before in recognizing the historical conditioning of the formulations of church dogma." Among other things, it acknowledges that "sometimes a dogmatic truth is expressed only incompletely, needing at a later date, and in a broader context of faith and knowledge, a fuller and more perfect expression."[51] This kind of acknowledgment will be required if ministerial ordination is ever to attain a fuller and more perfect expression.

---

[50] Raymond E. Brown, *Biblical Reflections on Crises Facing the Church* (New York: Paulist Press, 1975), p. 60n.

[51] Ibid., p. 66.

PART IV

Eucharist and social ethics

7 | The eucharistic transformation of culture

The purpose of this chapter is to reconsider H. Richard Niebuhr's book *Christ and Culture* by developing its implications for the eucharist.[1] More precisely, the intention is more the reverse, namely, to ask how the eucharist might bear on Niebuhr's question of Christ and culture. Although the eucharist was far from his mind, elements of Niebuhr's thought can be moved in this direction. A eucharistic relocation of the idea of Christ transforming culture promises not only to disclose weaknesses in Niebuhr's reasoning, but also to secure some of its strengths. Beyond Niebuhr, the goal is to sketch a eucharistic understanding of social ethics grounded in the meaning of the sacrament itself.

Reconsidering *Christ and Culture*

Ever since being proposed in the mid-twentieth century, H. Richard Niebuhr's idea of Christ transforming culture has enjoyed a remarkably favorable reception. Not surprisingly so, for it held out at least three advantages.

First, it moved beyond a narrowly individualistic notion of conversion. The prospect of transforming culture appealed to many who felt that there was more to the relevance of the gospel than simply converting the individual soul. Cultures, not just individuals, were in need of reform and renewal.

---

[1] H. Richard Niebuhr, *Christ and Culture* (New York: Harper & Row, 1951).

Second, it broke with Protestant individualism more broadly. The human self, on Niebuhr's view, was always a social self, not a solitary self. Individuals never existed apart from a complex network of social and cultural conditions by which they were shaped. The integrity of the gospel depended on seeing persons as persons in relation.

Finally, Niebuhr's idea offered an ennobling vision. The project of cultural transformation contrasted with other less appealing options: with every form of narrow withdrawal, every compromising social accommodation, every inducement toward weak resignation, every utopian excess. At a time of chronic anxiety about Christianity's status in the modern world, the thought of being called to transform the culture was, for many, an inspiring prospect.

The heart of Niebuhr's argument – his account of the five types by which Christ and culture had been related throughout history – only served to highlight the attractions of the conversionist option. Although Niebuhr would always find something worthwhile to notice in each type, little doubt could exist about his final preference.

Roughly speaking, Niebuhr evaluated the substance of his five types as follows.

- The sectarian type of cultural withdrawal (Christ against culture) was too antagonistic and severe, as well as too naive about the possibilities of escape from social sin.
- On the other hand, the accommodationist type (Christ of culture) was much the reverse, being too untroubled (ultimately) about the status quo and its possibilities for improvement.
- In turn, the synthetic type (Christ above culture), by presuming to build from culture to Christ, was at once too credulous about culture and too conciliatory about Christ, lacking an adequate sense of divine judgment.
- Meanwhile, like the sectarians, the dualists (Christ and culture in paradox) were too pessimistic about prospects for cultural betterment.

- Only the conversionists (Christ transforming culture) struck a proper balance between judgment and hope, being neither as suspicious toward culture as some (sectarians and dualists) nor as sanguine about it as others (accommodationists and synthesists).

Niebuhr's typology, however, has had its critics. The main objections fall into four points: his definition of culture was inadequate, his doctrine of Christ was defective, he was vague about the meaning of transformation, and he was unfair to the sectarian outlook. Before turning to the eucharist, a few observations are in order.

The charge that Niebuhr did not do justice to the sectarian type was advanced most forcefully by John Howard Yoder.[2] According to Yoder, all the other types relaxed the radical moral imperatives of Jesus in a way that only the sectarianians properly resisted. By finding something to affirm in each type, Niebuhr's very inclusiveness was finally a form of capitulation. The sectarian type, by contrast, withstood the drift toward relativism and compromise by insisting, against Niebuhr, that the gospel offered binding revelation, assured knowledge, and unyielding moral precepts (p. 81).

Moreover, these fixed certainties did not require Niebuhr's supposedly "monolithic" approach to culture, for culture was not one thing but many different things. "Each setting, each event, each relationship will open for us a set of options and challenges," insisted Yoder, "where we shall need to decide how to love our enemies, how to feed the hungry, how to keep our promises, how to make the earth fruitful, how to celebrate community, how to remember our heritage" (p. 89). Rather than wielding political power and permitting Christian involvement in the military,

[2] John Howard Yoder, "How H. Richard Niebuhr Reasoned: A Critique of *Christ and Culture*," in Glen H. Stassen, D. M. Yeager, and John Howard Yoder (Nashville: Abingdon, 1996), pp. 31–89. (Hereafter page numbers cited in text.)

sectarian Christians would resort to non-participation in order to remain loyal to Jesus. But within those limits, they would work for cultural betterment on an *ad hoc* basis.

Not published until 1996, though first drafted in 1958, Yoder's reflections on Niebuhr's *Christ and Culture* went through a long gestation period. Despite many fine observations, however, Yoder failed to consider a crucial point. In the end Niebuhr's typology was arguably less about substantive positions than it was about patterns of thought. Yoder made much of the charge that a figure like Tertullian did not conform perfectly to Niebuhr's sectarian type, and that Niebuhr was therefore wrong to imply inconsistency on Tertullian's part.

Niebuhr knew very well, however, and often remarked, that in practice no one represented a pure type. His point was not to squeeze mixed positions into little boxes called "types," but rather to illumine any given position with regard to its various modes of thought, some dominant, and others perhaps countervailing. By setting forth the basic logical options in the form of ideal types, Niebuhr offered categories of discernment by which the internal complexities of any position could be picked out. When his typology is seen less as a catalogue of substantive options and more as a formal analytical device, it becomes clear that Niebuhr was not pushing for unreasonable uniformity. There would seem to be no obstacle, for example, to taking Yoder's *ad hoc* counter-proposal on a case-by-case basis and subjecting it to a Niebuhrian typological analysis.

Culture, as Niebuhr defined it, was a highly differentiated phenomenon. In contrast to nature, it was the result of human efforts and purposes. It involved the full spectrum of arts, sciences, traditions, and social organizations. Two points in particular interested Niebuhr. First, culture was a repository of human values. It embodied an array of different and sometimes competing human goods as well as policies for attaining and conserving them. Second, culture was both temporal and pluralistic. A driving concern of *Christ and Culture* was how to relate "Christ" as something eternal, singular, and absolute to "culture" as something temporal, pluralistic, and relative.[3]

Certain difficulties in *Christ and Culture* emerge at this point. For Niebuhr, "Christ" was often little more than a cipher for "the absolute" while "culture" was a cipher for "the relative." Posed in this way, the problem addressed by the book was perhaps artificial. Because the absolute could never be fully accommodated by the relative, every strategy as represented by the five types had not only a certain limit but also a certain validity. But can the problem of "Christ and culture" really be grasped as that of relating the absolute to the relative?

Moreover, Niebuhr's "Christ" often seemed far from the ecumenical standards of Nicaea and Chalcedon.[4] In this book Christ functioned mainly to reveal the twin "absolutes" of God and the moral law. In turn, the God so revealed often seemed more like a cross between Fate and the Unconditioned than like the Holy Trinity of received dogma. Similarly, Christ himself seemed to have no clear trinitarian status. For Niebuhr, Christ was more nearly the center of loyalty than the object of faith. He was the revelation of God but not the person of God in self-revelation. He was more clearly the church's companion, prototype, and source than the incarnate Savior who died for our sins and rose again from the dead. He was fully human, perhaps divinely human, but in the end, it would seem, also merely human, though the matter was never really made clear.[5]

---

[3] Niebuhr, *Christ and Culture*, pp. 29–39.

[4] A colleague who knew him told me: "He was more orthodox in spirit than in theology."

[5] For a sympathetic account of this ambiguity, see Hans W. Frei, "The Theology of H. Richard Niebuhr," in *Faith and Ethics*, ed. Paul Ramsey (New York: Harper & Row, 1965), pp. 115–16. Frei points to a place in *Christ and Culture* where Niebuhr allows that his essentially "moral analysis" of Christ's character would not necessarily be incompatible with a "metaphysical" analysis of Christ's person.

To be sustained, the idea of Christ transforming culture would require a more robust understanding of Christ. It would also require a more robust understanding of two other matters, namely, transformation and the church. In Niebuhr's book the church was relegated largely to the margins. What role it might play in Christ's transformation of culture was never terribly clear. If anything, it was supposed to relate the absolute to the relative according to one of the types. Nevertheless, in his chapter on "Christ the Transformer of Culture," another possibility for the church became visible, if only by implication.

The dominant impression left by Niebuhr's book was that transforming culture should be a prime task of social ethics. However, though little noticed, another prospect was opened up with respect to the conversionist type. The transformation of culture – was that essentially something the church did, or something the church was? Niebuhr's example of Augustine as the "theologian of cultural transformation" (p. 208) pointed in the latter direction.

Augustine was praised for honing his Roman rhetorical skills to fit the service of Christ, for humanizing his previous Neoplatonism by subjecting it to the gospel, and for rethinking Ciceronian morals in the light of grace. He himself was "an example of what conversion of culture means" (p. 209). But if so, he himself "transformed culture" not by going forth and changing the world, but by reworking cultural materials to serve the needs of the church. "The Christian life," wrote Niebuhr at one point, "is cultural life converted" (p. 205). Transformed culture, from this point of view, would find its primary locus not in the world but in the church.

On this slender basis Frei asserts that Niebuhr's christology would "meet the test" of conforming to Chalcedon (p. 115). Frei is on more solid ground when he suggests that Niebuhr leaves us with little more than an "economic Trinitarianism," a polite way of saying "modalism" (p. 98). In any case his impressive essay is still arguably the best analysis we have of Niebuhr's theology.

The ensuing discussion will develop the following ideas.

- Christ himself is the transformer of culture.
- The transformation of culture is something the church is before it is something the church does.
- The church embodies, attests, and mediates Christ's saving work of cultural transformation, first as a status, then as a task.
- The central place where Christ takes earthly historical form as the transformer of culture is the eucharist.

The eucharist as a counter-cultural event

Although the relationship between "liturgy and ethics" has been the topic of many studies, they often lean in an instrumentalist direction. When described in more or less secular (as opposed to theological) terms, liturgy ends up being portrayed as the means to an end. The eucharist is depicted as a "source" or "influence" that has (or ought to have) beneficial social consequences. Social ethics becomes the overriding goal to which the eucharist is subordinate. Human agency and social influences end up dominating the discussion, with Christ being relegated to the shadows. Though Christ's eucharistic "presence" is never denied, his unique saving work gets short shrift, and the eucharist is not valued as an end in itself.

A good place to consider the social significance of the eucharist is Paul's discussion in 1 Cor. 11:17–34. Paul clearly expected the Corinthian celebration of the Lord's Supper to be a counter-cultural event. Yet instead of exemplifying the cultural transformation effected in Christ, the Corinthian eucharist served only to reproduce social divisions that prevailed in the surrounding culture. Paul's censure was severe.

Recent sociological research has clarified some of the more enigmatic aspects of this passage. It seems that the community would assemble in a wealthy member's house, where the Lord's Supper would be celebrated in conjunction with another meal.

Though many details remain obscure, at least this much can be surmised:

> The church at Corinth was composed of people from different social strata, the wealthy and the poor, as well as slaves and former slaves. It was customary for participants in the Lord's meal to bring from home their own food and drink. The wealthy brought so much food and drink that they could indulge in gluttony and drunkenness [in conformity with existing social customs]. The poor who came later, however, had little or nothing to bring, with the result that some went hungry ...
>
> The Corinthians' meal ... had become a social problem for the Christian community: (1) The meal made beforehand was apparently different in quantity and quality. (2) Some members [the wealthier] began eating before the others arrived and before the Lord's supper took place. (3) ... The ones who arrived late [i.e., slaves, former slaves, and the poor] found no room in the *triclinium*, which was the dining room [a privileged place] where regularly only twelve could recline for the meal.[6]

The end result was a pattern of hierarchical seating prior to the Lord's Supper, with the best seats reserved for those of higher rank. Disparities in food and drink were openly in evidence, in quality as well as quantity, with some persons having more than enough while others had next to nothing. The community was sundered by a display of conspicuous consumption at the expense of the poor and needy.

The celebration of the Lord's Supper at Corinth was thus disfigured, as Paul saw it, by a sorry spectacle of inequalities: inequalities of class (haves / have nots) (v. 21), of status (high/low) (vv. 21–22), of consumption (excess/want) (v. 21), and most disturbingly of regard (honor/shame) (v. 22).

---

[6] Panayotis Coutsoumpos, *Paul and the Lord's Supper: A Socio-Historical Investigation* (New York: Peter Lang, 2005), p. 105.

Paul analyzed the disorder into two parts, a lesser and a greater. The lesser disorder was the conjunction of the two meals, and the solution was simply to disjoin them. Other meals, Paul urged pointedly, should take place at home (v. 22). While not directly denouncing the gastronomic excesses of the privileged, Paul left little doubt that he saw them as contrary to the gospel, and especially to the eucharist.

The more grievous disorder struck a blow at the heart of the community. Humiliating the poor, neglecting the needy, and conspicuous consumption in the context of the eucharistic assembly were an affront to the gospel. Christ's sacrificial sharing of himself, under the eucharistic forms of his body and blood (vv. 23–26), had social implications.[7] It required believers not only to conform to Christ in his sacrificial self-giving (cf. Eph. 5:2), but also to rise above cultural antagonisms of religion, ethnicity, status, and gender: "for all of you are one in Christ Jesus" (Gal. 3:28). In the eucharistic assembly, deeds of humiliation, neglect and self-indulgence were beyond appalling. They were self-destructive.

Humiliating those who had nothing (v. 22) threatened the community by splitting it into factions (v. 19). The Corinthians had enmeshed themselves in a tangle of contradictions between Christ and culture. By deferring to the wealthy at the expense of the poor, they could only dishonor the church. "Or do you despise the church of God?" (v. 22). They were virtually excommunicating themselves from the sacrament. "When you meet together, it is not the Lord's supper that you eat" (v. 20). Above all, they could not abuse the poor in their midst while leaving the Lord himself unscathed. A literal translation would read: "Whoever ... eats the bread or drinks the cup of the Lord in an unworthy manner will be guilty of the Lord's body and blood" (v. 27). Contrary to much

---

[7] "Paul reminds us that the Master gave up everything, including himself, for us, whereas we are reluctant even to share a little food with our fellow believers." John Chrysostom, *Homilies on the Epistles of Paul to the Corinthians* 27.5.

traditional interpretation, the "unworthy partaking" was not a matter of inward disposition or general moral behavior, but precisely a matter of communal behavior in the eucharistic assembly. Humiliating the needy was the offense, and doing so at the Lord's Supper was tantamount to crucifying Christ. You will be guilty, Paul warned the offending social elite, of his body and blood.

The Corinthians had failed in *discerning the body* and therefore brought judgment down upon their heads (v. 29). While the phrase "discerning the body" referred essentially to reconciliation as the community's *raison d'être*, it carried a wider resonance at the same time. Having failed to discern that they were all one body, one community, in Christ (cf. 1 Cor. 12:12–13), what the Corinthians had failed to see was that they belonged inseparably to one another, that they were committed to one another's care (cf. 1 Cor. 10:24).

At the same time, however, as the body *of Christ*, they belonged not to themselves but to another (Rom. 7:4), namely, to the crucified and risen Lord. Therefore, the phrase "discerning the body" gestured also toward the risen Christ and his death.

Moreover, since Christ was offering himself eucharistically in the form of his body and blood, an allusion to the consecrated elements cannot be ruled out. The gift of the eucharist was precisely the gift of participating in his body, which had been given over to death for their sakes (v. 24). The threefold failure of discernment was therefore communal, christological, and eucharistic; for Christ, the community, and the eucharist finally coalesced into one indivisible body, a seamless web of unity-in-distinction.

Although it may seem implausible to modern sensibilities to suppose that weakness, sickness, and death could result from this failure of discernment (v. 31), Paul was essentially making a spiritual point. The body of Christ in Corinth was imperiled by a sickness unto death. By entering into contradiction with themselves, the Corinthians had also entered into contradiction with Christ and the eucharist. They could not undo their baptism, their union with one another and with Christ; they could only offend against it.

For Paul, their communal identity as the body of Christ was an indicative before it was an imperative. It could be resisted or restored but not escaped. When they entered into contradiction with it, it could only boomerang against them, bringing dire consequences in its train. Where once life had been offered and received, the eucharist became an omen of death (v. 29). The signs of divine judgment in Corinth were meant to be remedial, Paul warned, leading to repentance before it was too late (vv. 31–32).

Undergirding the social significance of the eucharist for Paul was his understanding of the blood of Christ. Christ's blood, as offered under the eucharistic form of the cup, was the divinely ordained means of reconciliation, both vertically and horizontally. By its outpouring on the cross, the world had been reconciled to God. Peace had been established, sins had been forgiven, and the walls of social hostility had been broken down. The solidarity of humankind in sin had been displaced by a solidarity in grace. Christ's blood was not (as some have claimed) the blood of martyrdom, but the blood of expiation. It was not essentially an example to be imitated, but a mystery to be honored and confessed. Its significance was exclusively unique to itself.

Significantly, Paul often wrote about these themes in the aorist and the perfect tenses. For him reconciliation in Christ was to be grasped as Gospel first and Law second – a fact before it was a demand. Reconciliation was fully worked out *extra nos* (apart from us) before it was effected *in nobis* (in and among us). It was a divine gift, finished and perfect in itself, and only then a corresponding task. Whether vertically or horizontally, reconciliation was not something to be supplemented, but something to be received; not something to be repeated, but something to be attested; not something in which to collaborate, but something in which to participate. It could only be mediated for what it was – a *fait accompli* prior to ensuing possibilities, the "already" that grounded the "not yet." It was not an ideal but a divine reality.

Even the horizontal dimension of reconciliation – its social aspect – was not primarily a matter of ethics. The most important declaration of this point appeared in Ephesians:

> But now in Christ Jesus you who once were far off have been brought near by the blood of Christ. For he is our peace; in his flesh he has made both groups into one and has broken down the dividing wall, that is, the hostility between us. He has abolished the law with its commandments and ordinances, that he might create in himself one new humanity in place of the two, thus making peace, and might reconcile both groups to God in one body through the cross, thus putting to death that hostility through it.
>
> (Eph. 2:13–16)

According to apostolic teaching, the costly work – the shed blood – by which entrenched divisions[8] have been overcome belongs to Christ alone (v. 13). He has put them to death in his person – "in his flesh" (v. 14) – that he might then remove them from the world (vv. 15–16). Implicit in this teaching is a complex eschatology. What has been overcome in principle is being mediated here and now, and is yet to be unveiled in its final form. Christ has caused a social transformation by his blood that finds its initial expression in the community of faith. The church is essentially a fellowship of reconciliation, which (despite its failings) stands as the provisional sign of that which is promised to all.

While Christ is spoken of in the active voice, those addressed are spoken of in the passive voice (v. 13). The groups in conflict are the objects of Christ's saving work (vv. 14–16). Certainly the grammar does not imply that those in need of reconciliation are expected to remain merely passive, but it does make them receptive and dependent. The reconciled community can arise only from a posture of prayer. What it cannot in fact achieve of itself – the breaking down of dividing walls – it receives by grace.

---

[8] Symbolized most basically by the Jew/Gentile division, though not restricted to it.

Grace is never manipulative though it is always constitutive. It allows a measure of cooperation without ceasing to be what it is as the true origin and cause. Social ethics without grace would be a contradiction in terms, because it would leave the central acting subject out of account. Believers are called to manifest among themselves the unity achieved in Christ – that is, to take the gift and become what they are. Conversely, they are called to resist and banish every impulse toward social division and humiliation.

> For in the one Spirit we were all baptized into one body – Jews or Greeks, slaves or free – and we were all made to drink of one Spirit.
>
> (1 Cor. 12:13)

> There is no longer Jew or Greek, there is neither slave or free, there is neither male and female; for all of you are one in Christ Jesus.
>
> (Gal. 3:28)

> We, who are many, are one body in Christ, and individually we are members one of another.
>
> (Rom. 12:5)

> Because there is one bread, we who are many are one body, for we all partake of the one bread.
>
> (1 Cor. 10:17)

The community is called to attest, mediate, and anticipate the unity of Christ in the eucharistic assembly. It does so only as Christ attests, mediates, and anticipates himself as the host who distributes the sacramental gifts (cf. 1 Cor. 10:4). As suggested in a previous chapter, mediation, attestation, and anticipation are essentially functions of Word and Sacrament. If the Word (Scripture and preaching) is associated primarily with bearing witness, and the Sacrament (baptism and the Lord's Supper) primarily with mediation, and both with anticipation, then it might be said that the Word mediates what it attests, while the Sacrament attests what it mediates, while both anticipate the promised future. The differences would be merely relative. The Sacrament would be a visible Word, and the Word an audible Sacrament.

Moreover, suppose that witness gives us the identity of Jesus Christ, while mediation gives us his presence, and both impart the promised future. If so, then both Word and Sacrament would attest Christ's identity, mediate his presence, and anticipate his future, though in each in its own way. This difference might be captured, to some extent, as that between hearing and seeing.[9] The Word would have the particular advantage of allowing us to hear that which cannot be seen.

In 1 Cor. 11:24–26, Paul states that the cup is to be drunk in *remembrance* of Christ, and the Lord's death *proclaimed* until he comes. Remembering and proclaiming (*anamnesis* and *kataggellein*), even as expressed in symbolic actions, would be impossible apart from the Word.[10] The eucharistic elements are obviously mute in themselves, and the symbolic actions of the sacrament would not be self-interpreting apart from the liturgical words that accompany them. Proclaiming and remembering depend essentially on the Word, even in the course of the liturgy.

At the same time, the reverse is also true. Just as the meal is interpreted by the Word, so also is the Word interpreted by – and embodied in – the meal. "For as often as you eat this bread and drink the cup, you proclaim the Lord's death until he comes" (1 Cor. 11:26). The Supper is itself a proclamation of the gospel.[11]

---

[9] Of course, the sacramental elements, being palpable as well as visible, involve more senses than merely seeing; the word as read on the scriptural page is visible to the naked eye, and so on.

[10] "The *anamnesis* of Christ ... takes place in the 'proclaiming' of Christ ... For *kataggellein* is always a matter of the word." Otfried Hofius, "The Lord's Supper and the Lord's Supper Tradition: Reflections on 1 Corinthians 11:23b–25," in *One Loaf, One Cup*, ed. Ben F. Meyer (Macon: Mercer University Press, 1991), pp. 108, 107.

[11] For the idea of the Supper itself as the proclamation of the gospel, see Beverly Roberts Gaventa, "'You Proclaim the Lord's Death': 1 Corinthians 11:26 and Paul's Understanding of Worship," *Review & Expositor* 80 (1983), pp. 377–87.

It is proclamation in the form of a deed. The Lord's death is proclaimed in its saving significance, and therefore also in its cultural relevance, by the eucharist. The eucharist embodies the gospel as a sacramental and cultural event.[12]

The death of Christ is the death of death, and therefore of the things that make for death. By virtue of the Holy One who died, this death involves a transvaluation of all values, or distorted "values," and a repudiation of what Paul calls "the flesh." The "flesh" finds cultural expression in every form of social humiliation and injustice. Yet, in the death of Christ, death dies, humiliation is humiliated, and social injustice is exposed for what it is. The lost, the humiliated, and the needy are taken up, by the cross, into the body of Christ, in whom they are restored, exalted, and filled with good things. To turn the sacrament into an occasion for re-humiliating the poor or once again disregarding the hungry would be tantamount to re-crucifying Christ. For the crucified Christ has made the poor and the needy his own.

Just as the Word belongs to the eucharist, and the eucharist depends on the Word, so also does the oneness of the community. It belongs to the eucharist and depends on the Word. The unity of the community is an article of faith. The reality and promise of that unity are attested by the Word even when contradicted by communal practices. The eucharist in itself does not create the community, though it does nurture and sustain it. It is Christ who creates the community through Word and Sacrament. And he does so primarily through the Word, since the Word is prior to, embedded in, and more extensive than the Sacrament, though by the same token it might also be said that the Sacrament is more

---

[12] The idea of the eucharist as a form of proclamation is endorsed by both John Paul II and the Lima document. At the same time they affirm that the relevant proclamation is a matter of both Word and Sacrament. See *Ecclesia de Eucharistia* (Nos. 4, 5, 10, 14, 41), in *Origins* 32 (May 1, 2003), pp. 753, 755–68; and *Baptism, Eucharist and Ministry*, Faith and Order Paper No. 111 (Geneva: World Council of Churches, 1982) (E 3, 7, 27).

intensive, more graphic, and more corroborative than the Word. The primacy of the Word is such that it is efficacious apart from the Sacrament in a way that the Sacrament, for all its density, is not efficacious apart from the Word. The Word is fulfilled by the Sacrament, while the Sacrament is elucidated by the Word. Yet strictly, it is only the Word, not the Sacrament, that is absolutely necessary for salvation. Normally, however, the two are mutually reinforcing and mutually interdependent, so that either would suffer without the other.

Paul's reprimand is a case in point. In order to restore the community in its conduct of the eucharist, Paul had to reach beyond the Sacrament itself. Recalling the eucharistic words of institution was essential though not enough (vv. 23–25). Strong words of admonition were also needed (vv. 17–18, 27–34). Through them the presence of an authority beyond his own was invoked. Paul believed his apostolic authority was grounded in a center beyond itself. As we read in a different context, it was a matter of "God ... making his appeal through us" (2 Cor. 5:20). The words of admonition were the words of the apostle, but the voice was the voice of Christ.

Therefore, the Word at once grounded the efficacy of the Sacrament while also extending beyond it. The witness of the Word was needed to mediate the presence of Christ when the eucharistic assembly went astray. The eucharist could do many things. Like the Word, it attested Christ's presence and mediated it while also anticipating the eschatological banquet. Over and above the Word, it enhanced Christ's presence by giving it physical, sacramental form. When properly conducted, the eucharist displayed the shape of the new community as a counter-cultural event. "All of you are one in Christ Jesus" (Gal. 3:28). But the Sacrament by itself, so rich in symbolic concentration, could neither elaborate on the full range of the gospel nor rectify its own abuse.

The eucharistic assembly was called to be a counter-cultural community, because it was essentially an eschatological community. Its eager expectation was based on memory, while its remembering was filled with hope, because it looked beyond itself to the risen, ascended, and coming Christ. The community could contradict itself though not destroy itself, for its life was "hidden with Christ in God" (Col. 3:3). At the same time it could never do more than approximate the new social being it was called to represent. It was always dependent on the vital surplus of the Word in proclamation and hope, by which it and its surrounding culture were directed to that which was not yet seen.

In short, the community was kept by the Word even when the Word was not kept by the community.[13] Despite every form of willful corruption, whether within itself or without, the eucharistic assembly had been appointed to be and become a beacon of hope. It testified by its very existence – in the Sacrament and under the Word – that the entrenched social divisions of the present time were "not worthy to be compared with the glory which shall be revealed in us" (Rom. 8:18, KJV).

The eucharist as Christ transforming culture

The eucharist has more commonly been regarded as entailing a transformation of nature than of culture. The parallels, however, can be instructive. An admirable account of nature's eucharistic transformation appears in the work of Eric Mascall.

It is a strength of Mascall's important, if now neglected, work *Corpus Christi*[14] that it regards eucharistic sacrifice as inseparable from eucharistic communion. There is, nevertheless, a notable

---

[13] See Karl Barth, *Church Dogmatics*, vol. II, part 1 (Edinburgh: T. & T. Clark, 1956), pp. 172–78, esp. p. 176.
[14] E. L. Mascall, *Corpus Christi: Essays on the Church and the Eucharist* (London: Longmans, Green, & Co., 1953). (Page references cited in the text. Capital letters are sometimes dropped in the quotations.)

weakness insofar as eucharistic communion is made subordinate to the sacrifice; for that would be to elevate the means over the end, if indeed Christ's sacrifice is the door to eternal life in communion with God. In any case, for Mascall, there is no eucharistic sacrifice that does not lead to communion, and no eucharistic communion that does not depend on the sacrifice made present in the eucharist.

Accordingly, Mascall distinguishes "three great moments" within a eucharistic liturgy: the offertory, the consecration, and the communion. In the offertory, the church solemnly lifts up the bread and wine as a gift to God. In the consecration, these gifts are transformed into Christ's body and blood. And in the communion, the gifts are then given back to the church as supernatural food. Mascall's orientation, though more vertical than horizontal, deserves to be taken seriously.

The vertical element is indispensable. The eucharistic sacrifice presupposes that fellowship with God (vertical) is the necessary ground of fellowship among human beings (horizontal). At the same time, of course (though underdeveloped by Mascall), the reverse is also true: human fellowship is a necessary concomitant of fellowship with God, a point that has been stressed and to which we will return. Whether vertically or horizontally, however, everything in the eucharist depends on the community's participation in Christ's sacrificial self-offering to God.

Mascall suggests that in the offertory the human creature assumes the role of being "nature's priest." Since Christ's work is cosmic in scope, the material creation needs, no less than humankind, "to be brought into the sphere of divine redemption, to be re-made by Christ and in Christ. And this is surely what happens in the eucharist." The material objects of bread and wine are offered to God in order that they may become part of Christ's sacrifice and thereby "transformed by the divine acceptance" (pp. 179–80). Thus, writes Mascall, the eucharist is "the sacramental and eschatological representation" not only of the redeemed community, but also of "the restored and transfigured universe" (p. 180).[15]

The eucharistic consecration is the moment of transformation. In it the bread and wine, as fruits of the earth, "pass not only through the hands of nature's priest but through the hands of the supernatural priest, the Incarnate Lord, acting through the organs of his mystical priestly body the church" (p. 180). Bread and wine, produced from the earth out of grain and grape, are appointed by Christ to become his body and blood.

Mascall's account of the liturgy would be strengthened if it took the Holy Spirit more fully into account. The offertory, the consecration, and the communion all depend on the *epiclesis*, for they all take place not only by the Word but in the Spirit. For it is in the Spirit that the gifts are offered through the Son and to the Father. Again, it is in the Spirit that communion with the Father is effected through the Son. Finally, it is in and through the Spirit that the gifts of bread and wine become Christ's body and blood as the vehicles of offering and communion. At the same time, it is in the Spirit that past and future, cross and feast, are made sacramentally available in the eucharist, as *anamnesis* and *prolepsis*.

If the offertory is seen as a passage of the sacramental gifts from earth to heaven, and the communion as their reverse transmission from heaven to earth – each time in the Word and by the Spirit – then the consecration is the transitional point at which the inexpressible takes place. It is "the transformation by God's acceptance of the gifts that are offered to him" (p. 184). Natural gifts are elevated into the supernatural. The ordinary is transfigured into the ineffable. Earthly food and drink become Christ's life-giving flesh and blood. The consecration of the bread and wine includes the promise that the whole earth is to be made new. "Behold,

---

[15] Though beyond the scope of this chapter, the idea of care for the earth and respect for the integrity of creation might be developed in this context.

I make all things new" (Rev. 21:5, KJV). The eucharist gives the sacramental expression to Christ transforming nature.

> Love is that liquor sweet and most divine,
> Which my God feels as blood; but I, as wine.
>
> (George Herbert)

Mascall's three moments of the liturgy pertain likewise to the community. When the gifts of bread and wine are offered to God, the community simultaneously offers itself in a sacrifice of thanks and praise. As Augustine noted: "The church herself is offered in the offering she makes to God."[16] In the eucharist the community offers itself to God in Christ and through the Spirit, even as by the Spirit Christ offers himself in and through the community. Again Augustine:

> Thus, he is both the priest who offers and the sacrifice which is offered; and he intended that there should be a daily sign of this in the sacrament of the church's sacrifice. For the church, being the body of which he is the head, is taught to offer herself through him.[17]

The point was restated by Luther with Christ at the center as the chief acting subject. It is not so much we who offer Christ as a sacrifice, observed Luther, as Christ who offers us.

> And in this way it is permissible, yes, profitable, to call the mass a sacrifice; not on its own account, but because we offer ourselves as a sacrifice along with Christ. That is, we lay ourselves on Christ ... and do not otherwise appear before God with our prayer, praise and sacrifice except through Christ and his mediation ... Not that we offer the sacrament, but that by our praise, prayer and sacrifice

---

[16] Augustine, *City of God*, x.6. From Augustine, *City of God against the Pagans*, ed. R. W. Dyson (Cambridge: Cambridge University Press, 1998), p. 400.

[17] Augustine, *City of God*, x.20; ibid., p. 422.

we move him and give him occasion to offer himself for us in heaven and ourselves with him.[18]

In the consecration of the gifts, as explained by Mascall, it was their acceptance by God that transformed the elements into Christ's body and blood. Likewise, we may say that in the consecration, it is the community's acceptance by God, by the Word and in the Spirit, that transforms its members into Christ's mystical body. That the people might be transformed with the gifts is the regular subject of eucharistic prayer. All the prayers suggest, however, that the transformation of culture has a vertical as well as a horizontal dimension.

Culture's vertical transformation occurs as Christ liberates the Gentiles from idolatry (Rom. 1:25) and the Jews from religious boasting (Rom. 2:17) – "for all have sinned and fall short of the glory of God" (Rom. 3:23) – by instituting eucharistic worship (1 Cor. 11:23–25). Through being united with Christ in his sacrifice, the newly formed fellowship of reconciliation, the undivided community of Jews and Gentiles, is made to be the mystical body of which Christ himself is the head. The gifts, the reconciled community, and Christ himself are all made to be one in the eucharistic sacrifice (in a differentiated unity). As the community offers itself to God in and with the gifts, Christ offers the community to God, in the Spirit, in and with the paschal sacrifice of his body and blood. As accepted by God, the consecrated gifts of Christ's body and blood are then given back to the community as the means of his union with them and of their communion with him.

When the faithful come up to the altar to receive Holy Communion, the truth is not so much that the body and blood of Christ are being given to them for their sanctification as that they are being drawn up into Christ for the building of his body; the

---

[18] Martin Luther "Treatise on the New Testament," in *Luther's Works*, vol. 35 (Philadelphia: Fortress Press, 1960), p. 99. Again, it would be possible for Luther's point to be restated by making the Spirit explicit.

sacrament does not disperse Christ among the faithful, it unites the faithful in Christ.

(p. 183)

It is precisely as worship that the eucharist is the sacrament of Christ transforming culture. The cultural transformation effected by Christ is first of all liturgical. "It is indeed our highest privilege and our most insistent duty that we should worship God," writes Mascall, "but it is salutary that when we come to worship him we should be reminded in the most forceful way that his response to our worship is to give a blessing to us" (p. 175). Human culture, as everywhere infused with corruptions of idolatry, and human religion, as disfigured by the futility of self-justification (even under the divine covenant with Israel and not least in the church[19]), are defeated by Christ on the cross and transformed by his institution of the eucharist.

When the community offers itself to God in the eucharist, with a sense of its own unworthiness, in and through the mediation of Christ and by his Spirit, it is acting not only as nature's priest but also as culture's priest. The community's priestly self-offering – and its inclusion in the self-offering of Christ the great High Priest – occurs at once for its own sake and yet also and all the more for the sake of the world. The eucharist is a liturgical foreshadowing of that liberation from idolatry and religious superiority which is slated to come to all. It is the sacramental expression – at the most primal and comprehensive level, that is, the religious level – of Christ transforming culture.

> All the ends of the earth shall remember
>   and turn to the LORD;
> and all the families of the nations
>   shall worship before him. (Ps. 22:27)

---

[19] And especially in the stiff-necked church, in all its factions and self-satisfied forms, as it resists the repentance necessary for reunion.

For all the gods of the peoples are idols,
   but the LORD made the heavens ...
Worship the LORD in holy splendor;
   tremble before him, all the earth. (Ps. 96:5, 9)

Then I looked, and I heard around the throne and the living creatures and the elders the voice of many angels, numbering myriads of myriads and thousands of thousands, saying with a loud voice, "Worthy is the Lamb who was slain, to receive power and wealth and wisdom and might and honor and glory and blessing!" And I heard every creature in heaven and on earth and under the earth and in the sea, and all there in, saying, "To him who sits on the throne and to the Lamb be blessing and honor and glory and might forever and ever!"

(Rev. 5:11–13, RSV)

Eucharistic sacrifice, as presented by Mascall, becomes a focal point around which many bewildering complexities can be sorted out. The eucharist looks forward in anticipation as well as backward in remembrance. It looks upward to worship in heaven as well as sideward to culture on earth. It actualizes a promise not only personal but social, and not only social but cosmic. It looks to Christ in his priestly office as well as to Christ in his royal office, and to both as proclaimed in his prophetic office. The altar at which it is celebrated is also a table. It anticipates a Messianic Banquet while making present a once-for-all sacrifice. These apparent polarities are united by Mascall in a beautiful image of the end of all things:

They [the apostles] will be seated with their Master, who is himself the Apostle of the Father, at the messianic banquet, which, because it is the banquet of his crucified and ascended body and blood, is at the same time the perpetual liturgy wherein the Father is glorified by the eucharistic offering of him who is the Son by nature and who includes within himself all those who, because they are his

269

members, are [children] of the Father by grace and adoption, and who in their organic unity are his mystical body and bride, the catholic church, one flesh with him. And in this perpetual liturgy, wherein the church will for ever contemplate and adore the Father, gazing at him as it were through the eyes of Christ who is her head, everything will be transformed but nothing will be destroyed.

(pp. 30–31)

Royal motifs are here combined with priestly motifs, those of the Messianic Banquet with those of the eucharistic offering. The banquet is a perpetual liturgy in which the Father is worshipped through the Son and in the Spirit. The office of the true King is fulfilled along with that of the great High Priest, according to the order of Melchizedek (cf. Heb. 5:10; 7:1). The people of God are incorporated by the Spirit into the Son's eternal self-offering to the Father in an act of perpetual adoration and praise.

The cultural transformation embodied in the eucharist thus ends as it began in worship, and worship that takes the form of a paschal meal. The banquet is a liturgy, even as the liturgy is an everlasting eucharist. Christ's body and blood – once sacrificed on the cross, then transfigured into consecrated gifts – are the center that unifies all things, in an endless self-giving by the Son to the Father in the Spirit, and so also by us, and of the Father to the Son in the Spirit, and so also to us. The eucharist as celebrated on earth participates here and now in the liturgy of heaven above while receiving all its substance from the Messianic Banquet yet to come.

"You must sit down," says Love, "and taste my meat."
So I did sit and eat.

(George Herbert)

What Mascall does not adequately bring out is that the consecrated elements are meant not only to be offered but also to be shared. Offering may be thought of as an upward or Godward movement on the vertical axis between heaven and earth. It is essentially a priestly act that relies centrally on Christ's unique mediation. As our High Priest, the incarnate Son has offered himself in the Spirit to the Father, once and for all, in our stead and for our sakes. He has lived out the life of faithfulness to God that we have failed to live, and he has taken the consequences of our disobedience to himself in order that we may live.

> [We have a high priest] who in every respect has been tested as we are, yet without sin.
>
> (Heb. 4:15)

> For our sake he made him to be sin who knew no sin, so that in him we might become the righteousness of God.
>
> (2 Cor. 5:21)

> He was wounded for our transgressions,
>   crushed for our iniquities;
> upon him was the punishment that made us whole,
>   and by his bruises we are healed.   (Isa. 53:5)

Mascall rightly sees that in the eucharist "the whole sacrificial action of Christ, centered in the cross ... is made sacramentally present in his church ... present in the unique mode of a sacrament" (p. 96). He sees that "the Mass is therefore neither a new sacrifice, nor part of the one sacrifice; it *is* the one sacrifice in its totality, present under a sign" (p. 97).[20]

By contrast, however, eucharistic sharing may be thought of as a double movement along two axes. It is at once a downward movement along the vertical axis, running from heaven to earth, from Christ in the Spirit to us, as well as a sideward movement

---

[20] Whether Mascall entirely grasps the once-for-all significance of Christ's saving death, however, is open to question. He rightly sees the continuity of the eucharist with Christ's sacrifice on the cross yet underestimates their asymmetry and distinction. He underestimates what T. F. Torrance has called "the dimension of depth."

along the horizontal axis within the community, from one human being in the Spirit to another. It is Christ's sharing of himself with the community through the consecrated gifts of bread and wine, and our sharing of ourselves in the eucharistic community with one another, through the kiss of peace and works of love. "Bread is meant to be shared," writes Xavier Léon-Dufour, "especially with the hungry; this sharing is the fundamental characteristic of the righteous."[21] Eucharistic sharing marks precisely that moment of communion which Mascall mentions but fails to develop.

Near the end of his *First Apology*, Justin Martyr writes:

> Those who have the means help all those who are in want, and we continually meet together. And over all that we take to eat we bless the creator of all things through God's Son Jesus Christ and through the Holy Spirit. And on the day named after the sun all, whether they live in the city or countryside, are gathered together in unity. Then the records of the apostles or the writings of the prophets are read as long as there is time. When the reader has concluded, the presider in a discourse admonishes and invites us into the pattern of these good things. Then we all stand together and offer prayer. And, as we said before, when we have concluded the prayer, bread is set out to eat, together with wine and water. The presider likewise offers up prayer and thanksgiving, as much as he can, and the people sing their assent saying the *amen*. There is a distribution of the things over which thanks have been said and each person participates, and these things are sent by deacons to those who are not present. Those who are prosperous and who desire to do so, give what they wish, according to each one's own choice, and the collection is deposited with the presider. He aids orphans and widows, those who are in want through disease or through another cause, those who are in prison, and foreigners

---

[21] Xavier Léon-Dufour, *Sharing the Eucharistic Bread* (New York: Paulist Press, 1987), pp. 58–59.

who are sojourning here. In short, the presider is a guardian to all who are in need.

(*1 Apology* 67)[22]

Where idolatry and self-justification are banished by the power of Christ's sacrificial love, indifference to the needy also necessarily disappears.

Never turn away those in need, but always share all things with your brother [or sister], and never say that your possessions are exclusively your own, because if you share in eternal things, how much more in things that are temporary.

(*Didache* 4.8)

According to the *Didache*, notes Stevenson, "confession of sins and reconciliation" were seen as "a regular feature of the eucharistic assembly." The "pure" or "undefiled" eucharistic offering "must not be despoiled by dissensions in the community."[23] The eucharist was expected to express the overcoming in Christ of every cultural division, especially those rooted in enmity, while at the same time committing all who partook of it to sharing with the poor.

Three illustrations may help to make the point. The first is taken from my personal experience with the International Protestant Church of Zurich (IPC).[24] The IPC is a member of the Association of International Churches in Europe, the Middle East and Africa (AICEMEA), a worldwide association of English-speaking congregations. It includes, by its own description, "believers from six continents – business people, expatriates, diplomats, refugees, missionaries, and students. What brings them all together is the English language and their love for Christ."[25]

[22] As translated by Gordon W. Lathrop, *Holy Things: A Liturgical Theology* (Minneapolis: Fortress Press, 1993), p. 45.

[23] Kenneth W. Stevenson, *Eucharist and Offering* (New York: Pueblo, 1986), p. 15.

[24] Website at www.ipc-zurich.org/index.html.

[25] As described on the AICEMEA website: www.aicemea.net.

During the year of my involvement with the Zurich congregation, I found the eucharist to be particularly moving. Members of the congregation would come forward in groups, one after the other, to assemble around the table at the front of the sanctuary, as room allowed, until all were served. A circle would be formed and the gifts would be distributed. For the occasion, many participants would dress in their festive native garb, especially from Africa, Asia, and Latin America. In a vivid way this assembled global diversity symbolized Christ's eucharistic transformation of culture while preserving from each what was best. "Many will come from east and west and will eat with Abraham and Isaac and Jacob in the kingdom of heaven" (Matt. 8:11).

The second is an anecdote told by Harvey Cox. It concerns a communion service celebrated in 1963 at the Williamston, North Carolina, jail, where Cox had been locked up because of a civil rights demonstration. Although the jail was segregated, all those arrested, including the white demonstrators, were consigned along with the black demonstrators to the already overcrowded Negro bloc. It happened that while they were there, a local preacher came by to hold a communion service. At the appropriate time, prisoners lined up to receive the bread, demonstrators and non-demonstrators alike. Taking the loaf from the minister on one side of the bars, they passed it around among themselves. When they came to the end, on the other side stood the white Sheriff. A black man was the last in line. With an awkward pause, he hesitated, then offered the bread through the bars. The Sheriff took the bread from the black man and ate it along with the prisoners.[26]

---

[26] I am grateful to Dr. Cox for confirming the details of this story, which I heard from him orally, though it does not appear in his published accounts of the incident. See Harvey Cox, "Letter from Williamston," *The Christian Century* 80 (1963), pp. 1516–18; and Cox, *Just As I Am* (Nashville: Abingdon Press, 1983), pp. 76–82.

Finally, mention may be made of *Take This Bread: A Radical Conversion* by Sara Miles.[27] This is a beautiful story of how, among other things, one congregation made the transition from eucharistic sharing to feeding the poor. The congregation is the St. Gregory of Nyssa Episcopal Church in San Francisco, about whose liturgy more is said in the Conclusion. Their feeding of the poor, a modern-day concretion of Justin Martyr's vision, began modestly but insistently after Miles, a self-described atheist, was unexpectedly struck by grace one Sunday during the eucharist. Wanting to serve the poor without humiliating them, a food pantry was established that gave away surplus food from the eucharistic altar, with no forms to fill out and no questions asked. Each week food for about 300 families is distributed. The program, which began in 2000, has spread throughout the city. "Doing the Gospel rather than just quoting it," writes Miles, "was the best way I could find out what God was up to" (p. 265).

Stories like these can be sentimentalized. They might be written off as trivial, offering grist to the mill of religion as the opiate of the people. Folk dressing up in festive costumes will not overcome bloody divisions of war and barbarism outside the walls of the sanctuary. An awkward religious moment in a segregated jail from the civil rights movement of over forty years ago does little to remove the continuing scandal of racial injustice in the United States today (not excluding its being abetted by ongoing racism in the white churches). Distributing food to the poor does nothing, in itself, to rectify structural injustices. The truth in such perceptions can be granted while still allowing that stories like these belong finally to another context – one determined rather by the gospel than the law.

From the gospel's standpoint, it would need to be acknowledged that prophetic criticism can easily slip from authenticity into

---

[27] Sara Miles, *Take This Bread: A Radical Conversion* (New York: Ballantine Books, 2007). (Hereafter cited in the text.) www.saintgregorys.org/Community/Outreach/FoodPantry/Open.html.

posturing if it becomes too self-exempting. In the eucharist it is acknowledged that if we had received justice instead of mercy we would all be on the road to perdition.[28] From an evangelical perspective, the contents of such stories may be taken as sacramental signs. They point to real-life eucharistic embodiments of the promised future. They offer a momentary glimpse, if no more, into a reality which is not yet seen. As living icons of the eschaton, they mediate what they provisionally attest of a cultural transformation yet to come. "With righteousness he shall judge the poor, and decide with equity for the meek of the earth" (Isa. 11:4).

Conclusion: the eucharist and social ethics

If the eucharist is the earthly historical form of Christ transforming culture, in the time between the times, then the community is called to a twofold task in social ethics. The first involves the ordering of its own common life; and the second, its action in the world. Ecclesial ordering and secular intervention are not mutually exclusive, and at times they may overlap. Nonetheless they are ordered in a particular way.

Priority belongs in principle to shaping the community's life.[29] As has been famously said, the community does not *have* a social ethic so much as it *is* a social ethic.[30] A community whose common life merely reflects the disorders of the surrounding culture is

---

[28] Cf. Miroslav Volf, *Exclusion and Embrace* (Nashville: Abingdon, 1996); Volf, *Free of Charge: Giving and Forgiving in a Culture Stripped of Grace* (Grand Rapids: Zondervan, 2006).

[29] This priority seems to be reflected in Justin Martyr's comments about the eucharist as quoted above. Even if what he offers is an idealized picture, the eucharistic community as he describes it seems to represent a reprise and a reversal of the divisive social situation confronted by Paul in 1 Cor. 11:17–32.

[30] Stanley Hauerwas, *The Peaceable Kingdom* (Notre Dame: University of Notre Dame Press, 1983), p. 99.

not strongly situated for social action. To some degree – and where is this not the case? – the gospel must progress in spite of the church, and always against its failures.

Social action, of course, cannot necessarily wait for the proper ordering of the community's internal affairs. The community must proceed on several fronts at once. Nevertheless, the shared bread of the eucharist commits the community to being an assembly that cares for the poor, the needy, and the humiliated within its own ranks. It cannot credibly work for social change in the outside world if its common life fails to reflect a new social order in its own right. "By this everyone will know that you are my disciples, if you have love for one another" (Jn. 13:35). Racial reconciliation, gender equality, and environmental responsibility – beginning but not ending at the local level – are imperatives to which the community can respond creatively, for example, without waiting for others to change. A church whose policies, structures, and internal relations gave more evidence of an alternative society would make a greater impact on the larger world. This aspect of Christian social ethics has too often suffered neglect.[31]

At the same time Yoder is undoubtedly correct that the community's approach to the surrounding culture will be differentiated rather than monolithic.

Some elements of culture the church categorically rejects (pornography, tyranny, cultic idolatry). Other dimensions of culture it accepts within clear limits (economic production, commerce, the graphic arts, paying taxes for peacetime civil government). To still other dimensions of culture Christian faith gives a new motivation and coherence (agriculture, family life, literacy, conflict resolution, empowerment). Still others it strips of their claims to possess autonomous truth and value, and uses them as vehicles of

---

[31] For an exception, see William T. Cavanaugh, *Torture and Eucharist* (Oxford: Basil Blackwell, 1998).

communication (philosophy, language, Old Testament ritual, music). Still other forms of culture are created by the Christian churches (hospitals, service of the poor, generalized education).[32]

At least two further points may be mentioned. First, as an alternative social order, the eucharistic community must be prepared for situations where faithfulness to Christ means noncompliance with the world. The withholding of consent is an elementary, if potentially costly, way for the community to maintain its integrity while engaging in social witness. Noncooperation is an important strategy in waging non-violent struggle. Boycotts, disinvestment, and conscientious objection to unjust wars are only some of the more familiar forms that this strategy may assume. Combining a high view of the eucharist with something like the social witness of historic peace churches would seem to be a matter of urgency for ecumenical progress in the twenty-first century.[33]

Finally, whether in actions of boldness or modesty, the community will always be chastened in its quest for social responsibility. It will always need to be informed by a sense of its own finitude and indeed its own sin. Cultural transformation, in the largest sense, is not something the community is called to accomplish. In an ineffable way it has already been accomplished by Another. The eucharist as celebrated by forgiven sinners is a living reminder of what can only be attested in humility and hope with respect to cultural transformation. In a difficult world, it is a gift of grace. But grace without the corresponding action is not grace.

---

[32] Yoder, "How H. Richard Niebuhr Reasoned," p. 69 (*supra* n. 2).
[33] A good example would be the work of the Mennonite Central Committee: http://mcc.org.

8 | Nicene Christianity, the eucharist, and peace

Nicene Christianity finds two of its most distinguished representatives – one from the fourth century, the other from the eleventh – in Athanasius and Anselm. As exponents of Nicene Christianity, they stood for a high view of the Trinity in connection with equally high views of the Incarnation and the atonement. Also central for them, though in different ways, were baptism and the eucharist as high ecclesial sacraments.

Less well known is that each theologian contributed to the peace witness of the ecumenical church. In light of recent charges leveled against Nicene Christianity, these contributions seem important to retrieve. Nicene Christianity has been accused of being an impediment to social welfare. Not only historically, but also because of its substance – that is, in its teachings and sacraments – it is alleged to promote abuse and obstruct peace.[1]

These charges, it is argued here, are overly broad. Counter-evidence exists not only regarding Athanasius and Anselm, but also regarding Nicene Christianity more generally, down to and including the present day. Although its record is far from perfect, Nicene Christianity has more than once functioned in ways contrary to what critics would allege. At its best, Nicene Christianity

---

[1] The criticisms of J. Denny Weaver, which are broadly representative of this trend, may serve as a useful summary and point of reference. See Weaver, *The Nonviolent Atonement* (Grand Rapids: Wm. B. Eerdmans, 2001). See also his "Christology, Atonement, and Peace" (2005), unpublished ms., which provides a convenient precis and expansion of the argument in his book; Weaver, "Violence in Christian Theology," *Cross Currents* 51 (2001), pp. 150–76.

has upheld justice, obstructed violence, and promoted peace. The picture is more varied than has been allowed. Since most of the world's 2.15 billion Christians belong to communities that embrace some form of Nicene Christianity, retrieving another side of the story might contribute to prospects for peace.

The special rank and function of the Nicene Creed must not be overlooked. According to the Faith and Order Commission of the World Council of Churches (WCC), "it is the one common creed which is most universally accepted as formulation of the apostolic faith by churches in all parts of the world, where it primarily serves as the confession of faith in the eucharistic liturgy."[2] Because of its biblical integrity, its conciliar authority, its temporal and geographical universality, and its liturgical usage in the eucharist, it deserves to be called "the Ecumenical Creed" (pp. 192–93).

It should be remembered how well this Creed has served millions of Christians, with whom we are also bound together in the unity of the Church, in the past. Its brief statement of the essential faith has provided at least formally a thread of unity down through the centuries. In one form or another, this Creed has been used by the Orthodox churches, by the Roman Catholic and Anglican churches, and by most of the churches of the Protestant Reformation, and in all parts of the world. It has helped the churches to affirm their fundamental belief in God, in the Lord Jesus Christ and his saving action, in the Holy Spirit and the Church, in the life of the kingdom to come. Some have used it as a baptismal confession, others as a central standard of doctrine. It has been read and sung

---

[2] See "Towards the Common Expression of the Apostolic Faith Today (1982)," in *Documentary History of Faith and Order, 1963–1993* (Faith and Order Paper No. 159), ed. Günter Gassmann (Geneva: WCC Publications, 1993), pp. 191–200; on p. 191. (References cited hereafter in the text.) See also *Confessing the One Faith: An Ecumenical Explication of the Apostolic Faith As It Is Confessed in the Nicene-Constantinopolitan Creed (381)*, Faith and Order Paper 153 (Geneva: World Council of Churches, 1991).

at the eucharist and other liturgical services and has been used as a statement of belief at the ordination of church ministers.

(p. 192)

By articulating "the integral unity of the Christian faith," it stands as the only "common expression" of the apostolic faith that can connect the member churches of the WCC (p. 195). Without a common recognition of the Nicene Creed, it is difficult to see how the divided church will ever advance toward the essential goal of becoming one, visible, eucharistic fellowship (p. 192).

> The first condition for a true communion between the churches is that each church makes reference to the Niceno-Constantinopolitan Creed as the necessary norm of this communion of the one Church spread throughout the whole world and across the ages.[3]

What follows will be divided into four parts: (1) Nicene Christianity and the eucharist, (2) Athanasius and the Incarnation, (3) Anselm and the atonement, and (4) the peace witness of Nicene Christians. These are large topics which cannot be pursued in detail. As far as the examples permit, special attention will be devoted to the eucharist. Historical cases will be considered with an eye toward contemporary relevance.

Nicene Christianity and the eucharist

While there is more to Nicene Christianity than the eucharist, the eucharist is central to Nicene Christianity. That is because Nicene

---

[3] Joint Orthodox–Roman Catholic International Commission, "Faith Sacraments and the Unity of the Church" (1987), in *The Quest for Unity: Orthodox and Catholics in Dialogue*, ed. John Borelli and John H. Erickson (Crestwood: St. Vladimir's Seminary Press, 1996), pp. 93–104; on p. 98. See also Gayraud S. Wilmore, "Black Christians, Church Unity and One Common Faith" in *Black Witness to the Apostolic Faith*, ed. David T. Shannon and Gayraud S. Wilmore (Grand Rapids: Wm. B. Eerdmans, 1985), pp. 9–17.

Christianity begins and ends in worship. Nicene worship is always eucharistic, directly or indirectly, even as it is always also baptismal and kerygmatic. These three liturgical elements – baptism, eucharist, and proclamation – are inseparable from one another. Just as the Word grounds baptism and the eucharist, so also they in turn symbolize and mediate the Word. The eucharist always presupposes baptism while mediating the reconciliation that the Word proclaims.

At the same time the centrality of the Nicene eucharist carries missional implications. Where the gospel is rightly preached, and then rightly embodied in the eucharist, the mission imparted to the church is necessarily one of reconciliation and peace. Because it is God's enemies who are the objects of God's love – "while we were enemies, we were reconciled to God through the death of his Son" (Rom. 5:10) – enemy-love can never be marginal. Enemy-love stands at the heart of the gospel, at the heart of the eucharist, and therefore at the heart of mission. It presupposes the solidarity of all human beings in sin as overmastered by their solidarity in grace.

"Of all the forms of love," writes John Zizioulas, "the most significant from the viewpoint of both the eucharist and of the last times is *love for our enemies.*"[4] Patristic interpretations of the eucharist tended to place "an almost excessive emphasis" on the forgiveness of enemies (p. 41). From its earliest times the church saw "reconciliation with our enemies as an inviolable pre-condition" for participating in the Lord's Supper. "First be reconciled to your brother or sister, and then come and offer your gift" (Matt. 5:24) (p. 42).

In the eucharist others are encountered as they are in Christ, Zizioulas explains, and that means not as they are in themselves, but as they will be in the promised future. It is that future "which gives all things their substance" (p. 42).

---

[4] John Zizioulas, "The Eucharist and the Kingdom of God" (Part III), *Sourozh* 60 (1995), pp. 32–46; on p. 40. (Hereafter references cited in the text.)

The eschatological orientation of the eucharist, Zizioulas continues, creates its own ethos:

> [It creates] the *eucharistic* ethos, the ethos of forgiveness, which is not merely an inner state but is experienced as a *gathering* and *coexistence with the person who has hurt us*, in a future which we do not control and which has no end, the "age which does not end or grow old." In order for the eucharist to be "for the forgiveness of sins and unto eternal life" for those who take part in it and receive communion, it must also be for forgiveness on our part of the sins of others and "unto eternal life" *with them* in the gathering of the kingdom.
>
> (p. 42)

Understood in this way, the eucharist serves as a kind of liturgical bridge, mediating between proclamation and mission. It liturgically enacts the gospel of reconciliation while communicating an ethos of peace to the church, and through the church to the world. The ethos of enemy-love and forgiveness as eucharistically embodied and mediated functions not only vertically but also horizontally; not only individually but also communally; not only in worship but also in witness. The ethos imparted by the eucharist to mission is an ethos of reconciliation and peace.[5]

Athanasius and the Incarnation

No one looking for material that might bolster the peace witness of the ecumenical church could fail to be struck by a late section

---

[5] The link between proclamation and mission also needs to be facilitated by Christian education. Without opportunities within the congregation for instruction, discussion, disagreement, and prolonged consideration, the ethos of reconciliation imparted by the eucharist is unlikely to bear as much fruit as it should.

of *De Incarnatione* by Athanasius.[6] Having discussed the soteriological reasons for the Incarnation, in a way that has instructed the church for centuries, Athanasius turns to their ethical consequences.

Christ came, he states, for the sake of peace – both vertically (reconciliation with God) and horizontally (peace with one another). He has united "those who hated each other," making himself "the common Savior of all."[7] To show that the peace which Christ brought is more than just inward, Athanasius cites Isaiah:

> They shall beat their swords into plowshares,
>   and their spears into pruning hooks;
> nation shall not lift up sword against nation,
>   neither shall they learn war any more. (Isa. 2:4).

Athanasius comments on how great a reversal this is in temporal affairs. Warfare is linked in his mind with dispositions and worship. Those whose dispositions are brutal are the very ones who worship demonic powers. They rage against one another "and cannot bear to be a single hour without weapons."[8] It is to "barbarians" such as these, he writes, that the gospel comes.

> When they hear the teaching of Christ, they immediately turn from war to farming, and instead of arming their hands with swords they lift them up in prayer; and, in a word, instead of waging war among themselves, from now on they take up arms against the devil and the demons, subduing them by their self-command and integrity of soul.[9]

---

[6] Athanasius, *Contra Gentes and De Incarnatione*, ed. Robert W. Thomson (Oxford: Clarendon Press, 1971). See also *St. Athanasius on the Incarnation*, tr. and ed. by CSMV (New York: Macmillan, 1946). I sometimes follow the CSMV translation where it is more vivid or closer to the Greek.

[7] *De Incarn.* 52; Thomson, p. 265; CSMV, p. 90.   [8] *De Incarn.* 52; CSMV, p. 91.

[9] *De Incarn.* 52; Thomson, p. 265; CSMV, p. 91 (combining elements from each translation).

What this great reversal shows, Athanasius writes, is the Savior's Godhead. "What human beings were unable to learn from idols they have learned from him."[10] Christ's followers have ceased from mutual fighting. By their renewed hearts and peaceable lives, they oppose demonic powers. "When they are insulted, they are patient, when robbed they make light of it, and most amazingly, they scorn death in order to become martyrs of Christ."[11] Believers, writes Athanasius, are those who would prefer to die "rather than deny their faith in Christ."[12] In this way they show their love for him who "by his own love underwent all things for [the world's] salvation."[13]

Athanasius saw no conflict between worshipping Christ and following him. How could Christ be worshipped if he were not fully God? Yet how could he be followed if he were not fully human? In the high mystery of the Incarnation, these affirmations could only remain in tension. Some aspects of Christ's saving office belonged uniquely to his person alone, while others were such that his disciples were invited to emulate them. Christ could not be worshipped without being followed, or followed without being worshipped. To drive a wedge between worship and discipleship, or between Christ's deity and his humanity, disparaging the one while affirming the other, could only wreak havoc on the gospel.[14]

A Christian, according to Athanasius, was someone who, by faith in Christ, was given a share in the eternal life of the Holy Trinity. Faith in Christ meant believing in him as the eternal Son, who became flesh to deliver us from the corruptions of sin and death, in which we were hopelessly entangled, and from which we had no power to extricate ourselves. What the Word enjoys in

---

[10] *De Incarn.* 52; Thomson, p. 265 (translation revised).
[11] *De Incarn.* 52; Thomson, p. 265–66; CSMV, p. 91.
[12] *De Incarn.* 27; Thomson, p. 199; CSMV, p. 57.   [13] *De Incarn.* 52; CSMV, p. 90.
[14] Cf. Weaver: "the deity of Christ makes it impossible for mere humans to accept his teaching and example as the basis for Christian ethics" ("Christology, Atonement, amd Peace," ms. p. 8 [*supra* n. 1]).

himself by nature, namely, eternal life, we receive in the power of the Holy Spirit, through our union with Christ by faith. For Athanasius, what it meant to be a Christian could not be stated apart from an interlocking nexus of trinitarian, incarnational, and soteriological affirmations.[15]

Like other early Greek patristic theologians, Athanasius took it for granted that the ethos of the gospel tended toward non-violence and peace. "For the truth is not proclaimed with swords or arrows or soldiers, but by persuasion and advice."[16] Although in Athanasius references to the eucharist are not often explicit, the eucharistic presuppositions of his theology are implicitly evoked by the language of "offering" and "sacrifice."[17] This language, which for him extends from the cross to the eucharist, is the principal idiom by which Christ's saving significance is interpreted.[18] The peaceable ethos of the gospel, for Athanasius, is grounded in the self-offering of Christ's sacrifice, with its double reference to the cross and the eucharist.

The connection that Athanasius saw between the Incarnation, the renunciation of warfare, and peaceable coexistence was not necessarily absolute, but it was nonetheless strong and significant. A similar connection can also be found in the proceedings of both Nicaea and Chalcedon. It hardly seems adequate for anyone to vilify these venerable standards as "failing to challenge violence" while ignoring relevant passages from the original proceedings themselves.[19]

---

[15] See, for example, Athanasius, *Against the Arians*, Discourse III, Ch. XXV, sec. 25, in *St. Athanasius: Select Works and Letters*, ed. Philip Schaff and Henry Wace, *A Select Library of Nicene and Post-Nicene Fathers*, vol. 4 (Grand Rapids: Wm. B. Eerdmans, 1980), p. 407.

[16] Athanasius, *History of the Arians* 33; quoted in *Athanasius*, ed. Khaled Anatolios (London: Routledge, 2004), p. 35 (translation slightly altered).

[17] See Anatolios in ibid., p. 59.

[18] Anatolios, *Athanasius: The Coherence of His Thought* (London: Routledge, 1998), p. 75.

[19] Weaver, "Christology, Atonement, and Peace," ms. p. 9 (*supra* n. 1).

Let me cite two conciliar canons and then comment on them. From the First Ecumenical Council of Nicaea (AD 325):

CANON XII: As many as were called by grace, and displayed the first zeal, having cast aside their military girdles, but afterwards returned, like dogs, to their own vomit (so that some spent money and by means of gifts regained their military stations); let these, after they have passed the space of three years as hearers, be for ten years prostrators.[20]

From the Fourth Ecumenical Council of Chalcedon (AD 451):

CANON VII: Those who have entered the clergy or have been tonsured into the monastic state may no longer serve in the army or accept any civil charge; otherwise those who have dared do so, and who have not repented and returned to their prior occupation for the love of God, shall be anathemized.[21]

It would be hard to deny that the ecumenical churches have had a checkered career with respect to their peace traditions. Nevertheless, while most communions have not adopted the rigor found in the historic peace churches, there is no reason to believe that they have not struggled with these issues from the beginning. The canons cited from Nicaea and Chalcedon are cases in point. While their letter may be archaic, their spirit is not. It is a spirit that abhors participation in military bloodshed and that rejects it for the highest expressions of the Christian life. To put it in the terms of the critics, but to reverse their point, violence is here not condoned but challenged – by the very councils they would seek to dismiss. At the same time, military participation is seen as a difficult problem that admits no easy solution. Apart from an

---

[20] *The Seven Ecumenical Councils of the Undivided Church*, ed. Henry R. Percival, in *A Select Library of Nicene and Post-Nicene Fathers*, vol. 14 (Grand Rapids: Wm. B. Eerdmans, 1983), p. 27.
[21] Ibid., p. 272.

honorable minority, as represented by the historic peace-church tradition, the solution for most ecumenical churches has undoubtedly been messy, often less than satisfying, and open to further deliberation.

It seems far-fetched, however, to blame the worst excesses of church history on these ecumenical standards themselves.[22] Peace-loving critics of Nicene Christianity would do well to consider that there are pacifist Christians all through the Eastern and Western communions of the ecumenical church. While Nicaea may be held in low esteem in certain circles, it is otherwise valued as the one standard commonly embraced throughout the worldwide church, including by pacifist Christians. Indeed, for major ecclesial communions Nicaea is non-negotiable, and for good reasons.[23] It is a sign of isolation when little understanding is evidenced of what those reasons might be.

Those who would disparage Nicaea, while wishing to take part in the ecumenical movement, are going to have to explain why their trinitarian and christological alternatives do not degenerate into Arianism.[24] We need this explanation from the critics of

[22] According to Professor Weaver, "violence" is "contained in the classic or standard creeds and formulas of christology and atonement" (e.g., Nicaea, Chalcedon, and Anselm) ("Christology, Atonement, and Peace," ms. p. 6). "The classic formulas" have not only "accommodated violence," but have also "acquiesced to the violence of racism and slavery" ("Christology, Atonement, and Peace," ms. p. 9 [supra n. 1]).

[23] Although the Chalcedonian Definition has not enjoyed the same universal acceptance as the Nicene-Constantinopolitan Creed, its reception is still very widespread, and the historic objections to it are arguably finally more semantic than substantive. For an indication of recent progress, see the important documents of the Oriental Orthodox–Roman Catholic Ecumenical Consultations in Syriac Dialogue, Nos. 1–5 (Vienna: Pro Oriente, 1994–2003). See also the WCC Faith and Order Document, "The Council of Chalcedon and Its Significance for the Ecumenical Movement (1971)," in Gassmann, Documentary History, pp. 226–35 (supra n. 2).

[24] Although there is more than one way for a theology to be "Arian," I use the term here for any position that denies the full and eternal deity of the incarnate Son. The suspicion of Arianism can hardly be allayed by referring vaguely to Jesus as "the presence of God." If Professor Weaver wishes to affirm the full deity of Jesus

Nicene Christianity. While the christological picture in their writings is not unmixed, it often displays definite Arian undercurrents.[25] After paying lip service to what they may call "ontological" questions – which they seem to regard as fairly worthless – the only thing that seems left for them is an exemplarist christology[26] in liberationist dress. What they regard as the "meaning" of the Incarnation and of faith would be unrecognizable to most of the ecumenical church on account of its being so reductionist.[27]

It is of course laudable, as all Christians would agree, to want to stand with the victims of injustice and alleviate their suffering. No doubt liberation theology has much to teach us here. There is a big difference, however, between Jesus as God Incarnate and Jesus as merely the "incarnation" (i.e., symbolic presence) of God's reign. If critics of Nicene Christianity cannot upgrade their christologies to meet Nicene standards, their ecumenical prospects are not bright. They will fail to make the contribution for which they are especially equipped, and from which the entire ecumenical church would benefit.

Christ, he needs not only to make that clear, but also to give it a central place in his soteriology. An exemplarist christology can get along very well without it.

[25] For the modern period this is a problem that emerges at least as early as Schleiermacher, when he wrote: "For the person of Christ began only when he became a human being." See Friedrich Schleiermacher, *The Christian Faith* (Edinburgh: T. & T. Clark, 1928, 1956), p. 473 (translation altered). This statement would seem to echo the Arian slogan, "There was when he was not." This famous slogan, though condemned by the Council of Nicaea in 325, was omitted from the postscript to the Nicene Creed as revised by the Council of Constantinople in 381.

[26] By "exemplarist christology" I mean any position which sees the significance of Jesus primarily in terms of his being a moral example for us to imitate.

[27] It should be noted that from the standpoint of Nicene Christianity Schleiermacher's christology would appear to be reductionist without being strictly exemplarist. For Schleiermacher, Jesus is not primarily a moral example, but rather the bearer of the Spirit, i.e., of a high-potency God-consciousness, which he transmits to the church. To perform this function, Jesus is not, and does not need to be, God Incarnate.

When the bishops met at Nicaea and then again at Chalcedon, to resolve controversies that were wracking the church, they gathered in a room around an open Bible. It was clear to them in a way that was not always clear to later generations, including modernist historians of doctrine, that what they were engaged in was not "metaphysical" speculation, but trying to understand Holy Scripture. The question on which everything hinged, in one way or another, was whether the New Testament called Jesus God. The resort to the language of *ousia* at Nicaea and then to *phusis* at Chalcedon was designed to uphold the full deity of Christ (and then later his full humanity as well) – in no uncertain terms. These terminological choices were essentially hermeneutical in significance. Their relative validity has been affirmed by generations of ecumenical Christians ever since, right down to the present day.[28]

A clue to why Christ's unabridged deity was seen as so important may be found in the one sentence that Nicaea and Chalcedon hold in common, since Chalcedon adopted it from its precursor: "For us human beings and our salvation." Nicaea and Chalcedon, in other words, were intended to function not only as hermeneutical decisions but also as soteriological guidelines. As the late Hans W. Frei liked to say, Nicaea and Chalcedon were best understood as "conceptual redescriptions of the narratives."[29]

---

[28] Among many exegetical discussions see Raymond E. Brown, "Does the New Testament Call Jesus God?" *Theological Studies* 26 (1965), pp. 545–73; I. Howard Marshall, "Incarnational Christology in the New Testament," in *Christ the Lord*, ed. Harold H. Rowdon (Downers Grove: InterVarsity Press, 1982), pp. 1–16; N. T. Wright, *The Climax of the Covenant* (Minneapolis: Fortress Press, 1992), ch. 4; Martin Hengel, *Studies in Early Christology* (Edinburgh: T. & T. Clark, 1995, 2004), ch. 7; Larry Hurtado, *Lord Jesus Christ: Devotion to Christ in Earliest Christianity* (Grand Rapids: Wm. B. Eerdmans, 2005). Without affirming, as it does, the need "to accept our Lord Jesus Christ as God and Savior," the World Council of Churches would lack ecumenical credibility.

[29] I do not know if he wrote this anywhere, but I remember him saying it more than once in personal conversation.

They were interpretive lenses through which the gospel narratives had to be read if their saving significance was not to be missed. They were second-order rules for reading those narratives. They were not replacements for the narratives, but attempts to make visible the deep structure within them, making explicit what was implicit. They made clear what was more often implied than stated in the New Testament witness to Jesus Christ.

The core soteriological themes that Nicaea and Chalcedon sought to safeguard are captured in the new catechism of the Presbyterian Church (USA). They are themes of salvation, revelation, and worship.

> Question 33. What is the significance of affirming that Jesus is truly God?
>
> Only God can properly deserve worship. Only God can reveal to us who God is. And only God can save us from our sins. Being truly God, Jesus meets these conditions. He is the proper object of our worship, the self-revelation of God, and the Savior of the world.[30]

What Nicaea and Chalcedon sought to uphold about the meaning of our salvation has been affirmed through the centuries by all major branches of the ecumenical church, and is still affirmed by them today. If they have something to learn from the historic peace churches, and from those who would criticize Nicene Christianity out of social concerns, as they arguably do, then it cannot be at the expense of these historic, biblical, and non-negotiable convictions. Any strategy that would pose a forced choice between these convictions and a deeper commitment to justice and peace seems doomed to fail, especially if it threatens to introduce an open or secret Arianism in its train.

---

[30] *The Study Catechism: Full Version* (Louisville: Witherspoon Press, 1998), p. 18.

Anselm and the atonement

Some critics of Nicene Christianity are even more severe, if possible, on Anselm and the atonement. Whereas, by their lights, Nicaea and Chalcedon fail to challenge violence, the standard versions of the atonement in the history of doctrine are even worse. "All of the standard atonement images harbor or actually model unjust suffering and divine violence."[31] "The logic of satisfaction atonement," we read, "makes God the chief avenger or the chief punisher ... It makes God a divine child abuser."[32] Violence is "intrinsic" to standard atonement doctrines.[33] The only way out, according to such critics, would be to abandon everything Anselm and the tradition ever stood for on the atonement in favor of an exemplarist *Christus victor* model reconstructed along liberationist and perhaps pacifist lines.

Of course it should be noted that not all *Christus victor* interpretations of the atonement are merely "exemplarist." Indeed, few of them are. From Greek and Latin patristic theology down to Luther and Calvin and on to Barth, von Balthasar, Torrance, and Schmemann, *Christus victor* views have been affirmed in connection with a high ("Chalcedonian") doctrine of Christ's person that accommodates a strong "objective" aspect to his saving work. They have little or no historic connection with Arianism or semi-Arianism. Nor, in these theologians, are they thought to be incompatible with "priestly" views that entail ideas of exchange (*admirabile commercium*), substitution, expiation, and the shedding of blood. The atonement needs to be described from the standpoint of Christ's priestly office as well as from that of his royal office. It needs to be

---

[31] Weaver, "Christology, Atonement, and Peace," ms. p. 9 (*supra* n. 1).

[32] Ibid., ms. p. 12. This criticism, along with others like it, is overly broad. The rule is *abusus non tollit usum* (wrong use does not preclude proper use). The antidote to abuse is not disuse but proper use.

[33] Ibid., ms. p. 14.

described from the standpoint of the *Christus patiens* or *Christus vicarius* – of the Christ who is High Priest and sacrifice in one: the paschal Lamb of God who takes away the sin of the world – as well as from that of the *Christus victor*. The royal and priestly offices are complementary, both expressing the mystery of Christ's one atoning sacrifice as a whole.

The most serious breakdown in this treatment of Anselm on the atonement is, from a Nicene standpoint, the utter lack of any feeling for a robust doctrine of the Trinity.

Nicene Christians would revere St. Anselm – in whom brilliance and devotion were combined to the highest degree – as one of the very great teachers in the history of the church. They would thus welcome the more judicious assessment of his views offered by Hans Urs von Balthasar. Having long since thrown Nicaea overboard, the critics have no trinitarian frame in which to understand the atonement.[34] Their disregard for the trinitarian sensibility that Anselm brings to his doctrine is far-reaching. For Anselm, as von Balthasar observes, everything depends on the trinitarian framework.

According to Anselm, the decision involved in the atonement was not taken by a remote and vengeful Father and inflicted upon an innocent child. To ascribe such a view to Anselm is to depart from the truth. On the contrary, as von Balthasar notes, for Anselm "this decision is a voluntary one, originating in the Son just as much as in the Father and in the Spirit."[35] Anselm traces everything back "to the Father's mercy and the Son's free self-surrender."[36] What the cross represents is the trinitarian mercy of

---

[34] In his book Professor Weaver touches on how the Trinity might bear on Anselm's argument, but can finally make nothing of it. See Weaver, *The Nonviolent Atonement*, pp. 203–4 (*supra* n. 1).

[35] Hans Urs von Balthasar, *Theo-Drama: Theological Dramatic Theory*, vol. IV (San Francisco: Ignatius Press, 1994), p. 258.

[36] Ibid., p. 265.

God for the sake of the world. It involves a suffering grounded entirely in freedom for the sake of love.

> What, indeed, can be conceived of [as] more merciful than that God the Father should say to a sinner condemned to eternal torments and lacking any means of redeeming himself, "Take my only-begotten Son and give him on your behalf," and that the Son himself should say, "Take me and redeem yourself."[37]

> God ... did not force Christ to die ... Rather he underwent death of his own accord [sponte].[38]

> Christ, along with the Father and the Holy Spirit, had determined that the way in which he would demonstrate the exaltedness of his omnipotence should be none other than through his death.[39]

> Since no one else could perform the deed ... the Son was willing to die for the sake of the world.[40]

> The Father did not coerce Christ to face death against his will ... Christ himself of his own volition underwent death in order to save humankind.[41]

"This recurrent *sponte* ['voluntarily']," comments von Balthasar, "is the leitmotif of the dramatic action."[42] Anselm time and again describes the Son's obedience as an action of spontaneous freedom. Even the will of God the Father seems increasingly to take the form of ratifying what the Son has chosen in order to bring mercy to the world. "The human race ... could not have been saved by

---

[37] Anselm, "Why God Became Man" (Bk. 2, ch. 20) in *Anselm of Canterbury: The Major Works*, ed. Brian Davies and G. R. Evans (Oxford: Oxford University Press, 1998), p. 354.

[38] Ibid. (Bk. 1, ch. 9), p. 277.   [39] Ibid. (Bk. 1, ch. 9), p. 278.

[40] Ibid. (Bk. 1, chs. 9, 10), p. 279.   [41] Ibid. (Bk. 1, ch. 8), p. 275.

[42] Von Balthasar, *Theo-Drama*, p. 258.

any other means than by his death ... He died not under any compulsion but of his own free will."[43] "Absolute and true obedience," explained Anselm, "is that which occurs when a rational being, not under compulsion but voluntarily, keeps to a desire which has been received from God."[44] For Anselm, as for much of the ecumenical tradition, the atonement represents "a trinitarian transaction of consent within history between the Father and the Son in the Holy Spirit."[45]

Von Balthasar concludes:

It is clear from [these] and similar passages how foolish it is to accuse Anselm of having invented a cruel Father-God, who, in order to restore his honor, demanded that his Son should be slaughtered. Anselm himself rejects such a repulsive picture of God.[46]

Anselm explicitly denied that God could delight in the blood of an innocent human being, or would actually need it. He denied that God could or would pardon the guilty only after killing the innocent.[47] These views cannot responsibly be ascribed to him. Nevertheless, it is not surprising that Arian-leaning critics would have difficulty in understanding his doctrine of the atonement as a matter of voluntary suffering and inner-trinitarian consent.

Anselm's critics are incorrect if they associate the view of "penal substitution" with Anselm.[48] While penal substitution became a

---

[43] Anselm, "Why God Became Man" (Bk. 1, ch. 10), p. 281.

[44] Ibid. (Bk. 1, ch. 10), p. 280.

[45] Von Balthasar, "Die neue Theorie von Jesus als dem 'Sündenbock,'" *Internationale katholische Zeitschrift* "Communio" 9 (1980), pp. 184–85; on p. 185.

[46] Von Balthasar, *Theo-Drama*, p. 259 n. 12. "The events of the Cross can only be interpreted against the background of the Trinity and through faith." *Theo-Drama*, p. 319 (*supra* n. 35).

[47] Anselm, "Why God Became Man" (Bk. 1, ch. 10), p. 282 (*supra* n. 37).

[48] Weaver, "Christology, Atonement, and Peace," ms. p. 11 (*supra* n. 1). He suggests that penal substitution is "an extension of Anselm's own logic." Professor Weaver's discussion of Anselm's relation to penal substitution seems more balanced in his book than in this paper. See Weaver, *The Nonviolent Atonement*,

predominant idea in post-Reformation Protestant theology, two things need to be remembered, namely, that penal views of the atonement are not necessarily substitutionary, while, in turn, substitutionary views are not necessarily penal. In one respect Anselm represents the first option; Athanasius represents the second.

Anselm's doctrine of the atonement was a doctrine of compensation. The dishonor done to God by human sin had to be recompensed for the sake of justice. Recompense, as Anselm understood it, meant either punishment or some other form of payment. "God cannot remit a sin unpunished, without recompense," he wrote, "that is, without the voluntary paying off of a debt."[49] Unless sin's debt were repaid, the state of blessedness intended for humankind could not be obtained. But since sin against God was of infinite weight, no mere mortal was sufficient to pay it off. Hence the necessity of the Incarnation: "If the recompense of which we have spoken is not paid – which no one can pay except God, and no one ought to pay except man – it is necessary that a God-Man should pay it."[50]

God chose to do for sinners what they could not do for themselves. By an infinite mercy, God elected to suffer in his own person (in the person of the God-Man) so that the debt of sin might be repaid. The debt was repaid not by punishment but by infinite merit. The Son's voluntary suffering on the cross was a gift of inestimable worth. Since the Father wished to reward the Son for this gift, but the Son, being divine, had no need of reward, he was able to have his merit transferred over to the faithful. The debt was repaid not by vicarious but by meritorious suffering.

---

pp. 192, 195 (*supra* n. 1). For a good discussion of how satisfaction in Anselm differs from penal substitution in the Reformers, see Robert B. Strimple, "St. Anselm's *Cur Deus Homo* and John Calvin's Doctrine of the Atonement," in *Anselm, Aosta, Bec and Canterbury*, ed. D. E. Luscombe and G. R. Evans (Sheffield: Sheffield Academic Press, 1996), pp. 348–60.

[49] Anselm, "Why God Became Man" (Bk. 1, ch. 19), p. 302 (*supra* n. 37).
[50] Ibid. (Bk. 2, ch. 6), p. 320 (slightly modified).

Anselm's account was not without its ambiguities. Some statements seemed to suggest for example, that punishment played a role in satisfaction after all. The Father wished the Son to endure death as an act of obedience "even though he did not like his punishment" (*Cur Deus Homo*, I.10; *quamvis poenam eius non amaret*). God's justice "does not allow anything to be given in repayment for sin except punishment" (1.24; *iustitiae illus, quae non nisi poenam permittit reddi propter peccatum*). Christ did not need to suffer punishment for himself but for others (II.18; *pro aliis, quibus nihil nisi poenam debebat*). In any case, regardless of what role punishment may or may not be assigned, Anselm essentially gives us a theory of propitiation without expiation, because while the Father's wrath was indeed propitiated, the Son's meritorious sacrifice was compensatory rather than expiatory.[51] It removed a debt (by supererogation), not a state of corruption (by vicarious substitution).[52]

Anselm's view of the atonement thus involved penal elements without being substitutionary.[53] By contrast, for Athanasius, who was following a Greek patristic tradition, Christ's death was substitutionary but not penal. I do not mean to suggest that Athanasius' view of the atonement was merely substitutionary, only that it involved substitutionary elements. He clearly believed that Christ died the death of sin in our place in order to destroy death for our sakes. He believed that Christ became a curse for us and that

---

[51] For a careful distinction between expiation and propitiation, see Frances M. Young, *The Sacrifice and Death of Christ* (London: SPCK, 1975), p. 72. It is important to note, however, that propitiation can be thought to occur also by expiation, not only by compensation. Propitiation need not mean merely "appeasement."

[52] For the standard interpretation that paying satisfaction was neither penal nor substitutionary, but a supererogatory act of perfect homage, see David Brown, "Anselm on Atonement," in *The Cambridge Companion to Anselm*, ed. Brian Davies and Brian Leftow (Cambridge: Cambridge University Press, 2005), pp. 279–302; Daniel Deme, *The Christology of Anselm of Canterbury* (Burlington: Ashgate, 2003).

[53] Von Balthasar makes a similar point when he observes that Anselm "undervalued" the patristic theme of the "great exchange." See *Theo-Drama*, pp. 260–61, 317 (*supra* n. 35).

sin was condemned in his flesh. He combined a substitutionary view with equally strong, if not stronger, elements of our participation in Christ. He saw no conflict between substitution and participation; indeed for him the two were complementary and coinherent.[54]

The contrast between Athanasius and Anselm should not be overstated. Broadly speaking, they held certain key themes in common. Like Anselm, Athanasius affirmed the Incarnation as indispensable to the saving significance of Christ's death.[55] Like Anselm, he too could employ the imagery of a debt that needed to be paid (though he laid far less stress on it).[56] And like Anselm, he viewed Christ's saving death as the very heart of the gospel. Christ's death, he wrote, is "the chief point of our faith" and the main reason for the Incarnation.[57] For reasons like these, Athanasius' *De Incarnatione* has been described as "the nearest patristic parallel to Anselm's *Cur Deus Homo*."[58]

---

[54] In supposing that Athanasius taught a view of "vicarious atonement," I follow John Henry Newman, Archibald Robertson and T. F. Torrance. See especially the recent works by Anatolios: *Athanasius: The Coherence*, p. 75; and *Athanasius*, pp. 56–61, 69–76 (*supra*, nn. 18, 16). See also George D. Dragas, "St. Athanasius on Christ's Sacrifice," in *Sacrifice and Redemption*, ed. S. W. Sykes (Cambridge: Cambridge University Press, 1991), pp. 73–100.

[55] *De Incarn.* 19; Thomson, p. 181; CSMV, p. 48 (*supra* n. 6): "He who ... suffered in the body was not simply a man, but the Son of God and Savior of all."

[56] *De Incarn.* 20; Thomson, p. 183; CSMV, p. 49: Christ surrendered himself to death for us, "since the debt owed by all human beings still had to be paid."

[57] *De Incarn.* 19; Thomson, p. 181; CSMV, p. 48: *to kephalaion tes pisteos hemon.* For an interesting distinction between "baptismal soteriology" and "eucharistic soteriology," see George Huntston Williams, "The Sacramental Presuppositions of Anselm's *Cur Deus Homo*," *Church History* 26 (1957), pp. 245–74. Although Williams plausibly associates the former with Athanasius and the latter with Anselm, the contrast would be overdrawn unless it were acknowledged that Anselm's view of salvation is also baptismal, even as Athanasius' view is also eucharistic, though each of course in different ways. Williams has the merit of pointing to the parallels between the Athanasius and Anselm on the saving significance of Christ's death. See also Williams, *Anselm: Communion and Atonement* (St. Louis: Concordia Publishing House, 1960), which expands upon his essay.

[58] Williams, "Sacramental Presuppositions," p. 249.

If Athanasius and Anselm are correct, then the contemporary disapproval of the atonement, as represented by social critics of Nicene Christianity – on quasi-Arian, exemplarist, and "politically correct" grounds – amounts, in effect, to an assault on the historic faith of the ecumenical church.[59] Where the doctors of the church saw mercy, today's alienated theologians see abuse. Certainly, as von Balthasar and other sympathetic critics have observed, Anselm's idea of punishment as the condition that satisfies God's righteousness was unfortunate.[60] Yet the patristic and biblical idea of the great exchange (*admirabile commercium*), and therefore of vicarious substitution, does not depend on this notion of punishment.[61]

The idea of Christ's substitutionary death cannot be rejected without departing from profoundly Judaic elements in the apostolic witness.[62] This is a point that can hardly be overstressed.

---

[59] The attack is also reminiscent of Socinus. See von Balthasar, *Theo-Drama*, pp. 268–69, 274 n. 5 (*supra* n. 35).

[60] Von Balthasar, *Theo-Drama*, pp. 260–61, 390, 499; cf. pp. 337–38. For a judicious handling of the punishment theme, see Karl Barth, *Church Dogmatics*, vol. IV, part 1 (Edinburgh: T. & T. Clark, 1969), pp. 252–55. Like Athanasius, Barth saw Christ's death as substitutionary but not as penal (or only as secondarily so). What satisfies the righteousness of God, Barth argued, is not punishment but precisely expiation, where "expiation" is understood as the sinner's abolition and removal in Christ when he died for our sakes and in our place (which of course is then followed by a restitution in Christ through his resurrection). Barth's rich discussions of God's mercy and righteousness, and of Christ's substitutionary though non-penal death, are a highpoint in the history of doctrine. See *Church Dogmatics*, vol. II, part 1 (Edinburgh: T. & T. Clark, 1957), pp. 368–406; vol. IV, part 1, pp. 211–83.

[61] Professor Weaver's assertion that "it is possible to interpret Paul in non-satisfaction ways" is unfortunate in its formulation (ms. p. 28). Nor does it inspire confidence that he approaches the question with an open mind. For an example of careful exegesis that supports the line of argument taken here, see Otfried Hofius, *Paulusstudien* (Tübingen: Mohr Siebeck, 1989), pp. 1–174. A good survey in English may be found in I. Howard Marshall, "The Death of Jesus in Recent New Testament Study," *Word and World* 3 (1983), pp. 12–21.

[62] For an affirmation of the substitution theme by a contemporary Jewish theologian, with reference to its strong bearing on Christianity, see Jon Levensen, *The Death and Resurrection of the Beloved Son* (New Haven: Yale University Press, 1993), pp. 163, 208.

Sweeping dismissals of substitution, though common in the modern period, are an unfortunate sign of Gentile thinking. They are in danger of rejecting the paschal mystery of Christ as present in the eucharist. They cut the church off from its Judaic and eucharistic roots. When carried through by the critics of Nicene Christianity, the threat of Arianism is compounded by that of Marcionism.

As in the case of Nicaea and Chalcedon, it hardly seems reputable to disparage Anselm of Canterbury while paying little attention to his actual record. Anselm need not be enlarged in death beyond what he was in life. Like anyone he had his short-comings, not least in matters of politics and peace.[63] Yet to overlook his disapproval of the First Crusade, his opposition to slavery, and his moving prayers, as if they did not exist, adds little to the credibility of his detractors.

Anselm was a conscientious objector to the First Crusade (1095–100). At a time when most church leaders defended it as necessary, he himself demurred. He was "skeptical about, if not openly hostile to the holy war."[64]

As one historian sums up:

Anselm ... opposed the clergy embarking on crusade. Monks, above all, should stay in the monastery and not go outside on crusade. Any monk joining the crusade would surely be damned, he argued. Furthermore, he took the same stance that the early Church Fathers had taken toward the military: He urged that no Christian should be involved in bloodshed because the military often engages in profane wars. Instead, the Christians should join the peaceful *Militia Christi*, which engages in spiritual warfare.[65]

---

[63] See for example R. W. Southern, *Saint Anselm: A Portrait in a Landscape* (Cambridge: Cambridge University Press, 1990), pp. 221–27, 289–307.

[64] James A. Brundage, "St. Anselm, Ivo of Chartres and the Crusade," ch. IX in *The Crusades, Holy War and Canon Law* (Aldershot: Variorum, 1991), p. 183.

[65] Brian Irby, "From Peace to War: The Formulation of the Idea of Crusade," *Central Arkansas Historical Review* (Spring 1997).

Anselm was no absolute pacifist, but he rejected enthusiasm for the crusade, because he did not consider the use of military force "appropriate for spiritual purposes."[66] This sort of cool rejection was by no means to be taken for granted. As Eamon Duffy points out:

> The response to Urban II's proclamation of what came to be known as the First Crusade was staggering ... Apocalyptic preaching by zealots like the diminutive evangelist from Picardy, Peter the Hermit, fueled popular excitement, and all over Europe tens of thousands flocked to take the crusade vow ... From every country in Europe wave upon wave of armed men ... flooded toward Constantinople, the normal route to the Holy Land.[67]

We may be grateful that in the midst of this riot of enthusiasm, there was at least one major figure who stood in solitary witness and pointed to a better way.

It also needs to be noted that at the Council of London-Westminster (1102) – convened and presided over by Anselm – the slave trade that existed between England and Ireland was officially condemned.[68] The Canon against slavery denounced that "wicked trade by which human beings were bought and sold as though they were beasts that perish."[69] This Canon was later known and cited by Harriet Beecher Stowe. Thus did the eleventh-century Archbishop offer support and encouragement to the nineteenth-century Christian abolitionist.[70]

---

[66] Brundage, "St. Anselm," p. 183.

[67] Eamon Duffy, "The Holy Terror," *New York Review of Books*, 53/16 (October 19, 2006), p. 44.

[68] See Joseph Clayton, *Saint Anselm: A Critical Biography* (Milwaukee: Bruce Publishing Company, 1933), pp. 105–6.

[69] Ibid.

[70] See Harriet Beecher Stowe, *Key to Uncle Tom's Cabin* (Boston, MA: John P. Jewett & Co., 1854), p. 472.

Like Augustine in his *Confessions,* Anselm sometimes composed his treatises in the form of a prayer. Here is an excerpt from his *Proslogion* on the theme of justice and mercy:

> Although it is difficult to understand how your mercy is not lacking in your justice, still I must believe that it is in no way opposed to justice, since it flows from your goodness, which is not goodness without justice. This means that mercy and justice are in harmony with one another. For, if you are merciful because you are supremely good, and cannot be supremely good unless you are supremely just, it must follow then that you are merciful precisely because you are supremely just. Help me, O just and merciful God, whose light I seek, help me, so that I may understand what I have just said: Namely, that you are merciful precisely because you are just.[71]

A prayer that Anselm once wrote for his enemies includes these lines:

> O Lord, you alone are powerful. You alone are merciful. Whatever you bid me desire for my enemies, give it to them and give it back also to me. And if what I ask at any time for them should be outside the rule of charity ... do not give this to them nor give it back to me ... May I not be the occasion of death for my brothers [or sisters]. May I not be a scandal or a stumbling block to them. My own sin is quite enough for me ... May [my enemies] be reconciled to you, and through you to me.[72]

It is hard to see how historical and devotional matters like these can be ignored. St. Anselm's portrayal as the emblem of violence and abuse by his politically correct detractors cannot be sustained.

---

[71] Anselm, *Proslogion,* 9. As translated by William H. Shannon, *Anselm: The Joy of Faith* (New York: Crossroad, 1999), p. 160.

[72] Anselm, *Prayer for Enemies.* As translated by Shannon, *Anselm,* pp. 125–26 (slightly revised).

Whether from the standpoint of his atonement doctrine, or his practices, or his prayers, he deserves better.

Finally, it should be noted that the argument of *Cur Deus Homo* is laced with liturgical and sacramental allusions. According to George Huntston Williams, Anselm was the first theologian to think through the medieval doctrine of the eucharist. His view of the atonement, Williams suggests, should be seen not merely as rationalistic speculation, but more importantly as an exercise in sacramental theology, and especially in eucharistic soteriology. To a large degree the distinctive ideas in Anselm's doctrine of the atonement − like mercy, justice, sacrifice, honor, and debt − all have a eucharistic resonance. It seems plausible to posit that the peaceable attitudes in his practices and prayers are traceable, in no small degree, to the ethos of eucharistic mediation.[73]

To sum up: It has been charged that Nicene Christianity not only has failed to challenge violence, but is inherently incapable of doing so. Against this charge, some counter-examples have been set forth.

- The great defender of the Nicene Creed, Athanasius himself, has been shown not only to have challenged violence and to have commended a peaceable way, but to have done so out of his most basic convictions, both soteriological and sacramental.[74]
- Canons from the First Ecumenical Council (Nicaea) and the Fourth Ecumenical Council (Chalcedon) have been adduced. These Canons show church discipline being exacted of Nicene Christians for violating God's love by subjecting themselves, in certain respects, to military participation and imperial hostilities. These are the very councils that have supposedly made it

---

[73] See Williams, "Sacramental Presuppositions," and *Anselm: Communion and Atonement* (*supra* n. 57).

[74] For a judicious assessment of Athanasius' character, see Anatolios, *Athanasius*, pp. 33–39 (*supra* n. 16). See also Duane W. H. Arnold, *The Early Episcopal Career of Athanasius of Alexandria* (Notre Dame: Notre Dame University Press, 1991).

impossible for Nicene Christianity to challenge violence and abuse.

No claim is being made that Nicene Christianity has always lived up to its highest ideals. Too often it has not. These examples are sufficient, however, to refute the charge that Nicene Christianity has no such ideals, or that it is inherently incapable of putting them into practice.

Another accusation, even more serious, is that the atonement doctrine of Nicene Christianity, particularly as found in Anselm, not only has failed to challenge violence and abuse, but has actually instigated it. Violence and abuse are said to be intrinsic to Anselm's doctrine and therefore to be warranted by it. Against these accusations, the following observations have been offered.

• At its heart Anselm's atonement doctrine is a matter of voluntary suffering. Unimaginable suffering for the sake of unworthy others is freely undertaken from a motivation of infinite love. It has nothing to do with coercion, cruelty or capriciousness. From beginning to end, it is governed by the framework of inner-trinitarian consent. To misrepresent Anselm and his doctrine as instigating abuse can only be regarded as unfounded.[75]

• The similarities between Anselm and Athanasius on the saving significance of Christ's death suggest that the charges against Anselm involve an attack on Nicene Christianity as a whole. The exemplarist christologies of the critics veer in the direction of Arianism, while the rejection of substitutionary atonement – as

---

[75] Beyond authorizing abuse, a closely related problem would be that of submitting to abuse, unwisely or uncritically. Atonement doctrines have been thought to authorize this sort of servile submission, but are misused when interpreted in this way. The question is beyond the scope of this discussion. See Marie M. Fortune, *Keeping the Faith: Guidance for Christian Women Facing Abuse* (San Francisco: HarperSanFrancisco, 1995), and Fortune, *Sexual Violence: The Sin Revisited* (Cleveland: Pilgrim Press, 2005).

embedded in the paschal mystery of the eucharist – veers in the direction of Marcionism.

• Anselm's conscientious objection to the First Crusade, his conciliar success in condemning slavery, and his unsurpassed prayers concerning mercy, justice, and love for enemies, all suggest that his eucharistic soteriology, of which his atonement doctrine forms but a part, cannot fairly be charged with the indignity of authorizing abuse.

Again no need exists to depict Anselm and his doctrine as any better than they were. But it is a matter of simple fairness not to make them guilty of offenses for which they cannot be truly held responsible.

The peace witness of Nicene Christians

Since most ecumenical Christians are Nicene Christians, and since Nicene Christians include some distinguished witnesses for peace, any attempt to discredit Nicaea as soft on violence would also, it seems, reflect upon the faith of these Christians. Would it not be better to look for what is best in Nicaea and its adherents, in order to encourage others, than to engage in ill-considered tactics of disparagement?

Consider some important names: Dorothy Day, Helmut Gollwitzer, Jim Forest, Oscar Romero, Sr. Helen Prejean, André Trocmé, William Stringfellow, Dom Helder Camera, Mother Maria Skobtsova, Lech Walesa, Paul Schneider, Sr. Ita Ford, Kim Dae-jung, Desmond Tutu, Dietrich Bonhoeffer, Fanny Lou Hamer and Karl Barth. These are among the many twentieth-century Christians known for their commitment to justice and peace. They are all Nicene Christians. Some of them are martyrs. The corrupting effects ascribed to their confession apparently escaped them.[76]

---

[76] See Alexander F. C. Webster, *The Pacifist Option: The Moral Argument Against War in Eastern Orthodox Moral Theology* (San Francisco: International Scholars

In what follows, two twentieth-century cases will be examined, one from the Anabaptist tradition, the other from the Reformed tradition. The Anabaptist representative will be the late Dale Aukerman, whose affiliation was with the Church of the Brethren, a historic peace church. The Reformed representative will be André Trocmé, a leader in the French Reformed Church. Both were pastors, writers, and peace activists. Both affirmed the full deity of Christ and substitutionary atonement. In part because neither was an academic theologian, no technical or extensive evidence of their doctrinal commitments is to be expected; yet in each case the contours of their faith reflected historic ecumenical convictions.[77]

Dale Aukerman labored for peace and against the death penalty throughout his ministry. *Hope Beyond Healing: A Cancer Journal* is the moving record of his final, more personal battle with death.[78] Among his writings was *Darkening Valley: A Biblical Perspective on Nuclear War*,[79] perhaps the most important work on Christian discipleship since Bonhoeffer.[80]

Scattered throughout his works are indications of the faith by which he was sustained. They are often incidental, more at the level of governing convictions than topics of direct focus, since his concern was with the meaning of discipleship in a culture of death. It is clear, however, that he held a high view of the

Publications, 1998); *American Catholic Pacifism: The Influence of Dorothy Day and the Catholic Worker Movement*, ed. Anne Klejment and Nancy L. Roberts (Westport: Praeger, 1996); Ronald Musto, *The Catholic Peace Tradition* (Maryknoll: Orbis, 1986).

77 Much the same must be said of their eucharistic views. Little is known of them. We may be as certain of their regular participation in the Lord's Supper as of their relatively low church understandings. For them the paschal mystery would have been more a matter of scriptural teaching than of liturgical expression.

78 Dale Aukerman, *Hope Beyond Healing: A Cancer Journal*, Forward by Jim Wallis (Elgin: Brethren Press, 2000).

79 Aukerman, *Darkening Valley: A Biblical Perspective on Nuclear War* (New York: Seabury Press, 1981). References to this work are cited by page number in the text.

80 See my review in *The Christian Century* 99 (January 6–13, 1982), pp. 34–35.

Incarnation,[81] a high view of Christ's resurrection,[82] and a high view of the atonement. Because the latter point is especially contested, it deserves special attention. Aukerman quoted with approval James Denney on 2 Cor. 5:14 "We are convinced that one has died for all; therefore all have died": "This clause puts as plainly as it can be put the idea that his death was the equivalent to the death of all. In other words, it was the death of all [human beings] which was died by him" (p. 44). Again quoting Denney: "It is our death that Christ died on the cross" (p. 45). Aukerman added: "Because the full magnitude of God dwelt in him, he could take to himself and know the full magnitude of human hate, killing and death ... The slaughters, the hate and guilt of multitudes throughout all history converged on him" (p. 44). With theologians like Athanasius and Anselm, as well as with the humblest of believers, Aukerman affirmed: "In Jesus, God did what no one else could do" (p. 197). For Aukerman as for the historic church, everything stood or fell with Christ's saving death in our place and for our sakes.

Far from seeing substitutionary atonement an impediment to peace or an incitement to abuse, Aukerman saw it as the foundation for an ethic of non-violence.[83] Christians were called "to meet enemies as God in Christ had met them" (p. 180). They were to meet hostility not with retaliation or vengeance, but with the

---

[81] "God narrowed himself down into Jesus Christ. The Incomprehensible and Inscrutable became a human person in our midst" (*Darkening Valley*, p. 109). In accord with the Nicene Creed, he affirmed that the Son was the Son "from all eternity" (ibid., p. 148; quoting von Balthasar). It is not my intention to collect every such statement that he made, but only to illustrate his views.

[82] "Jesus was raised from the tomb with a changed body; his crucified body and the matter in it were recreated, transformed" (ibid., p. 121).

[83] He also worked with *Christus victor* imagery quite extensively. But it never occurred to him to suppose that the imagery of Christ's royal work (defeating hostile powers) conflicted with imagery of Christ's priestly sacrifice (the Lamb bearing sin and death vicariously for our sakes). These were, in effect, two complementary perspectives on Christ's one, indivisible saving office.

"scandalous defenselessness" of love (p. 180). They were called not to save the world from sin and death, but to bear witness, through non-violence, to the One who had. For Aukerman, as for all ecumenical Christians, Jesus was first of all the Lord and Savior, and only then also the Exemplar.

The uniqueness of Christ as the Savior, as Aukerman saw it, placed a healthy limit on the possibility of imitating him. It served to free the disciples of Christ from all impulses to moralism, self-righteousness, and self-justification. "Self-justification before God and security through weapons over against enemies are the inner and outer culminations of our human attempt to save ourselves" (p. 149).[84] The free gift of grace, for Aukerman, meant the end of all need to defend ourselves.

He could turn this insight into a challenge. "The Anabaptist tradition," he wrote, "has been strongly oriented toward practice and not that much toward matters of faith about God and Christ ... Yet the whole of the New Testament ... makes emphatically clear ... that right belief is crucial, and indeed foundational for right practice."[85] He noted the complaint of a fellow anabaptist pastor: "I could preach every Sunday on salvation by grace, and the majority of my people would still believe in salvation by works."[86] With a theologian of his church, he agreed that when anabaptists condemned others as "warmongers" who did not share their outlook on peacemaking, it was a matter of "simplistic

---

[84] In 1982 Aukerman spoke at New Brunswick Theological Seminary at my invitation. In line with the remark just cited, he presented the Reformation doctrine of justification to my students as the basis for an ethic of non-violence. For a similar argument from the Lutheran side, see Hans Werner Bartsch, "The Foundation and Meaning of Christian Pacifism," in *New Theology No. 6*, ed. Martin E. Marty and Dean G. Peerman (New York: Macmillan, 1969), pp. 185–98.

[85] Dale Aukerman, "Anabaptist Peacemaking for a New Century," *Brethren Life and Thought* 39 (1994): 203–9; on p. 208.

[86] Dale Aukerman, "BVS – Reminiscence and Rumination," *Brethren Life and Thought* 3 (1958), pp. 39–46; on p. 44. The same complaint could be made, of course, from within other traditions.

moralism." Pacifists, Aukerman concluded, need "to give a careful, charitable hearing to persons with other points of view."[87]

André Trocmé was a Reformed pastor, who during the Nazi occupation of France led a non-violent resistance movement in Le Chambon, a remote mountain village in southern France. With his fellow villagers, he helped to save the lives of an estimated 2,500– 5,000 Jews, many of whom were children. After the war he served as European secretary for the Fellowship of Reconciliation. Like Dale Aukerman after him, Trocmé was essentially a Nicene Christian of pacifist convictions. Like Aukerman, he held a high view of the Incarnation and the atonement – though almost always as background convictions from which he drew non-violent implications. Like Aukerman, he was thus a pastor of orthodox beliefs who put them into extraordinary practice in difficult times. In an article in 1955 he wrote:

> Basic truth has been taught to us by Jesus Christ. What is it? The person of any one man is so important in the eyes of God, so central to the whole of His creation, that the unique perfect being, Jesus, (a) sacrificed his earthly life for that one man in the street, and (b) sacrificed his perfection [by assuming the burden of that person's sins] in order to save that single man. Salvation has been accomplished without any regard to the moral value of the saved man.[88]

Trocmé here grounds respect for the dignity of every person, regardless of moral worth, in the Incarnation and cross of Christ. For Trocmé, the Incarnation meant that Jesus was a unique and perfect being; the cross, that he had assumed to himself the whole burden of human sin; and salvation, that he had accomplished something for us, at terrible cost, that we could not do for ourselves.

---

[87] Dale Aukerman, "A Response to Vernard Eller," *Brethren Life and Thought* 34 (1989), pp. 43–47; on p. 43.

[88] André Trocmé, "The Law Itself Was a Lie!," *Fellowship* magazine (January 1955), p. 4. Quoted by Philip Hallie, *Lest Innocent Blood Be Shed: The Story of Le Chambon and How Goodness Happened There* (New York: Harper & Row, 1979), p. 160.

Trocmé derived an ethic of non-violence from Jesus' "sacrifice on the cross."[89] His explanation of that sacrifice could at times assume Anselmian overtones.[90] He saw Jesus as the *goel*, a Hebrew word for "avenging kinsman," appointed to stand in and stand up for the fallen human race. But in Jesus the law of retaliation was fulfilled by being overturned. Although God's demand for righteousness could never be abolished, in Jesus God's judgment against sin was borne "by God himself, by the God who is the *goel* of his people in the person of his Son" (p. 9). In Jesus God redeemed the guilty by redirecting their judgment to himself (p. 68). Jesus was the Lamb of God, the *goel*, who took away the world's sin (p. 135). Though innocent, he took the place of the guilty that they might live and not be destroyed. Evil was overcome by redemptive love when God liberated his people by dying for them (p. 68).[91]

For Trocmé the indicative of the cross led to the imperative of non-violence.

> By choosing to save at the cost of his life, Jesus forever joined two realities: redemption and nonviolence. Because Jesus is the Redeemer, no one can any longer save by killing or kill to save. Life alone, life given, not life exacted from others, can save life.
>
> (p. 133)

Non-violence thus thrusts itself on those who would follow Jesus. It was "an article of faith, a mark of obedience, a sign of the kingdom to come" (p. 143). In Le Chambon Trocmé embodied what he believed about Jesus. He "would not separate himself from

---

[89] André Trocmé, *Jesus and the Nonviolent Revolution* (Maryknoll: Orbis Books, 2004), p. 143. (References hereafter cited in the text.)

[90] These were elsewhere counterbalanced by *Christus victor* motifs.

[91] Trocmé's substitutionary theme is curiously forced by Professor Weaver in a non-substitutionary direction. Not only does he mix the ideas of "penal substitution" and "satisfaction atonement" indiscriminately, but he clearly has no concept of non-penal (expiatory) substitution ("Christology, Atonement, and Peace," ms. p. 28).

Jesus," wrote Philip Hallie, "by hating and killing his fellowman."[92] He became a *goel* for endangered Jews in his witness to Jesus, whom he confessed as the *goel* of the world.

Conclusion

Aukerman and Trocmé represent the peace witness of Nicene Christians at their best. Accusations that associate the logic of Nicaea with indifference, and atonement doctrines with abuse, are more than challenged by their life and thought.

Nevertheless, the concerns of socially minded critics of Nicene Christianity are by no means to be dismissed. They are perhaps best taken as a call to self-examination and repentance. Who among us can say that we or our various traditions have cared enough about the victims of violence and oppression or done enough for justice and peace? How can one appeal to the best representatives of Nicene Christianity if one is not prepared to follow in their train?

While few ecumenical traditions are likely to embrace outright pacifism, all can move closer to a chastened non-pacifism,[93] to just peacemaking,[94] and to creative non-violence[95] – for the sake of

---

[92] Hallie, *Lest Innocent Blood*, p. 84 (*supra* n. 88).

[93] See George F. Kennan, *The Nuclear Delusion* (New York: Pantheon, 1982). Note especially pp. xxviii–xix, where Kennan, the political realist, makes an eloquent plea for the abolition of war.

[94] "Just peacemaking" is an important attempt to move beyond the impasse between the just-war tradition and pacifism. See Glen H. Stassen, *Just Peacemaking: Transforming Initiatives for Justice and Peace* (Louisville: Westminster/John Knox Press, 1992); *Just Peacemaking: Ten Practices for Abolishing War*, ed. Glen Stassen (Cleveland: Pilgrim Press, 2004, 2nd edn.).

[95] See Gene Sharp, *The Politics of Nonviolent Action*, 3 parts (Boston, MA: Porter Sargent, 1972–85); *Waging Nonviolent Struggle: 20th Century Practice and 21st Century Potential*, ed. Gene Sharp (Boston, MA: Extending Horizons Books, 2005); Marshall B. Rosenberg, *Nonviolent Communication: A Language of Compassion* (Encinitas: PuddleDancer Press, 2003).

Christ and for the sake of the world. After a long, terrible, and bloody twentieth century, which saw tens of millions of combatants and civilians being slaughtered without mercy, aerial bombardments of cities, indiscriminate killings, the burning of villages, the erection of death camps, the commission of genocides, the refinement and proliferation of torture, the widespread incidence of rapes and pillagings, it is more than ever incumbent on the church to recover her traditions of peace. *Let love be genuine; hate what is evil, hold fast to what is good; love one another with mutual affection; outdo one another in showing honor* (Rom. 12:9–10).

Conclusion: let us keep the feast

The strategy of this book has been both pragmatic and principled. It has attempted to develop a set of proposals that could be achieved in practice without involving any tradition in unacceptable compromises. The proposals, if adopted, would arguably bring greater enrichment than loss. They would facilitate genuine ecumenical convergence toward eucharistic sharing. They would open up new avenues for healing the notorious divisions that have beset the sacrament of unity.

The argument is addressed primarily to the Reformed churches and through them to the wider *oikumene*. If they were to adopt these proposals (or something like them), it would be an act of witness, showing how one tradition can benefit from heeding the admonitions of others. It would show how hard truths can lead to renewal, bringing not regret but an enhanced level of fellowship and faithfulness. Have not the Reformed always affirmed the principle of ongoing reformation – *ecclesia reformata et semper reformanda secundum verbum dei* – the church reformed and always being reformed according to the Word of God? What better use could there be of this principle than to apply it to Reformed views of the Lord's Supper? Ecumenical conversion begins at home.

On the quixotic premise that the Reformed might actually adopt some such proposals, admonitions were ventured to the high sacramental churches as well. The Reformed family could hardly expect the sacramental churches to pay attention to its admonitions if it were not prepared to heed their concerns in turn. At the same time, what was mentioned in the Introduction needs to be reiterated here. I am at a loss when it comes to coordinating these proposals with churches in burgeoning anabaptist, pentecostal, charismatic, and parachurch movements, and related ecclesial formations. Ecumenical convergence does not seem possible without affirming Nicene Christianity, a high view of the eucharist, and some sort of episcopal polity. The question has been how to facilitate this outcome for the Reformed in accord with their theological convictions.

The proposals will now be summarized. At the same time, they will be brought into relationship with appropriate sections from agreed statements by the Eastern Orthodox / Roman Catholic US Consultation,[1] the *Catechism of the Catholic Church* (1994),[2] and certain representative Orthodox discussions.

An attempt has been made, as mentioned, to keep the Reformed in alignment with the Eastern Orthodox on those points where they cannot follow the Roman Catholics, and where, as far as the Catholics are concerned, the Orthodox view does not seem to be church-dividing. At points where disagreement remains, but not so much as to prevent eucharistic sharing, there would obviously need to be continuing discussion and mutual forbearance, with no side condemning the views of the other. For example, the doctrine of transubstantiation would not be required of Eastern Orthodox and Reformed churches, but they would put it in the best light and not condemn Roman Catholicism for holding it.

---

[1] Documents included in *The Quest for Unity: Orthodox and Catholics in Dialogue: Documents of the Joint International and Official Dialogues in the United States, 1965–1995*, ed. John Borelli and John Erickson (Crestwood: St. Vladimir's Seminary Press / Washington, DC: US Catholic Conference, 1996), pp. 45–46 (Eucharist), 69–75 (BEM), 120–24 (Pastoral Office)

[2] *Catechism of the Catholic Church* (Vatican City: Libreria Editrice Vaticana, 1994).

The bread that we break

It is proposed:

(1) that the Reformed churches affirm, without equivocation, that the consecrated bread has become the body of Christ and the consecrated cup the blood of Christ.

(2) that the Reformed follow Vermigli, Bucer, and Cranmer (and possibly Calvin) insofar as they affirmed the eucharistic views on real presence represented by Theophylact (eleventh century). These views were in fact commonplace in the fourth and fifth centuries, in figures like the Cappadocians and Cyril of Alexandria, and they have standing in Eastern Orthodoxy today.

　(a) Specifically, it is proposed that the Reformed view the relationship between Christ's life-giving flesh and the consecrated elements as one of mutual indwelling (*koinonia*).

　(b) The technical name for this position is transelementation (*metastoicheiosis*).

　(c) It involves the elevation and objective conversion of the elements through their mystical union with Christ's flesh in the power of the Holy Spirit, but not a destruction of their "substance" so that only their "accidents" (or species) would remain.

(3) that the Reformed affirm that the signs truly become the reality they signify without ceasing to be signs, that the signs thus effectually mediate what they are and are what they mediate, since as bread and wine they are at the same time Christ's body and blood.

Points of convergence with the high sacramental churches

(1) "In this eucharistic meal, according to the promise of Christ, the Father sends the Spirit to consecrate the elements to be the body and blood of Jesus Christ and to sanctify the faithful"

("An Agreed Statement on the Holy Eucharist," No. 2; US Orthodox/Catholic Theological Consultation, 1969).

(2) "The mode of Christ's presence under the Eucharistic species is unique ... It is a substantial presence by which Christ, God and man, makes himself wholly and entirely present" (*Catechism*, No. 1374).

(3) "The symbol itself is a participant in the spiritual reality and is able or called upon to embody it ... It is the manifestation, the presence, the operation of one reality within the other."[3]

Points of clarification for the Reformed tradition

(1) The historic Reformed insistence on the integrity of Christ's body in heaven ("local presence") is not compromised by this position. Upholding that integrity is as important to the Orthodox and the Catholics as it is to the Reformed. (The technicalities were worked out admirably by Aquinas.)

(2) As has been noted, Calvin also taught the true, substantial, and ineffable presence of Christ's life-giving flesh in conjunction with the elements, and he was open to the patristic idea of their "secret conversion." While he did not teach "transelementation," he seemed, in some ways, to teach something not far from it. He regarded Vermigli's views on the eucharist to be exemplary.

(3) In transelementation, the relationship of Christ's life-giving flesh to the elements can be formally described as one of asymmetry, unity, and distinction. The Reformed, who have always insisted on the aspect of necessary distinction, would stretch only to adopt a stronger position on the aspect of mystical unity.

---

[3] Alexander Schmemann, *The Eucharist* (Crestwood: St. Vladimir's Seminary Press, 1988), p. 39.

The sacrifice we offer

It is proposed:

(1) that the Reformed affirm a position on eucharistic sacrifice that accords with the Reformation's insistence on monergism with respect to the work of salvation. The eucharistic sacrifice would in no sense be a meritorious work attributable to the priesthood or the church. Eucharistic sacrifice would be affirmed, while the central concern of the Reformation was upheld.

(2) that the consecrated elements of bread and wine be seen not only in their "downward" (or "humanward") significance as the means of communion, but also in their "upward" (or "Godward") significance as the means by which church is incorporated into Christ's offering of himself in eternal intercession on behalf of the faithful and the world. With this revision, the Reformed, while continuing to plead Christ's eternal sacrifice in thanks and praise, would give this plea a richer eucharistic location.

(3) that the eucharistic sacrifice be seen not only in its abiding distinction from Christ's sacrifice on the cross (the dimension of depth), but also in its inseparable unity with it.

   (a) that it be seen as a secondary and dependent form of the once-for-all sacrifice on the cross.

   (b) that it be seen as the actualization of that sacrifice in a sacramental mode.

   (c) that it be seen as neither a repetition of nor a supplement to that sacrifice.

   (d) that it be seen as a memorial (*anamnesis*) of that sacrifice, not as a merely mental event, but as a liturgical action and therefore as a communal participation in what is being remembered.

(e) that it be seen not just as a memorial (*anamnesis*) of a past event, but at the same time as a real anticipation (*prolepsis*) of the promised future, and therefore of the coming marriage feast of the Lamb, which is also the Banquet of the great High King.

(4) that the eucharistic sacrifice not be cut off from its essence as the paschal mystery and therefore from its role as the fulfillment of Passover in and through Christ's sacrifice on the cross.

(a) that it thus be seen not only in terms of participation but also in terms of substitution, according to the paschal mystery of exchange (*admirabile commercium*), whereby the just died for the unjust, the innocent for the guilty, and the Living for those in Adam who are dead, so that the latter might not merely be spared, but made just, holy, and alive eternally, through Christ.

Points of convergence with the high sacramental churches

(1) "The eucharistic sacrifice involves the active presence of Christ, the High Priest, acting through the Christian community, drawing it into his saving worship. Through celebration of the Eucharist the redemptive blessings are bestowed on the living and the dead for whom intercession is made" ("An Agreed Statement on the Holy Eucharist," No. 3; US Orthodox/Catholic Theological Consultation, 1969).

(a) Comment: In the belief that Christ intercedes for all the faithful, it may be presumed that he does so for both the living and the dead, on whom his redemptive blessings fall. It may also be presumed that he takes up the eucharistic intercessions of the church and sanctifies them. Insofar as the celebration of the eucharist is itself a sacramental form of Christ's one saving sacrifice, in which he is actively present as the High Priest, it is possible to affirm the statement about intercession cited above – but only on the premise of the centrality of Christ and the church's eucharistic *participatio Christi*.

(2) "The relationship between Christ's sacrifice and his presence in the eucharist requires further clarification, particularly in regard to his offering of himself to the Father and his giving of himself to us as spiritual food" ("An Agreed Statement on the LIMA Document: 'Baptism, the Eucharist and Ministry,'" Section II; US Orthodox/Catholic Theological Consultation, 1984).

    (a) Comment: If the proposal on eucharistic sacrifice developed in this book were adopted by the Reformed, presumably it would go some way toward alleviating this Orthodox/Catholic concern about a lack of clarity in the *BEM* document.

(3) "The whole community [participates] in the Lord's own sacrifice by means of the Eucharist" (*Catechism*, No. 1212). "We offer to the Father what he himself has given us: the gifts of his creation, bread and wine which ... have become the body and blood of Christ" (*Catechism*, No. 1357). "The sacrifice of praise to the Father is offered through Christ and with him, to be accepted in him" (*Catechism*, No. 1361). "The Eucharist is the memorial of Christ's Passover, the making present and the sacramental offering of his unique sacrifice in the liturgy of the Church ..." (*Catechism*, No. 1362). "When the Church celebrates the Eucharist, she commemorates Christ's Passover, and it is made present: the sacrifice Christ offered once for all ..." (*Catechism*, No. 1364). "The Church participates in the offering of her Head. With him, she herself is offered whole and entire" (*Catechism*, No. 1367). "Christ himself [is] the principal agent of the Eucharist" (*Catechism*, No. 1348).

(4) "Only God can save – precisely save – us, for our life needs salvation, and not simply help ... And he fulfills this in the ultimate, perfect, and all-embracing sacrifice in which he gave his only begotten Son for the salvation of the world ... In this

sacrifice everything is fulfilled and accomplished" (Schmemann, *Eucharist*, pp. 103–4). "The offering by ourselves of Christ, and in Christ of ourselves, makes possible and fulfills our commemoration" (ibid., p. 131).

Points of clarification for the Reformed tradition

(1) Schmemann, at least, seems clearer than the Catholic catechism that synergism is to be rejected with respect to salvation, because when it comes to effecting our salvation, God through Jesus Christ in the Holy Spirit is not merely the "principal" but the "exclusive" agent. In a way typical of the Orthodox, he eschews categories of causation in favor of those that are more personal and participatory.

(2) Schmemann also seems to uphold a more high-profile distinction between the sacrifice of the cross and the eucharistic sacrifice, though of course he affirms their sacramental unity as well.

(3) In its robust association of Passover with the eucharist, the Catholic catechism is exemplary. For the Orthodox the association is more nearly tacit though everywhere present in their understanding of the Divine Liturgy. For example, in the Liturgy of Preparation, a portion of the eucharistic bread, called "the Lamb," is cut out by the priest and consecrated to be the eucharist. The high sacramental churches have not lost vital priestly and sacrificial imagery through the erosion that has too often come to characterize the Reformed and other Protestant liturgies. The eucharist is indeed the joyful feast of the kingdom of God, but it is also the feast of the paschal mystery.

(4) In their teachings about the eucharist, neither the Catholics nor the Orthodox always place sufficient emphasis on Christ having died in our place, though this theme is indispensable to any properly paschal understanding of Christ's sacrifice, with its deep roots in the religion of Israel and the apostolic witness.

Here is an area where classical Reformation theology could make a contribution to the wider *oikumene* today. T. F. Torrance, for example, is strong on this theme with respect to the eucharist, as are also, more generally, Eberhard Jüngel and Karl Barth.

Eucharist and ministry

It is proposed:

(1) that the Reformed churches accept episcopal ordination as the ecumenical norm to which they will need to accommodate their polities.

(2) that the episcopacy be reconfigured along lines of collegiality, jurisdiction, and governance that correspond more nearly with current Eastern Orthodox than Roman Catholic understandings, though, should it ever come, the episcopal office in a reunited church is not likely to be entirely identical with any forms that now exist.

(3) that the primacy of the bishop of Rome, as the highest symbol and spokesperson of Christian unity, within a newly minted collegial structure, be welcomed with gladness by all Christian traditions and individuals.

(4) that the high sacramental churches find a theologically principled way of giving their blessing to the ministerial office as it now exists in the churches of the Reformation, despite the irregularities and deficiencies in ordination procedures that were historically unavoidable. Previous generations of church leadership could not, given the limitations of the times, prevent new divisions from arising in the church. If no tradition exempts itself from a share of responsibility for the divisions, a charitable resolution should be possible.

(5) that baptism be seen as the center out of which to think about ordination, so that ordination becomes a further specification,

321

for a particular ministry, of the charism received in baptism. All vocations in the church, whether necessitating ordination or not, would be seen as involving some such further specification of the baptismal charism, each in the way proper to it. This move would help to block various tendencies whereby the episcopacy is separated too sharply from the rest of the church.

(6) that it be affirmed that there is one ministry common to Christ and his church, so that all particular forms of ministry, whether ordained or not, are seen as particular modes of participating in the one, yet highly ramified, ministry of Christ.

(7) that in a divided church all traditions acknowledge that none can be without non-trivial defect regarding apostolic succession in its doctrinal aspect. All traditions need to subject themselves – through self-examination, dialogue, and prayer, under the sovereignty of the Word of God in the power of the Spirit – to the admonitions of others, and so ponder what they are called to learn from the Spirit's operation in traditions not their own.

Points of convergence and divergence with the high sacramental churches

(1) "We find helpful the treatment of the historical development of the three-fold ministry, as well as the delineation of the functions of bishop, presbyter, and deacon, [which] are adequately outlined and balanced" ("An Agreed Statement on the LIMA Document: 'Baptism, the Eucharist and Ministry,'" Section III; US Orthodox/Catholic Theological Consultation, 1984).

(2) "Apostolic succession is rightly interpreted as involving the total life of the Church. The view that ordained ministry is an integral part of the apostolic tradition is especially useful in advancing ecumenical discussion. Ordained ministry is thus understood as one of the expressions of the Church's apostolicity. This understanding, in our judgment, is confirmed by the act of ordination within the believing community which signifies the

bestowal of the gift of ministry through the laying on of hands of the bishop and the epiclesis of the Holy Spirit" ("An Agreed Statement on the LIMA Document: 'Baptism, the Eucharist and Ministry,'" Section III; US Orthodox/Catholic Theological Consultation, 1984).

(3) "While both bishop and presbyter share the one ministry of Christ, the bishop exercises authoritative leadership over the whole community. The presbyter shares in the pastoral office under the bishop" ("The Pastoral Office: A Joint Statement," No. 4; US Orthodox/Catholic Theological Consultation, 1976). "Catholic theologians have explained these elements in terms of character, priestly character. Similar elements are included in Orthodox understanding of priesthood as a charisma. Both character and charisma stress the relationship of the ordained to the gift of the Holy Spirit on which the exercise of his ministry in service to the community depends" ("The Pastoral Office: A Joint Statement," No. 8; US Orthodox/Catholic Theological Consultation, 1976).

(4) "Though the ecclesial Communities which are separated from us lack the fullness of unity with us flowing from Baptism, and though we believe they have not retained the proper reality of the eucharistic mystery in its fullness, especially because of the absence of the sacrament of Orders, nevertheless when they commemorate His death and resurrection in the Lord's Supper, they profess that it signifies life in communion with Christ and look forward to His coming in glory. Therefore the teaching concerning the Lord's Supper, the other sacraments, worship, the ministry of the Church, must be the subject of the dialogue" (Vatican II, "Decree on Ecumenism," *Unitatis Redintegratio*, 1965, No. 22).[4]

---

[4] "Decree on Ecumenism" (*Unitatis Redintegratio*), No. 22, in *The Documents of Vatican II*, ed. Walter Abbott (New York: Guild Press, America Press, Association Press, 1966), pp. 341–66; on p. 364.

(5) "The order of deaconesses seems definitely to have been considered an 'ordained' ministry during early centuries in at any rate the Christian East ... Some Orthodox writers regard deaconesses as having been a 'lay' ministry. There are strong reasons for rejecting this view. In the Byzantine rite the liturgical office for the laying-on of hands for the deaconess is exactly parallel to that for the deacon; and so on the principle lex orandi, lex credendi – the Church's worshipping practice is a sure indication of its faith – it follows that the deaconess receives, as does the deacon, a genuine sacramental ordination."[5]

"The traditional exclusion of women from ordination to the pastoral office affects both Catholic and Orthodox theologians, but in a differing way. Concerning this issue, Catholic theologians are examining biblical data, traditional practice, theological and anthropological data. Since they have not reached a consensus, the question remains disputed among them" ("The Pastoral Office: A Joint Statement," Section II, No. 2; US Orthodox/Catholic Theological Consultation, 1976).

Points of clarification for the Reformed tradition

(1) All churches, as has been stressed, will need to make difficult adjustments at some points for the good of the whole in obedience to Christ. For the Reformed churches, accepting an episcopal polity, even if in a decentralized, electoral, and collegial form, will not be easy. Adjusting to the scheme of bishop, presbyter, and deacon will pose special challenges, especially for those Reformed churches that ordain "ruling" as well as "teaching" elders.

---

[5] Bishop Kallistos Ware, "Man, Woman and the Priesthood of Christ," in *Women and the Priesthood*, ed. T. Hopko (Crestwood: St. Vladimir's Seminary Press, 1982), p. 16.

(2) In Reformed communities, the office of "ruling" elder will probably need to become more vocational and less formal, while the office of "teaching" elder will need to be enhanced in a more sacramental direction than is now the case. Ruling elders will need to be folded into a revised diaconate, teaching elders into the presbyteriate, and moderators of presbyteries and executive presbyters into the episcopate.

(3) A Porvoo-like process will need to be instituted. All ordained ministers will need to be folded, without prejudice, into the historic apostolic succession through the laying on of hands.

(4) The Reformed would then be in a better position within the wider *oikumene* to insist that while it may be the eucharist that fulfills the church, it is Holy Scripture that establishes it. The church lives by the freedom of grace, through the proclamation of the Word of God, or it does not live at all. The Reformed will stand for the centrality of Christ, as attested by Holy Scripture, and for the wind of the Spirit to blow where it will.

(5) A preaching office without its eucharistic complement in the weekly liturgy, however, would be like a head without a torso, while a sacramental priestly office without a robust liturgy of the Word would be much the reverse. It has been said, not without justice, that Protestants have their religion too much in their heads. If Calvin rather than Zwingli were our liturgical guide, he would be taken seriously when he wrote that the eucharist should be received "very often, and at least [*ad minimum*] once a week" (*Inst.* IV.17.43).

(6) The admonition of *defectus* with regard to the ministerial office in Reformational churches has been discussed at length in Part III. If, as is proposed here, this admonition is to be relativized and universalized, as opposed to being dismissed, the chances would be better if the Reformed adopted a new stance on real presence, eucharistic sacrifice, and episcopal governance.

(7) The remarks cited above from Bishop Ware make it sound as though ordaining women may be more of an open question

for the high sacramental churches than is apparently the case. For these churches to receive an infusion of verbal imagination, so that ordained ministers were seen as witnesses first and "iconic" representations second, if at all, would take a surprising work of the Spirit. Yet the arguments against women's ordination are weak, the arguments for it are strong, and hope must be kept alive against hope.

Concluding unscientific personal postscript

When I asked Donald Schell, co-rector of San Francisco's St. Gregory of Nyssa Episcopal Church, what I could read to learn more about their worship, his answer took me by surprise. "The book that got us started," he replied, "was *Liturgy and Architecture* by Louis Bouyer."[6] Having read the book, I can see why.

Whether it is realized it or not, function does indeed follow form. A sanctuary's architecture very largely determines what kind of worship can be held. Following Bouyer, St. Gregory's intends to make worship as participatory as possible. Without abolishing the distinction between the congregation and the presbyter, the congregation is given an unusually active role in the liturgy, not only (as in other liturgies) through recitation and song, but through movement, discussion, and even a form of eucharistic co-distribution. None of this would be possible in most sanctuaries as they have come to be known.

St. Gregory's building plan is adapted from the earliest Christian churches of Syria. In these sanctuaries, as Bouyer points out, the architecture maintained continuity with the Jewish synagogue, though in a Christianized form. When one walks in the door at St. Gregory's, what one sees first is the large D-shaped altar-table,

---

[6] Louis Bouyer, *Liturgy and Architecture* (Notre Dame: University of Notre Dame Press, 1967).

and beyond it the baptismal fount. The building is laid out in a rectangle of two equal squares.

To one's right is the western square, where the congregation will sit in rows of seats arranged in choir fashion, so that the people face one another across a long aisle. It is here that they celebrate the Liturgy of the Word.

The aisle leads up to a platform at the far wall, which holds a broad chair for the preacher, who delivers the homily from there while seated. Flanking the preacher on either side are chairs for the deacons and cantors. At the aisle's other end, but still in the western square, a lectern rises, almost at the building's center, from which the day's lessons from Holy Scripture are read.

To one's center-left (still as one walks in) is the eastern square, an open space with the altar-table standing alone in the center. Here, in the Liturgy of the Sacrament, the congregation will give thanks, feast, and dance together.

Throughout both parts of the service, the clergy preside among the people rather than opposite them. Following Bouyer, they face east, unifying both parts of the service in a common orientation.[7]

Bouyer's influence is felt at every point. He argued that early Christian worship in Syria was highly participatory, that the clergy presided among the people rather than over against them, and that they always faced east. The liturgy had three focal points: "the celebration of the word, the altar around which all are to be gathered as the effect of their response to the word, [and] the *parousia* toward which they are finally to be oriented."[8]

The traditional practice of praying toward the east was carried over from the synagogue, but invested with a new meaning. For

---

[7] For a feminist case against east-facing celebration, see Nancy Jay, *Throughout Your Generations Forever* (Chicago: University of Chicago Press, 1992). For a counter-argument in its favor, see Sarah Coakley, "The Woman at the Altar: Cosmological Disturbance or Gender Subversion?," *Anglican Theological Review*, 86 (2004), pp. 75–93.

[8] Bouyer, *Liturgy and Architecture*, p. 91.

the synagogue it had meant praying toward Jerusalem; for the church, praying toward the new Jerusalem. "The fact that the eucharistic celebration has an eschatological orientation, that it is not a final step but that it looks toward a further consummation, needs certainly to be emphasized in some way where Christians gather for the eucharist," wrote Bouyer.[9] An eschatological liturgy needs to be facilitated by the architecture. "An organization of the building, therefore, which leads toward the altar but does not stop at it, which points beyond it at some cosmic and supra-cosmic perspective, is greatly to be desired,"[10] according to Bouyer, a desire St. Gregory's admirably fulfills.

The Sunday morning worship begins when the music director calls everyone to gather around the altar. With the help of the choir he teaches the congregation a simple hymn, which they will sing as they move – or rather dance – toward their seats in the western area. At St. Gregory's, simple liturgical dances for the entire congregation are seen as one of the most profound parts of worship. They are adapted from ancient liturgical practice. Another simple line dance is taught (at least to newcomers who do not yet know it), as the entire congregation leaves the liturgy of the Word, again singing a hymn along with the dance, and reassembles in the eastern area to celebrate the eucharist.

It may seem that having both the celebrant and the congregation facing in the same direction, toward the east, would not be advantageous for the eucharist, but Bouyer argued quite the opposite. He contended that when the priest started facing the congregation, it led to a number of unfortunate developments. The eschatological orientation of the eucharist was lost, congregational participation declined, clericalization of the eucharist set in (leading eventually even to the private mass), and the liturgy became a show to be observed rather than a communal practice to take part in.

---

[9] Ibid., pp. 94–95. [10] Ibid., p. 95.

Over time it was all ratified by architecture. "The altar facing the people. historically ... far from having been ever intended for a common celebration, seems to have been both the effect and the cause of a substitution of a clerical celebration for a corporate worship."[11] Pews became immovable, no possibility remained for the congregation to move together during the service, and no room any longer existed for them to gather together as a community around the altar.

Bouyer's arguments have, it is noteworthy, caught the attention of the Pope. Pope Benedict XVI (then Cardinal Ratzinger) follows Bouyer in advocating that a proper sanctuary consists of two parts, one for the Word, the other for the Sacrament, and that in the course of the service the congregation should move from the one to the other. He also commends facing east.

> At the end of the Liturgy of the Word, during which the faithful stand around the bishop's seat, everyone walks together with the bishop to the altar, and now the cry resounds: *Conversi ad Dominum*, "Turn toward the Lord!" In other words, look to the east with the bishop, in the sense of the words from the epistle to the Hebrews: *[Look] ... to Jesus the pioneer and perfecter of our faith* (12:2). The Liturgy of the Eucharist is celebrated as we look up to Jesus. It *is* our looking up to Jesus. Thus, in early church buildings, the liturgy has two places.[12]

The Pope considers facing east for the eucharist to be of the highest importance. "A common turning to the east during the Eucharistic Prayer remains essential. This is not a case of something accidental, but of what is essential. Looking at the priest has no importance. What matters is looking together at the Lord."[13] The Pope realizes it will be difficult to recover this ancient liturgical

---

[11] Ibid., p. 60.
[12] Joseph Ratzinger, *The Spirit of the Liturgy* (San Francisco: Ignatius Press, 2000), p. 72.
[13] Ibid., p. 81.

practice without attending to architecture. "If the presence of the Lord is to touch us in a concrete way, the tabernacle must also find its proper place in the architecture of our church buildings."[14]

At St. Gregory's this process is already under way. They have restored a true common celebration by retrieving the necessary architecture. They have followed Bouyer when he writes that "the altar should never be lost in some inaccessible sanctuary but always be a short distance from the first ranks of the people. What is needed especially is, for the offering and the communion, that they may come as near to it as possible."[15] As Bouyer recommended, and the Pope concurs, at the time of the eucharistic prayer, the congregation gathers "in a more or less semi-circular way behind the celebrant."[16]

It is perhaps little wonder that after visiting St. Gregory's, Fr. John F. Baldovin, a liturgical scholar from the Weston School of Theology, commented: "I have just had the closest possible experience of what worship was like in the fourth century." A visitor from Africa remarked: "The church service here is the closest thing I've experienced in America to a village worship service in Africa."[17]

Other aspects of the great St. Gregory's experiment may be mentioned. An attempt at multiculturalism is evident at every turn. African outfits are worn by the priests, oriental gongs are sounded after the readings, the preacher's seat is a Thai elephant howdah, brightly colored pink and orange ceremonial umbrellas adorn the processions, the lectern is backed by a tree of lights (menorah) and a screen of Ethiopian crosses with streamers, the hymns include everything from shape note to Ralph Vaughan Williams to Dave Brubeck. Large dramatic icons grace the walls. Circling the dome above the altar is an unforgettable iconic

---

[14] Ibid., p. 91.

[15] Bouyer, *Liturgy and Architecture*, pp. 111–12 (*supra* n. 6). [16] Ibid., p. 112.

[17] Quoted in Trudy Bush, "Back to the Future," *The Christian Century* 199 (November 20, 2002), pp. 18–22. (The article, I assume, wrongly attributes to "John Baldwin" the comment by Fr. Baldovin.) See also Robert L. Woodbury, "An Empty Stage or Heaven Apprehended," *Sacred Architecture* 10 (2005).

representation of dancing saints, Christian and non-Christian alike, including figures as diverse as Elizabeth I, Malcolm X, Lady Godiva, Martin Luther, Abraham Joshua Heschel, Ella Fitzgerald, Buddha, and Muhammad.

Obviously not everything at St. Gregory's would be to everyone's taste. Its quirkiness extends into theology. The Nicene Creed is omitted from the liturgy for being "divisive," baptism is replaced by the eucharist as the rite of initiation, or even as the instrument of outreach, comments are allowed after the homily only if they are "experiential" but not if they are "substantive," favored biblical scholars are sometimes elevated over Scripture and tradition, and more. Brilliance does not always protect against idiosyncrasy.

On a personal note, I must confess that in some ways I liked the experiment's earlier version better. In the Episcopal Church at Yale, the main innovation was a wonderful blending of Eastern Orthodox elements with *The Book of Common Prayer*. The Trisagion, the Beatitudes, and the Lord's Prayer were sung to haunting Russian Orthodox settings. I later had them included in the service in which I was ordained. With the Orthodox element less in evidence, the experiment in its new form incorporates so many diverse and basically unintegrated components as often to seem jarring, but perhaps that is the point. In any case, I want to close by reflecting on something else.

Not being a liturgical scholar myself, I think I am not entitled to much more than merely stating my preferences. I like it best when there is a common loaf and a common cup. I like it when the bread is made from wholegrain flour, and the cup is filled with real wine. I like it when the whole congregation can go forward and gather round the altar-table. I like it when we all face east, and the cup is not withheld. I find St. Gregory's magnificent in that regard. I like it when the elements are passed from the celebrants to the congregants, and then by the congregants to one another, because I like it when the priesthood of all believers is symbolically enacted in that way. I like it when the elements are distributed randomly among those gathered so as to create a moment of holy chaos.

I like it when the Liturgy of the Sacrament takes place in a different space from the Liturgy of the Word, and I like it when both are celebrated in the worship service every week, if not more.

I don't mind other forms of celebration. Certainly Bouyer and St. Gregory's have made me see how much liturgy can be impaired by architecture – or enhanced by it. When there is not enough room at the front of the sanctuary, I like it when the congregation at least proceeds forward, in a line or by groups, to receive Holy Communion, the wine perhaps by intinction. Meanwhile, I hope the Pope will set a new standard for the architecture of eucharistic assemblies.

What I like least, I'm afraid, is the usual form of celebration in American Protestant churches like my own. What does it symbolize when little trays of pre-cut white bread are passed through the pews, to be followed by larger, more cumbersome trays with grape-juice-filled little cups (these days, more often than not, even disposable plastic cups). I feel embarrassed when these services are visited by ecumenical friends. How can they help musing that what is being symbolized here is the essence of Protestant individualism and privatized religion, the alone communing with the Alone (as Plotinus said), a deracinated form of community, giving new meaning to Rahner's phrase "anonymous Christians"?

In this book I have advocated a great deal that will be difficult to implement. Why not add one thing more? What I would hope for all churches everywhere is the recovery of a liturgy and an architecture like St. Gregory's.

> At the Lamb's high feast we sing
> praise to our victorious King ...
> praise we him, whose love divine
> gives his sacred Blood for wine,
> gives his Body for the feast,
> Christ the victim, Christ the priest. [18]

[18] From a Latin hymn, sixth or seventh century; tr. Robert Campbell, 1849.

Index

academic theology, 2–6, 7–8
accommodationist approach to culture and Christianity, 248
Acts 5:39, 200
admonition as well as affirmation involved in ecumenism, 195, 220, 231, 313
adoration of the host, 69, 83, 84
agency in eucharistic sacrifice, 160–76, 178
  harmonized interpretation of doctrine, 165–76, 178
  Reformation tradition of, 162–5
  Roman Catholic views of, 160
  Scotist approach to, 161
  Thomist approach to, 160
  through Word and sacrament, 184–5
  in trinitarian terms, 165
Alexy II (Russian Orthodox patriarch), 227
alienated theologians, 3, 299
Ambrose of Milan, 230
Anabaptist tradition, 11, 308, 314
anamnesis, 139–45, 156–8, 177, 184, 262
Anglican–Roman Catholic International Commission (ARCIC), 179–81, 218
Anglicans, *see* Episcopalians/Anglicans
Anselm of Canterbury, 226, 279, 292–305
Apostles, Ethiopic version of apocryphal *Epistle of the*, 132
apostolic succession and authority to ordain, 198–200, 228–31
Aquinas, *see* Thomas Aquinas
architecture of church and liturgy, 14, 323–4

ARCIC (Anglican–Roman Catholic International Commission), 179–81, 218
Arianism
  defined, 288
  modern liberal theology's tendency towards, 4
  of Nicene critics, 288–91, 292, 295, 299, 300, 304
  Schleiermacher and, 289
Aristotelian metaphysics implied by transubstantiation, 73, 75, 76
ascension of Christ
  Luther and Calvin on, 136
  Torrance on, 153–6
Ashley, Benedict M., 217
Assyrian Church of the East, eucharistic prayer of, 230
Athanasius (bishop of Alexandria), 150, 155, 279, 283–91, 296, 297–8, 303, 304
atonement, peace, and Nicene Christianity, 292–305, 307–8
Augustine of Hippo, 42, 252, 266, 302
Aukerman, Dale, 306, 307–8

Babylonian Captivity of the Church, The (Luther), 102
Baldovin, John F., 330
baptism and eucharist, 155, 282, 321
Baptism, Eucharist and Ministry (*BEM*; 1982 World Council of Churches), 78, 81–2, 89, 205, 207, 319, 322, 323–32
Barth, Karl, 5, 15–18, 292, 299, 305, 321
Behr-Sigel, Elisabeth, 237
Belgic Confession (1618), 49

333